Jordan Banking and Financial Market Handbook

Just The facts101
Textbook Key Facts

by Cram101
Texbook NOT Included

Table of Contents

Just The Facts101

Exam Prep for

Jordan Banking and Financial Market Handbook

Just The Facts101 Exam Prep

eAIN 464141

Foundations of Business

A business, also known as an enterprise, agency or a firm, is an entity involved in the provision of goods and/or services to consumers. Businesses are prevalent in capitalist economies, where most of them are privately owned and provide goods and services to customers in exchange for other goods, services, or money.

:: National accounts ::

__________ is a monetary measure of the market value of all the final goods and services produced in a period of time, often annually. GDP per capita does not, however, reflect differences in the cost of living and the inflation rates of the countries; therefore using a basis of GDP per capita at purchasing power parity is arguably more useful when comparing differences in living standards between nations.

Exam Probability: **Low**

1. *Answer choices:*

(see index for correct answer)

- a. Fixed capital
- b. Gross domestic product
- c. National Income

Guidance: level 1

:: Globalization-related theories ::

_________ is the process in which a nation is being improved in the sector of the economic, political, and social well-being of its people. The term has been used frequently by economists, politicians, and others in the 20th and 21st centuries. The concept, however, has been in existence in the West for centuries. "Modernization, "westernization", and especially "industrialization" are other terms often used while discussing _________ . _________ has a direct relationship with the environment and environmental issues. _________ is very often confused with industrial development, even in some academic sources.

Exam Probability: **High**

2. *Answer choices:*

(see index for correct answer)

- a. Economic Development
- b. postmodernism
- c. Capitalism

Guidance: level 1

:: International trade ::

An _________ is a good brought into a jurisdiction, especially across a national border, from an external source. The party bringing in the good is called an _________ er. An _________ in the receiving country is an export from the sending country. _________ ation and exportation are the defining financial transactions of international trade.

Exam Probability: **High**

3. *Answer choices:*

(see index for correct answer)

- a. Trade Act
- b. International Organisation of Employers
- c. Import
- d. Section 201

Guidance: level 1

:: Health promotion ::

_________ , as defined by the World _________ Organization , is "a state of complete physical, mental and social well-being and not merely the absence of disease or infirmity." This definition has been subject to controversy, as it may have limited value for implementation. _________ may be defined as the ability to adapt and manage physical, mental and social challenges throughout life.

Exam Probability: **Medium**

4. *Answer choices:*
(see index for correct answer)

- a. High-deductible health plan
- b. Integrated Management of Childhood Illness
- c. Health equity
- d. Black Report

Guidance: level 1

:: Management occupations ::

_________ ship is the process of designing, launching and running a new business, which is often initially a small business. The people who create these businesses are called _________ s.

Exam Probability: **High**

5. *Answer choices:*
(see index for correct answer)

- a. Pit manager
- b. Entrepreneur
- c. Sport management
- d. Business manager

Guidance: level 1

:: Business ::

The seller, or the provider of the goods or services, completes a sale in response to an acquisition, appropriation, requisition or a direct interaction with the buyer at the point of sale. There is a passing of title of the item, and the settlement of a price, in which agreement is reached on a price for which transfer of ownership of the item will occur. The seller, not the purchaser typically executes the sale and it may be completed prior to the obligation of payment. In the case of indirect interaction, a person who sells goods or service on behalf of the owner is known as a salesman or saleswoman or salesperson, but this often refers to someone _________ goods in a store/shop, in which case other terms are also common, including salesclerk, shop assistant, and retail clerk.

Exam Probability: **High**

6. *Answer choices:*

(see index for correct answer)

- a. Service recovery
- b. Viability study
- c. Price adjustment
- d. Business mileage reimbursement rate

Guidance: level 1

:: Currency ::

A _________ , in the most specific sense is money in any form when in use or circulation as a medium of exchange, especially circulating banknotes and coins. A more general definition is that a _________ is a system of money in common use, especially for people in a nation. Under this definition, US dollars , pounds sterling , Australian dollars , European euros , Russian rubles and Indian Rupees are examples of currencies. These various currencies are recognized as stores of value and are traded between nations in foreign exchange markets, which determine the relative values of the different currencies. Currencies in this sense are defined by governments, and each type has limited boundaries of acceptance.

Exam Probability: **Medium**

7. *Answer choices:*

(see index for correct answer)

- a. Unidad de Fomento
- b. Currency
- c. Swan diagram
- d. Non-decimal currency

Guidance: level 1

:: Industrial Revolution ::

The _________ , now also known as the First _________ , was the transition to new manufacturing processes in Europe and the US, in the period from about 1760 to sometime between 1820 and 1840. This transition included going from hand production methods to machines, new chemical manufacturing and iron production processes, the increasing use of steam power and water power, the development of machine tools and the rise of the mechanized factory system. The _________ also led to an unprecedented rise in the rate of population growth.

Exam Probability: **Medium**

8. *Answer choices:*
(see index for correct answer)

- a. Stott
- b. Ironworks
- c. Leawood Pump House
- d. Industrial Revolution

Guidance: level 1

:: Stock market ::

_________ is freedom from, or resilience against, potential harm caused by others. Beneficiaries of _________ may be of persons and social groups, objects and institutions, ecosystems or any other entity or phenomenon vulnerable to unwanted change by its environment.

Exam Probability: **Medium**

9. *Answer choices:*
(see index for correct answer)

- a. MoneyBee
- b. Central limit order book
- c. Security
- d. Purple chip

Guidance: level 1

:: Management ::

__________ is the practice of initiating, planning, executing, controlling, and closing the work of a team to achieve specific goals and meet specific success criteria at the specified time.

Exam Probability: **High**

10. *Answer choices:*

(see index for correct answer)

- a. Project management
- b. Mission critical
- c. Mobile sales enablement
- d. Cynefin

Guidance: level 1

:: Problem solving ::

In other words, __________ is a situation where a group of people meet to generate new ideas and solutions around a specific domain of interest by removing inhibitions. People are able to think more freely and they suggest as many spontaneous new ideas as possible. All the ideas are noted down and those ideas are not criticized and after __________ session the ideas are evaluated.The term was popularized by Alex Faickney Osborn in the 1953 book Applied Imagination.

Exam Probability: **High**

11. *Answer choices:*

(see index for correct answer)

- a. Rhetorical reason
- b. Syntegrity
- c. Calculation
- d. Brainstorming

Guidance: level 1

:: Analysis ::

_________ is the process of breaking a complex topic or substance into smaller parts in order to gain a better understanding of it. The technique has been applied in the study of mathematics and logic since before Aristotle , though _________ as a formal concept is a relatively recent development.

Exam Probability: **High**

12. *Answer choices:*
(see index for correct answer)

- a. Analysis
- b. Proximity analysis
- c. Gompertz constant
- d. Deviation analysis

Guidance: level 1

:: Financial statements ::

In financial accounting, a _________ or statement of financial position or statement of financial condition is a summary of the financial balances of an individual or organization, whether it be a sole proprietorship, a business partnership, a corporation, private limited company or other organization such as Government or not-for-profit entity. Assets, liabilities and ownership equity are listed as of a specific date, such as the end of its financial year. A _________ is often described as a "snapshot of a company's financial condition". Of the four basic financial statements, the _________ is the only statement which applies to a single point in time of a business' calendar year.

Exam Probability: **Low**

13. *Answer choices:*
(see index for correct answer)

- a. Financial report
- b. quarterly report
- c. Clean surplus accounting
- d. Balance sheet

Guidance: level 1

:: Business models ::

__________ es are privately owned corporations, partnerships, or sole proprietorships that have fewer employees and/or less annual revenue than a regular-sized business or corporation. Businesses are defined as "small" in terms of being able to apply for government support and qualify for preferential tax policy varies depending on the country and industry. __________ es range from fifteen employees under the Australian Fair Work Act 2009, fifty employees according to the definition used by the European Union, and fewer than five hundred employees to qualify for many U.S. __________ Administration programs. While __________ es can also be classified according to other methods, such as annual revenues, shipments, sales, assets, or by annual gross or net revenue or net profits, the number of employees is one of the most widely used measures.

Exam Probability: **Medium**

14. *Answer choices:*

(see index for correct answer)

- a. Meta learning
- b. Product-service system
- c. What if chart
- d. Small business

Guidance: level 1

:: Real estate ::

__________ s serve several societal needs – primarily as shelter from weather, security, living space, privacy, to store belongings, and to comfortably live and work. A __________ as a shelter represents a physical division of the human habitat and the outside .

Exam Probability: **Medium**

15. *Answer choices:*

(see index for correct answer)

- a. Buyer agency agreement
- b. Displaced sales
- c. Landed nobility
- d. Building

Guidance: level 1

:: Survey methodology ::

An _________ is a conversation where questions are asked and answers are given. In common parlance, the word " _________ " refers to a one-on-one conversation between an _________ er and an _________ ee. The _________ er asks questions to which the _________ ee responds, usually so information may be transferred from _________ ee to _________ er . Sometimes, information can be transferred in both directions. It is a communication, unlike a speech, which produces a one-way flow of information.

Exam Probability: **High**

16. *Answer choices:*

(see index for correct answer)

- a. Group concept mapping
- b. Survey research
- c. Interview
- d. Public opinion

Guidance: level 1

:: Social security ::

_________ is "any government system that provides monetary assistance to people with an inadequate or no income." In the United States, this is usually called welfare or a social safety net, especially when talking about Canada and European countries.

Exam Probability: **Medium**

17. *Answer choices:*

(see index for correct answer)

- a. Social security
- b. South African Social Security Agency
- c. Student benefit
- d. Social Security Board

Guidance: level 1

:: International trade ::

_________ involves the transfer of goods or services from one person or entity to another, often in exchange for money. A system or network that allows _________ is called a market.

Exam Probability: **Low**

18. *Answer choices:*

(see index for correct answer)

- a. Intervention stocks
- b. Strong dollar policy
- c. Food power
- d. Gains from trade

Guidance: level 1

:: Graphic design ::

An _________ is an artifact that depicts visual perception, such as a photograph or other two-dimensional picture, that resembles a subject—usually a physical object—and thus provides a depiction of it. In the context of signal processing, an _________ is a distributed amplitude of color.

Exam Probability: **Low**

19. *Answer choices:*

(see index for correct answer)

- a. Centerfold
- b. Communicate knowledge manifesto
- c. Image
- d. Graphis Inc.

Guidance: level 1

:: Debt ::

__________ is the trust which allows one party to provide money or resources to another party wherein the second party does not reimburse the first party immediately , but promises either to repay or return those resources at a later date. In other words, __________ is a method of making reciprocity formal, legally enforceable, and extensible to a large group of unrelated people.

Exam Probability: **Low**

20. *Answer choices:*

(see index for correct answer)

- a. Rule of 72
- b. Debit commission
- c. Sum certain
- d. Museum of Foreign Debt

Guidance: level 1

:: Meetings ::

A __________ is a body of one or more persons that is subordinate to a deliberative assembly. Usually, the assembly sends matters into a __________ as a way to explore them more fully than would be possible if the assembly itself were considering them. __________ s may have different functions and their type of work differ depending on the type of the organization and its needs.

Exam Probability: **High**

21. *Answer choices:*

(see index for correct answer)

- a. Annual general meeting
- b. Evoma
- c. Committee
- d. Extraordinary general meeting

Guidance: level 1

:: Regression analysis ::

A _________ often refers to a set of documented requirements to be satisfied by a material, design, product, or service. A _________ is often a type of technical standard.

Exam Probability: **High**

22. *Answer choices:*

(see index for correct answer)

- a. Guess value
- b. Poisson regression
- c. Specification
- d. Cross-sectional regression

Guidance: level 1

:: Accounting software ::

_________ is any item or verifiable record that is generally accepted as payment for goods and services and repayment of debts, such as taxes, in a particular country or socio-economic context. The main functions of _________ are distinguished as: a medium of exchange, a unit of account, a store of value and sometimes, a standard of deferred payment. Any item or verifiable record that fulfils these functions can be considered as _________ .

Exam Probability: **Medium**

23. *Answer choices:*

(see index for correct answer)

- a. Boeing Calc
- b. DHPOS
- c. E-accounting
- d. Money

Guidance: level 1

:: Marketing analytics ::

__________ is a long-term, forward-looking approach to planning with the fundamental goal of achieving a sustainable competitive advantage. Strategic planning involves an analysis of the company`s strategic initial situation prior to the formulation, evaluation and selection of market-oriented competitive position that contributes to the company`s goals and marketing objectives.

Exam Probability: **Medium**

24. *Answer choices:*

(see index for correct answer)

- a. marketing dashboard
- b. Marketing strategy
- c. Return on marketing investment
- d. Mission-driven marketing

Guidance: level 1

:: Cash flow ::

__________ s are narrowly interconnected with the concepts of value, interest rate and liquidity.A __________ that shall happen on a future day tN can be transformed into a __________ of the same value in t0.

Exam Probability: **Low**

25. *Answer choices:*

(see index for correct answer)

- a. Cash flow
- b. Invoice discounting
- c. First Chicago Method
- d. Operating cash flow

Guidance: level 1

:: Environmental economics ::

_________ is the process of people maintaining change in a balanced environment, in which the exploitation of resources, the direction of investments, the orientation of technological development and institutional change are all in harmony and enhance both current and future potential to meet human needs and aspirations. For many in the field, _________ is defined through the following interconnected domains or pillars: environment, economic and social, which according to Fritjof Capra is based on the principles of Systems Thinking. Sub-domains of sustainable development have been considered also: cultural, technological and political. While sustainable development may be the organizing principle for _________ for some, for others, the two terms are paradoxical . Sustainable development is the development that meets the needs of the present without compromising the ability of future generations to meet their own needs. Brundtland Report for the World Commission on Environment and Development introduced the term of sustainable development.

Exam Probability: **Medium**

26. *Answer choices:*

(see index for correct answer)

- a. Pigovian tax
- b. Sustainability
- c. Current solar income
- d. Good Country Index

Guidance: level 1

:: Unemployment ::

In economics, a _________ is a business cycle contraction when there is a general decline in economic activity. Macroeconomic indicators such as GDP , investment spending, capacity utilization, household income, business profits, and inflation fall, while bankruptcies and the unemployment rate rise. In the United Kingdom, it is defined as a negative economic growth for two consecutive quarters.

Exam Probability: **Medium**

27. *Answer choices:*

(see index for correct answer)

- a. Recession
- b. NAIRU

- c. Employment protection legislation
- d. Mount Street Club

Guidance: level 1

:: Training ::

__________ is teaching, or developing in oneself or others, any skills and knowledge that relate to specific useful competencies. __________ has specific goals of improving one`s capability, capacity, productivity and performance. It forms the core of apprenticeships and provides the backbone of content at institutes of technology . In addition to the basic __________ required for a trade, occupation or profession, observers of the labor-market recognize as of 2008 the need to continue __________ beyond initial qualifications: to maintain, upgrade and update skills throughout working life. People within many professions and occupations may refer to this sort of __________ as professional development.

Exam Probability: **High**

28. *Answer choices:*
(see index for correct answer)

- a. Training
- b. Screencast
- c. National Occupational Standards
- d. Endurance training

Guidance: level 1

:: Semiconductor companies ::

__________ Corporation is a Japanese multinational conglomerate corporation headquartered in Konan, Minato, Tokyo. Its diversified business includes consumer and professional electronics, gaming, entertainment and financial services. The company owns the largest music entertainment business in the world, the largest video game console business and one of the largest video game publishing businesses, and is one of the leading manufacturers of electronic products for the consumer and professional markets, and a leading player in the film and television entertainment industry. __________ was ranked 97th on the 2018 Fortune Global 500 list.

Exam Probability: **Low**

29. *Answer choices:*

(see index for correct answer)

- a. Arteris
- b. Microchip Technology
- c. CML Microcircuits
- d. Sony

Guidance: level 1

:: Systems theory ::

A _________ is a group of interacting or interrelated entities that form a unified whole. A _________ is delineated by its spatial and temporal boundaries, surrounded and influenced by its environment, described by its structure and purpose and expressed in its functioning.

Exam Probability: **Medium**

30. *Answer choices:*

(see index for correct answer)

- a. Viable System Model
- b. System
- c. process system
- d. co-design

Guidance: level 1

:: Logistics ::

_________ is generally the detailed organization and implementation of a complex operation. In a general business sense, _________ is the management of the flow of things between the point of origin and the point of consumption in order to meet requirements of customers or corporations. The resources managed in _________ may include tangible goods such as materials, equipment, and supplies, as well as food and other consumable items. The _________ of physical items usually involves the integration of information flow, materials handling, production, packaging, inventory, transportation, warehousing, and often security.

Exam Probability: **Medium**

31. *Answer choices:*
(see index for correct answer)

- a. Center for Transportation and Logistics Neuer Adler
- b. Savi Technology
- c. Medical Materiel
- d. Logistics

Guidance: level 1

:: Generally Accepted Accounting Principles ::

An _________ or profit and loss account is one of the financial statements of a company and shows the company's revenues and expenses during a particular period.

Exam Probability: **Low**

32. *Answer choices:*
(see index for correct answer)

- a. Management accounting principles
- b. Income statement
- c. Operating income before depreciation and amortization
- d. Indian Accounting Standards

Guidance: level 1

:: Stock market ::

A _________, equity market or share market is the aggregation of buyers and sellers of stocks, which represent ownership claims on businesses; these may include securities listed on a public stock exchange, as well as stock that is only traded privately. Examples of the latter include shares of private companies which are sold to investors through equity crowdfunding platforms. Stock exchanges list shares of common equity as well as other security types, e.g. corporate bonds and convertible bonds.

Exam Probability: **High**

33. *Answer choices:*
(see index for correct answer)

- a. P chip
- b. Stock market

- c. SPI 200 futures contract
- d. Open outcry

Guidance: level 1

:: Free trade agreements ::

A __________ is a wide-ranging taxes, tariff and trade treaty that often includes investment guarantees. It exists when two or more countries agree on terms that helps them trade with each other. The most common __________ s are of the preferential and free trade types are concluded in order to reduce tariffs, quotas and other trade restrictions on items traded between the signatories.

Exam Probability: **Low**

34. *Answer choices:*

(see index for correct answer)

- a. Trans-Pacific Partnership
- b. Trade, Development and Cooperation Agreement
- c. Trade agreement
- d. Investor-state dispute settlement

Guidance: level 1

:: Export and import control ::

" __________ " means the Government Service which is responsible for the administration of __________ law and the collection of duties and taxes and which also has the responsibility for the application of other laws and regulations relating to the importation, exportation, movement or storage of goods.

Exam Probability: **Medium**

35. *Answer choices:*

(see index for correct answer)

- a. Plant Protection and Quarantine
- b. Export Management and Compliance Program
- c. International Traffic in Arms Regulations
- d. Customs

Guidance: level 1

:: Production economics ::

In microeconomics, _________ are the cost advantages that enterprises obtain due to their scale of operation , with cost per unit of output decreasing with increasing scale.

Exam Probability: **High**

36. *Answer choices:*

(see index for correct answer)

- a. Productive capacity
- b. Partial productivity
- c. Limiting factor
- d. Economies of scale

Guidance: level 1

:: Telecommunication theory ::

In reliability theory and reliability engineering, the term _________ has the following meanings.

Exam Probability: **Low**

37. *Answer choices:*

(see index for correct answer)

- a. Black facsimile transmission
- b. Availability
- c. Round-trip delay time
- d. Bipolar signal

Guidance: level 1

:: Human resource management ::

_________ is the corporate management term for the act of reorganizing the legal, ownership, operational, or other structures of a company for the purpose of making it more profitable, or better organized for its present needs. Other reasons for _________ include a change of ownership or ownership structure, demerger, or a response to a crisis or major change in the business such as bankruptcy, repositioning, or buyout. _________ may also be described as corporate _________, debt _________ and financial _________.

Exam Probability: **High**

38. *Answer choices:*

(see index for correct answer)

- a. Management by objectives
- b. Dr. Marri Channa Reddy Human Resource Development Institute of Andhra Pradesh
- c. Four-day week
- d. Continuing professional development

Guidance: level 1

:: Management ::

A _________ describes the rationale of how an organization creates, delivers, and captures value, in economic, social, cultural or other contexts. The process of _________ construction and modification is also called _________ innovation and forms a part of business strategy.

Exam Probability: **High**

39. *Answer choices:*

(see index for correct answer)

- a. Job rotation
- b. Management buyout
- c. Management fad
- d. Earned value management

Guidance: level 1

:: Data management ::

_________ is a form of intellectual property that grants the creator of an original creative work an exclusive legal right to determine whether and under what conditions this original work may be copied and used by others, usually for a limited term of years. The exclusive rights are not absolute but limited by limitations and exceptions to _________ law, including fair use. A major limitation on _________ on ideas is that _________ protects only the original expression of ideas, and not the underlying ideas themselves.

Exam Probability: **Low**

40. *Answer choices:*

(see index for correct answer)

- a. Data processing system
- b. ISO 8000
- c. Distributed data store
- d. Copyright

Guidance: level 1

:: Auditing ::

_________, as defined by accounting and auditing, is a process for assuring of an organization`s objectives in operational effectiveness and efficiency, reliable financial reporting, and compliance with laws, regulations and policies. A broad concept, _________ involves everything that controls risks to an organization.

Exam Probability: **Medium**

41. *Answer choices:*

(see index for correct answer)

- a. Assurance services
- b. Internal control
- c. Management representation
- d. Software licensing audit

Guidance: level 1

:: Management ::

A _________ is when two or more people come together to discuss one or more topics, often in a formal or business setting, but _________ s also occur in a variety of other environments. Many various types of _________ s exist.

Exam Probability: **High**

42. *Answer choices:*

(see index for correct answer)

- a. Responsible autonomy
- b. Project management information system
- c. Concept of operations
- d. Meeting

Guidance: level 1

:: Financial markets ::

A _________ is a financial market in which long-term debt or equity-backed securities are bought and sold. _________ s channel the wealth of savers to those who can put it to long-term productive use, such as companies or governments making long-term investments. Financial regulators like the Bank of England and the U.S. Securities and Exchange Commission oversee _________ s to protect investors against fraud, among other duties.

Exam Probability: **High**

43. *Answer choices:*

(see index for correct answer)

- a. CUSIP-linked MIP code
- b. Subscription
- c. Financial market
- d. Capital market

Guidance: level 1

:: Customs duties ::

A _________ is a tax on imports or exports between sovereign states. It is a form of regulation of foreign trade and a policy that taxes foreign products to encourage or safeguard domestic industry. _________ s are the simplest and oldest instrument of trade policy. Traditionally, states have used them as a source of income. Now, they are among the most widely used instruments of protection, along with import and export quotas.

Exam Probability: **High**

44. *Answer choices:*

(see index for correct answer)

- a. You Are on Indian Land
- b. Canadian import duties
- c. Specific rate duty
- d. Duty-free shop

Guidance: level 1

:: Statistical terminology ::

_________ es can be learned implicitly within cultural contexts. People may develop _________ es toward or against an individual, an ethnic group, a sexual or gender identity, a nation, a religion, a social class, a political party, theoretical paradigms and ideologies within academic domains, or a species. _________ ed means one-sided, lacking a neutral viewpoint, or not having an open mind. _________ can come in many forms and is related to prejudice and intuition.

Exam Probability: **Medium**

45. *Answer choices:*

(see index for correct answer)

- a. Efficiency
- b. Bias
- c. Percentage point
- d. Realization

Guidance: level 1

:: ::

Business is the activity of making one's living or making money by producing or buying and selling products . Simply put, it is "any activity or enterprise entered into for profit. It does not mean it is a company, a corporation, partnership, or have any such formal organization, but it can range from a street peddler to General Motors."

Exam Probability: **Medium**

46. *Answer choices:*

(see index for correct answer)

- a. hierarchical perspective
- b. personal values
- c. functional perspective
- d. cultural

Guidance: level 1

:: Casting (manufacturing) ::

A _________ is a regularity in the world, man-made design, or abstract ideas. As such, the elements of a _________ repeat in a predictable manner. A geometric _________ is a kind of _________ formed of geometric shapes and typically repeated like a wallpaper design.

Exam Probability: **High**

47. *Answer choices:*

(see index for correct answer)

- a. Foundry sand testing
- b. Full-mold casting
- c. Riser
- d. Controlled permeability formwork

Guidance: level 1

:: Marketing techniques ::

__________ is the activity of dividing a broad consumer or business market, normally consisting of existing and potential customers, into sub-groups of consumers based on some type of shared characteristics. In dividing or segmenting markets, researchers typically look for common characteristics such as shared needs, common interests, similar lifestyles or even similar demographic profiles. The overall aim of segmentation is to identify high yield segments – that is, those segments that are likely to be the most profitable or that have growth potential – so that these can be selected for special attention .

Exam Probability: **Low**

48. *Answer choices:*

(see index for correct answer)

- a. Prize
- b. Market segmentation
- c. Stunt casting
- d. Precision marketing

Guidance: level 1

:: Financial regulatory authorities of the United States ::

The __________ is the revenue service of the United States federal government. The government agency is a bureau of the Department of the Treasury, and is under the immediate direction of the Commissioner of Internal Revenue, who is appointed to a five-year term by the President of the United States. The IRS is responsible for collecting taxes and administering the Internal Revenue Code, the main body of federal statutory tax law of the United States. The duties of the IRS include providing tax assistance to taxpayers and pursuing and resolving instances of erroneous or fraudulent tax filings. The IRS has also overseen various benefits programs, and enforces portions of the Affordable Care Act.

Exam Probability: **High**

49. *Answer choices:*

(see index for correct answer)

- a. Internal Revenue Service
- b. Federal Reserve Board
- c. National Credit Union Administration

- d. Municipal Securities Rulemaking Board

Guidance: level 1

:: Debt ::

__________ , in finance and economics, is payment from a borrower or deposit-taking financial institution to a lender or depositor of an amount above repayment of the principal sum , at a particular rate. It is distinct from a fee which the borrower may pay the lender or some third party. It is also distinct from dividend which is paid by a company to its shareholders from its profit or reserve, but not at a particular rate decided beforehand, rather on a pro rata basis as a share in the reward gained by risk taking entrepreneurs when the revenue earned exceeds the total costs.

Exam Probability: **High**

50. *Answer choices:*

(see index for correct answer)

- a. Debt crisis
- b. Debt wall
- c. gearing
- d. Internal debt

Guidance: level 1

:: Quality management ::

__________ ensures that an organization, product or service is consistent. It has four main components: quality planning, quality assurance, quality control and quality improvement. __________ is focused not only on product and service quality, but also on the means to achieve it. __________ , therefore, uses quality assurance and control of processes as well as products to achieve more consistent quality.What a customer wants and is willing to pay for it determines quality. It is written or unwritten commitment to a known or unknown consumer in the market . Thus, quality can be defined as fitness for intended use or, in other words, how well the product performs its intended function

Exam Probability: **Medium**

51. *Answer choices:*

(see index for correct answer)

- a. Test bay
- b. QC Reporting
- c. External quality assessment
- d. Management by wandering around

Guidance: level 1

:: Poker strategy ::

_________ is any measure taken to guard a thing against damage caused by outside forces. _________ can be provided to physical objects, including organisms, to systems, and to intangible things like civil and political rights. Although the mechanisms for providing _________ vary widely, the basic meaning of the term remains the same. This is illustrated by an explanation found in a manual on electrical wiring.

Exam Probability: **Low**

52. *Answer choices:*

(see index for correct answer)

- a. Fold equity
- b. Position
- c. Q-ratio
- d. M-ratio

Guidance: level 1

:: Business law ::

_________ is where a person`s financial liability is limited to a fixed sum, most commonly the value of a person`s investment in a company or partnership. If a company with _________ is sued, then the claimants are suing the company, not its owners or investors. A shareholder in a limited company is not personally liable for any of the debts of the company, other than for the amount already invested in the company and for any unpaid amount on the shares in the company, if any. The same is true for the members of a _________ partnership and the limited partners in a limited partnership. By contrast, sole proprietors and partners in general partnerships are each liable for all the debts of the business .

Exam Probability: **Medium**

53. *Answer choices:*
(see index for correct answer)

- a. Ladenschlussgesetz
- b. Business.gov
- c. Limited liability
- d. Lease

Guidance: level 1

:: Strategic management ::

_________ is a strategic planning technique used to help a person or organization identify strengths, weaknesses, opportunities, and threats related to business competition or project planning. It is intended to specify the objectives of the business venture or project and identify the internal and external factors that are favorable and unfavorable to achieving those objectives. Users of a _________ often ask and answer questions to generate meaningful information for each category to make the tool useful and identify their competitive advantage. SWOT has been described as the tried-and-true tool of strategic analysis.

Exam Probability: **Low**

54. *Answer choices:*
(see index for correct answer)

- a. SWOT analysis
- b. customer lock-in
- c. Keiretsu
- d. E-learning Maturity Model

Guidance: level 1

:: Classification systems ::

_________ is the practice of comparing business processes and performance metrics to industry bests and best practices from other companies. Dimensions typically measured are quality, time and cost.

Exam Probability: **Medium**

55. *Answer choices:*
(see index for correct answer)

- a. Genetypes
- b. Bautz-Morgan classification
- c. House numbering
- d. Stellar classification

Guidance: level 1

:: Market research ::

A __________ is a small, but demographically diverse group of people and whose reactions are studied especially in market research or political analysis in guided or open discussions about a new product or something else to determine the reactions that can be expected from a larger population. It is a form of qualitative research consisting of interviews in which a group of people are asked about their perceptions, opinions, beliefs, and attitudes towards a product, service, concept, advertisement, idea, or packaging. Questions are asked in an interactive group setting where participants are free to talk with other group members. During this process, the researcher either takes notes or records the vital points he or she is getting from the group. Researchers should select members of the __________ carefully for effective and authoritative responses.

Exam Probability: **Medium**

56. *Answer choices:*

(see index for correct answer)

- a. AQH Share
- b. Indian Readership Survey
- c. LRMR
- d. Focus group

Guidance: level 1

:: Fraud ::

In law, _________ is intentional deception to secure unfair or unlawful gain, or to deprive a victim of a legal right. _________ can violate civil law , a criminal law , or it may cause no loss of money, property or legal right but still be an element of another civil or criminal wrong. The purpose of _________ may be monetary gain or other benefits, for example by obtaining a passport, travel document, or driver`s license, or mortgage _________ , where the perpetrator may attempt to qualify for a mortgage by way of false statements.

Exam Probability: **Low**

57. *Answer choices:*
(see index for correct answer)

- a. Fraud Squad
- b. Customer not present
- c. Fraud
- d. Check washing

Guidance: level 1

:: Costs ::

In microeconomic theory, the _________ , or alternative cost, of making a particular choice is the value of the most valuable choice out of those that were not taken. In other words, opportunity that will require sacrifices.

Exam Probability: **Low**

58. *Answer choices:*
(see index for correct answer)

- a. Cost of poor quality
- b. Manufacturing cost
- c. Opportunity cost
- d. Cost curve

Guidance: level 1

:: Association of Southeast Asian Nations ::

The Association of Southeast Asian Nations is a regional intergovernmental organization comprising ten countries in Southeast Asia, which promotes intergovernmental cooperation and facilitates economic, political, security, military, educational, and sociocultural integration among its members and other countries in Asia. It also regularly engages other countries in the Asia-Pacific region and beyond. A major partner of Shanghai Cooperation Organisation, _________ maintains a global network of alliances and dialogue partners and is considered by many as a global powerhouse, the central union for cooperation in Asia-Pacific, and a prominent and influential organization. It is involved in numerous international affairs, and hosts diplomatic missions throughout the world.

Exam Probability: **High**

59. *Answer choices:*

(see index for correct answer)

- a. ASEAN Hymn
- b. Asian Monetary Unit
- c. ASEAN
- d. Enlargement of the Association of Southeast Asian Nations

Guidance: level 1

Management

Management is the administration of an organization, whether it is a business, a not-for-profit organization, or government body. Management includes the activities of setting the strategy of an organization and coordinating the efforts of its employees (or of volunteers) to accomplish its objectives through the application of available resources, such as financial, natural, technological, and human resources.

:: Management ::

In organizational studies, __________ is the efficient and effective development of an organization`s resources when they are needed. Such resources may include financial resources, inventory, human skills, production resources, or information technology and natural resources.

Exam Probability: **Low**

1. *Answer choices:*

(see index for correct answer)

- a. Project cost management
- b. Resource management
- c. Decentralized decision-making
- d. Logistics management

Guidance: level 1

:: ::

__________ is a kind of action that occur as two or more objects have an effect upon one another. The idea of a two-way effect is essential in the concept of __________, as opposed to a one-way causal effect. A closely related term is interconnectivity, which deals with the __________s of __________s within systems: combinations of many simple __________s can lead to surprising emergent phenomena. __________ has different tailored meanings in various sciences. Changes can also involve __________.

Exam Probability: **Low**

2. *Answer choices:*

(see index for correct answer)

- a. deep-level diversity
- b. functional perspective
- c. levels of analysis
- d. imperative

Guidance: level 1

:: Behavior modification ::

In psychotherapy and mental health, __________ has a positive sense of empowering individuals, or a negative sense of encouraging dysfunctional behavior.

Exam Probability: **Low**

3. *Answer choices:*

(see index for correct answer)

- a. Thought stopping
- b. Enabling

Guidance: level 1

:: Materials ::

A __________, also known as a feedstock, unprocessed material, or primary commodity, is a basic material that is used to produce goods, finished products, energy, or intermediate materials which are feedstock for future finished products. As feedstock, the term connotes these materials are bottleneck assets and are highly important with regard to producing other products. An example of this is crude oil, which is a __________ and a feedstock used in the production of industrial chemicals, fuels, plastics, and pharmaceutical goods; lumber is a __________ used to produce a variety of products including all types of furniture. The term "__________" denotes materials in minimally processed or unprocessed in states; e.g., raw latex, crude oil, cotton, coal, raw biomass, iron ore, air, logs, or water i.e. "...any product of agriculture, forestry, fishing and any other mineral that is in its natural form or which has undergone the transformation required to prepare it for internationally marketing in substantial volumes."

Exam Probability: **High**

4. *Answer choices:*

(see index for correct answer)

- a. Layered double hydroxides
- b. Propolis
- c. Latex
- d. Raw material

Guidance: level 1

:: Hospitality management ::

A _________ is an establishment that provides paid lodging on a short-term basis. Facilities provided may range from a modest-quality mattress in a small room to large suites with bigger, higher-quality beds, a dresser, a refrigerator and other kitchen facilities, upholstered chairs, a flat screen television, and en-suite bathrooms. Small, lower-priced _________ s may offer only the most basic guest services and facilities. Larger, higher-priced _________ s may provide additional guest facilities such as a swimming pool, business centre , childcare, conference and event facilities, tennis or basketball courts, gymnasium, restaurants, day spa, and social function services. _________ rooms are usually numbered to allow guests to identify their room. Some boutique, high-end _________ s have custom decorated rooms. Some _________ s offer meals as part of a room and board arrangement. In the United Kingdom, a _________ is required by law to serve food and drinks to all guests within certain stated hours. In Japan, capsule _________ s provide a tiny room suitable only for sleeping and shared bathroom facilities.

Exam Probability: **High**

5. *Answer choices:*

(see index for correct answer)

- a. Bed-making
- b. Swiss Hotel Schools Association
- c. Hotel
- d. Towel animal

Guidance: level 1

:: Management ::

In the field of management, _________ involves the formulation and implementation of the major goals and initiatives taken by an organization`s top management on behalf of owners, based on consideration of resources and an assessment of the internal and external environments in which the organization operates.

Exam Probability: **High**

6. *Answer choices:*

(see index for correct answer)

- a. Goal
- b. Managerial Psychology

- c. Supplier performance management
- d. Knowledge ecosystem

Guidance: level 1

:: ::

In a supply chain, a _________ , or a seller, is an enterprise that contributes goods or services. Generally, a supply chain _________ manufactures inventory/stock items and sells them to the next link in the chain. Today, these terms refer to a supplier of any good or service.

Exam Probability: **Low**

7. *Answer choices:*

(see index for correct answer)

- a. Sarbanes-Oxley act of 2002
- b. Vendor
- c. interpersonal communication
- d. corporate values

Guidance: level 1

:: ::

A _________ or GM is an executive who has overall responsibility for managing both the revenue and cost elements of a company`s income statement, known as profit & loss responsibility. A _________ usually oversees most or all of the firm`s marketing and sales functions as well as the day-to-day operations of the business. Frequently, the _________ is responsible for effective planning, delegating, coordinating, staffing, organizing, and decision making to attain desirable profit making results for an organization .

Exam Probability: **High**

8. *Answer choices:*

(see index for correct answer)

- a. personal values
- b. General manager
- c. process perspective
- d. Sarbanes-Oxley act of 2002

Guidance: level 1

:: Evaluation methods ::

In social psychology, _________ is the process of looking at oneself in order to assess aspects that are important to one`s identity. It is one of the motives that drive self-evaluation, along with self-verification and self-enhancement. Sedikides suggests that the _________ motive will prompt people to seek information to confirm their uncertain self-concept rather than their certain self-concept and at the same time people use _________ to enhance their certainty of their own self-knowledge. However, the _________ motive could be seen as quite different from the other two self-evaluation motives. Unlike the other two motives through _________ people are interested in the accuracy of their current self view, rather than improving their self-view. This makes _________ the only self-evaluative motive that may cause a person`s self-esteem to be damaged.

Exam Probability: **High**

9. *Answer choices:*

(see index for correct answer)

- a. Self-assessment
- b. Design science
- c. SAT Subject Tests
- d. Creative participation

Guidance: level 1

:: Scientific method ::

In the social sciences and life sciences, a _________ is a research method involving an up-close, in-depth, and detailed examination of a subject of study , as well as its related contextual conditions.

Exam Probability: **Medium**

10. *Answer choices:*

(see index for correct answer)

- a. Case study
- b. Causal research
- c. pilot project
- d. explanatory research

Guidance: level 1

:: Systems theory ::

A _________ is a set of policies, processes and procedures used by an organization to ensure that it can fulfill the tasks required to achieve its objectives. These objectives cover many aspects of the organization`s operations . For instance, an environmental _________ enables organizations to improve their environmental performance and an occupational health and safety _________ enables an organization to control its occupational health and safety risks, etc.

Exam Probability: **High**

11. *Answer choices:*

(see index for correct answer)

- a. subsystem
- b. co-design
- c. process system
- d. decentralized system

Guidance: level 1

:: Management ::

_________ is the identification, evaluation, and prioritization of risks followed by coordinated and economical application of resources to minimize, monitor, and control the probability or impact of unfortunate events or to maximize the realization of opportunities.

Exam Probability: **High**

12. *Answer choices:*

(see index for correct answer)

- a. Risk management
- b. Balanced scorecard
- c. Modes of leadership
- d. Energy management software

Guidance: level 1

:: Employment discrimination ::

A __________ is a metaphor used to represent an invisible barrier that keeps a given demographic from rising beyond a certain level in a hierarchy.

Exam Probability: **Low**

13. *Answer choices:*
(see index for correct answer)

- a. Marriage bars
- b. Employment discrimination law in the European Union
- c. Glass ceiling
- d. Employment Non-Discrimination Act

Guidance: level 1

:: Leadership ::

__________ Theory, or the __________ Model, is a model created by Paul Hersey and Ken Blanchard, developed while working on Management of Organizational Behavior. The theory was first introduced in 1969 as "life cycle theory of leadership". During the mid-1970s, life cycle theory of leadership was renamed " __________ Theory."

Exam Probability: **High**

14. *Answer choices:*
(see index for correct answer)

- a. Situational leadership
- b. Inspired Leadership Award
- c. Integral leadership
- d. Moral example

Guidance: level 1

:: Labor ::

The workforce or labour force is the labour pool in employment. It is generally used to describe those working for a single company or industry, but can also apply to a geographic region like a city, state, or country. Within a company, its value can be labelled as its "Workforce in Place". The workforce of a country includes both the employed and the unemployed. The labour force participation rate, LFPR , is the ratio between the labour force and the overall size of their cohort . The term generally excludes the employers or management, and can imply those involved in manual labour. It may also mean all those who are available for work.

Exam Probability: **Medium**

15. *Answer choices:*

(see index for correct answer)

- a. Strikebreaker
- b. Labor force
- c. Working Saturday
- d. Labour festival

Guidance: level 1

:: Unemployment ::

In economics, a _________ is a business cycle contraction when there is a general decline in economic activity. Macroeconomic indicators such as GDP , investment spending, capacity utilization, household income, business profits, and inflation fall, while bankruptcies and the unemployment rate rise. In the United Kingdom, it is defined as a negative economic growth for two consecutive quarters.

Exam Probability: **High**

16. *Answer choices:*

(see index for correct answer)

- a. Recession
- b. Waithood
- c. Youth unemployment
- d. Functional finance

Guidance: level 1

:: Survey methodology ::

An _________ is a conversation where questions are asked and answers are given. In common parlance, the word " _________ " refers to a one-on-one conversation between an _________ er and an _________ ee. The _________ er asks questions to which the _________ ee responds, usually so information may be transferred from _________ ee to _________ er . Sometimes, information can be transferred in both directions. It is a communication, unlike a speech, which produces a one-way flow of information.

Exam Probability: **High**

17. *Answer choices:*

(see index for correct answer)

- a. Sampling
- b. Swiss Centre of Expertise in the Social Sciences
- c. National Health Interview Survey
- d. World Association for Public Opinion Research

Guidance: level 1

:: Television commercials ::

_________ is a phenomenon whereby something new and somehow valuable is formed. The created item may be intangible or a physical object .

Exam Probability: **High**

18. *Answer choices:*

(see index for correct answer)

- a. Mountain
- b. Spongmonkeys
- c. Lamp
- d. Creativity

Guidance: level 1

:: ::

_________ is the administration of an organization, whether it is a business, a not-for-profit organization, or government body. _________ includes the activities of setting the strategy of an organization and coordinating the efforts of its employees to accomplish its objectives through the application of available resources, such as financial, natural, technological, and human resources. The term " _________ " may also refer to those people who manage an organization.

Exam Probability: **Medium**

19. *Answer choices:*

(see index for correct answer)

- a. Management
- b. open system
- c. corporate values
- d. Sarbanes-Oxley act of 2002

Guidance: level 1

:: Grounds for termination of employment ::

_________ is a habitual pattern of absence from a duty or obligation without good reason. Generally, _________ is unplanned absences. _________ has been viewed as an indicator of poor individual performance, as well as a breach of an implicit contract between employee and employer. It is seen as a management problem, and framed in economic or quasi-economic terms. More recent scholarship seeks to understand _________ as an indicator of psychological, medical, or social adjustment to work.

Exam Probability: **High**

20. *Answer choices:*

(see index for correct answer)

- a. No call, no show
- b. Absenteeism
- c. Sleeping while on duty
- d. Huffman v. Office of Personnel Management

Guidance: level 1

:: Organizational theory ::

Decentralisation is the process by which the activities of an organization, particularly those regarding planning and decision making, are distributed or delegated away from a central, authoritative location or group. Concepts of _________ have been applied to group dynamics and management science in private businesses and organizations, political science, law and public administration, economics, money and technology.

Exam Probability: **Medium**

21. *Answer choices:*

(see index for correct answer)

- a. Aston Group
- b. Organizational performance
- c. Mutual aid
- d. Decentralization

Guidance: level 1

:: Occupations ::

An _________ is a person who has a position of authority in a hierarchical organization. The term derives from the late Latin from officiarius, meaning "official".

Exam Probability: **Medium**

22. *Answer choices:*

(see index for correct answer)

- a. Officer
- b. Copyist
- c. Expeditor
- d. Interdisciplinarity

Guidance: level 1

:: Costs ::

In economics, _________ is the total economic cost of production and is made up of variable cost, which varies according to the quantity of a good produced and includes inputs such as labour and raw materials, plus fixed cost, which is independent of the quantity of a good produced and includes inputs that cannot be varied in the short term: fixed costs such as buildings and machinery, including sunk costs if any. Since cost is measured per unit of time, it is a flow variable.

Exam Probability: **High**

23. *Answer choices:*

(see index for correct answer)

- a. Average cost
- b. Prospective costs
- c. Sliding scale
- d. Total cost

Guidance: level 1

:: Data collection ::

A _________ is an utterance which typically functions as a request for information. _________ s can thus be understood as a kind of illocutionary act in the field of pragmatics or as special kinds of propositions in frameworks of formal semantics such as alternative semantics or inquisitive semantics. The information requested is expected to be provided in the form of an answer. _________ s are often conflated with interrogatives, which are the grammatical forms typically used to achieve them. Rhetorical _________ s, for example, are interrogative in form but may not be considered true _________ s as they are not expected to be answered. Conversely, non-interrogative grammatical structures may be considered _________ s as in the case of the imperative sentence "tell me your name".

Exam Probability: **Low**

24. *Answer choices:*

(see index for correct answer)

- a. Physical test
- b. Concrete slump test
- c. German General Social Survey
- d. Pop-up satellite archival tag

Guidance: level 1

:: Human resource management ::

__________ is the strategic approach to the effective management of people in an organization so that they help the business to gain a competitive advantage. It is designed to maximize employee performance in service of an employer`s strategic objectives. HR is primarily concerned with the management of people within organizations, focusing on policies and on systems. HR departments are responsible for overseeing employee-benefits design, employee recruitment, training and development, performance appraisal, and Reward management . HR also concerns itself with organizational change and industrial relations, that is, the balancing of organizational practices with requirements arising from collective bargaining and from governmental laws.

Exam Probability: **High**

25. *Answer choices:*

(see index for correct answer)

- a. Human resource management
- b. Contextual performance
- c. On-ramping
- d. Lego Serious Play

Guidance: level 1

:: Economic globalization ::

__________ is an agreement in which one company hires another company to be responsible for a planned or existing activity that is or could be done internally,and sometimes involves transferring employees and assets from one firm to another.

Exam Probability: **High**

26. *Answer choices:*

(see index for correct answer)

- a. Outsourcing
- b. global financial

Guidance: level 1

:: Marketing ::

_________ or stock control can be broadly defined as "the activity of checking a shop's stock." However, a more focused definition takes into account the more science-based, methodical practice of not only verifying a business' inventory but also focusing on the many related facets of inventory management "within an organisation to meet the demand placed upon that business economically." Other facets of _________ include supply chain management, production control, financial flexibility, and customer satisfaction. At the root of _________, however, is the _________ problem, which involves determining when to order, how much to order, and the logistics of those decisions.

Exam Probability: **Low**

27. *Answer choices:*

(see index for correct answer)

- a. Porter hypothesis
- b. Customer equity
- c. Pharmaceutical marketing
- d. Inventory control

Guidance: level 1

:: Strategic alliances ::

A _________ is an agreement between two or more parties to pursue a set of agreed upon objectives needed while remaining independent organizations. A _________ will usually fall short of a legal partnership entity, agency, or corporate affiliate relationship. Typically, two companies form a _________ when each possesses one or more business assets or have expertise that will help the other by enhancing their businesses. _________ s can develop in outsourcing relationships where the parties desire to achieve long-term win-win benefits and innovation based on mutually desired outcomes.

Exam Probability: **Low**

28. *Answer choices:*

(see index for correct answer)

- a. Defensive termination
- b. International joint venture

- c. Cross-licensing
- d. Strategic alliance

Guidance: level 1

:: Management ::

A __________ is a method or technique that has been generally accepted as superior to any alternatives because it produces results that are superior to those achieved by other means or because it has become a standard way of doing things, e.g., a standard way of complying with legal or ethical requirements.

Exam Probability: **High**

29. *Answer choices:*

(see index for correct answer)

- a. Court of Assistants
- b. Business rule mining
- c. Best practice
- d. Coworking

Guidance: level 1

:: Management occupations ::

__________ is the process of designing, launching and running a new business, which is often initially a small business. The people who create these businesses are called entrepreneurs.

Exam Probability: **Low**

30. *Answer choices:*

(see index for correct answer)

- a. Ceco
- b. Directeur sportif
- c. Pit manager
- d. Entrepreneurship

Guidance: level 1

:: Business law ::

A _________ is a business entity created by two or more parties, generally characterized by shared ownership, shared returns and risks, and shared governance. Companies typically pursue _________ s for one of four reasons: to access a new market, particularly emerging markets; to gain scale efficiencies by combining assets and operations; to share risk for major investments or projects; or to access skills and capabilities.

Exam Probability: **Low**

31. *Answer choices:*

(see index for correct answer)

- a. Process agent
- b. Trading while insolvent
- c. Joint venture
- d. OHADA

Guidance: level 1

:: ::

_________ is a means of protection from financial loss. It is a form of risk management, primarily used to hedge against the risk of a contingent or uncertain loss

Exam Probability: **Medium**

32. *Answer choices:*

(see index for correct answer)

- a. co-culture
- b. Sarbanes-Oxley act of 2002
- c. Insurance
- d. imperative

Guidance: level 1

:: Evaluation ::

_________ solving consists of using generic or ad hoc methods in an orderly manner to find solutions to _________ s. Some of the _________ -solving techniques developed and used in philosophy, artificial intelligence, computer science, engineering, mathematics, or medicine are related to mental _________ -solving techniques studied in psychology.

Exam Probability: **High**

33. *Answer choices:*
(see index for correct answer)

- a. Continuous assessment
- b. Educational evaluation
- c. Summative assessment
- d. Problem

Guidance: level 1

:: Management occupations ::

_________ ship is the process of designing, launching and running a new business, which is often initially a small business. The people who create these businesses are called _________ s.

Exam Probability: **Medium**

34. *Answer choices:*
(see index for correct answer)

- a. entrepreneurial
- b. Female entrepreneur
- c. Entrepreneur
- d. Pit manager

Guidance: level 1

:: Industrial Revolution ::

The _________ , now also known as the First _________ , was the transition to new manufacturing processes in Europe and the US, in the period from about 1760 to sometime between 1820 and 1840. This transition included going from hand production methods to machines, new chemical manufacturing and iron production processes, the increasing use of steam power and water power, the development of machine tools and the rise of the mechanized factory system. The _________ also led to an unprecedented rise in the rate of population growth.

Exam Probability: **Low**

35. *Answer choices:*

(see index for correct answer)

- a. Coalbrookdale by Night
- b. Grubb Family Iron Dynasty
- c. Industrial Revolution
- d. Torr Vale Mill

Guidance: level 1

:: ::

In organizational behavior and industrial/organizational psychology, proactivity or _________ behavior by individuals refers to anticipatory, change-oriented and self-initiated behavior in situations. _________ behavior involves acting in advance of a future situation, rather than just reacting. It means taking control and making things happen rather than just adjusting to a situation or waiting for something to happen. _________ employees generally do not need to be asked to act, nor do they require detailed instructions.

Exam Probability: **Medium**

36. *Answer choices:*

(see index for correct answer)

- a. Character
- b. Proactive
- c. deep-level diversity
- d. interpersonal communication

Guidance: level 1

:: ::

A _________ or sample _________ is a single measure of some attribute of a sample . It is calculated by applying a function to the values of the items of the sample, which are known together as a set of data.

Exam Probability: **Low**

37. *Answer choices:*

(see index for correct answer)

- a. interpersonal communication
- b. imperative
- c. hierarchical perspective
- d. Statistic

Guidance: level 1

:: Electronic feedback ::

_________ occurs when outputs of a system are routed back as inputs as part of a chain of cause-and-effect that forms a circuit or loop. The system can then be said to feed back into itself. The notion of cause-and-effect has to be handled carefully when applied to _________ systems.

Exam Probability: **Medium**

38. *Answer choices:*

(see index for correct answer)

- a. Positive feedback
- b. feedback loop

Guidance: level 1

:: Regression analysis ::

A _________ often refers to a set of documented requirements to be satisfied by a material, design, product, or service. A _________ is often a type of technical standard.

Exam Probability: **Low**

39. *Answer choices:*

(see index for correct answer)

- a. Path coefficient
- b. Quantile regression
- c. Specification
- d. Ordered logit

Guidance: level 1

:: Business law ::

A _________ is a group of people who jointly supervise the activities of an organization, which can be either a for-profit business, nonprofit organization, or a government agency. Such a board`s powers, duties, and responsibilities are determined by government regulations and the organization`s own constitution and bylaws. These authorities may specify the number of members of the board, how they are to be chosen, and how often they are to meet.

Exam Probability: **Low**

40. *Answer choices:*

(see index for correct answer)

- a. Official Assignee
- b. United Kingdom commercial law
- c. Board of directors
- d. Family and Medical Leave Act of 1993

Guidance: level 1

:: ::

_________ consists of using generic or ad hoc methods in an orderly manner to find solutions to problems. Some of the problem-solving techniques developed and used in philosophy, artificial intelligence, computer science, engineering, mathematics, or medicine are related to mental problem-solving techniques studied in psychology.

Exam Probability: **Low**

41. *Answer choices:*

(see index for correct answer)

- a. open system
- b. cultural
- c. levels of analysis

- d. hierarchical

Guidance: level 1

:: Logistics ::

__________ is generally the detailed organization and implementation of a complex operation. In a general business sense, __________ is the management of the flow of things between the point of origin and the point of consumption in order to meet requirements of customers or corporations. The resources managed in __________ may include tangible goods such as materials, equipment, and supplies, as well as food and other consumable items. The __________ of physical items usually involves the integration of information flow, materials handling, production, packaging, inventory, transportation, warehousing, and often security.

Exam Probability: **High**

42. *Answer choices:*
(see index for correct answer)

- a. Waybill
- b. Menlo Worldwide Logistics
- c. Freightos
- d. Logistics

Guidance: level 1

:: Human resource management ::

__________ involves improving the effectiveness of organizations and the individuals and teams within them. Training may be viewed as related to immediate changes in organizational effectiveness via organized instruction, while development is related to the progress of longer-term organizational and employee goals. While __________ technically have differing definitions, the two are oftentimes used interchangeably and/or together. __________ has historically been a topic within applied psychology but has within the last two decades become closely associated with human resources management, talent management, human resources development, instructional design, human factors, and knowledge management.

Exam Probability: **High**

43. *Answer choices:*

(see index for correct answer)

- a. Personal development planning
- b. Autonomous work group
- c. Organizational culture
- d. Income bracket

Guidance: level 1

:: Monopoly (economics) ::

A _________ is a form of intellectual property that gives its owner the legal right to exclude others from making, using, selling, and importing an invention for a limited period of years, in exchange for publishing an enabling public disclosure of the invention. In most countries _________ rights fall under civil law and the _________ holder needs to sue someone infringing the _________ in order to enforce his or her rights. In some industries _________ s are an essential form of competitive advantage; in others they are irrelevant.

Exam Probability: **Medium**

44. *Answer choices:*

(see index for correct answer)

- a. Eisenkammer Pirna
- b. Sherman Antitrust Act
- c. Patent
- d. Monopsony

Guidance: level 1

:: Teams ::

A _________ usually refers to a group of individuals who work together from different geographic locations and rely on communication technology such as email, FAX, and video or voice conferencing services in order to collaborate. The term can also refer to groups or teams that work together asynchronously or across organizational levels. Powell, Piccoli and Ives define _________ s as "groups of geographically, organizationally and/or time dispersed workers brought together by information and telecommunication technologies to accomplish one or more organizational tasks." According to Ale Ebrahim et. al. , _________ s can also be defined as "small temporary groups of geographically, organizationally and/or time dispersed knowledge workers who coordinate their work predominantly with electronic information and communication technologies in order to accomplish one or more organization tasks."

Exam Probability: **Low**

45. *Answer choices:*

(see index for correct answer)

- a. Team-building
- b. Virtual team

Guidance: level 1

:: Leadership ::

_________ /Management is a part of a style of leadership that focuses on supervision, organization, and performance; it is an integral part of the Full Range Leadership Model. _________ is a style of leadership in which leaders promote compliance by followers through both rewards and punishments. Through a rewards and punishments system, transactional leaders are able to keep followers motivated for the short-term. Unlike transformational leaders, those using the transactional approach are not looking to change the future, they look to keep things the same. Leaders using _________ as a model pay attention to followers` work in order to find faults and deviations.

Exam Probability: **High**

46. *Answer choices:*

(see index for correct answer)

- a. Sex differences in leadership

- b. Transactional leadership
- c. The Leadership Council
- d. Maintenance actions

Guidance: level 1

:: Game theory ::

To _________ is to make a deal between different parties where each party gives up part of their demand. In arguments, _________ is a concept of finding agreement through communication, through a mutual acceptance of terms—often involving variations from an original goal or desires.

Exam Probability: **High**

47. *Answer choices:*
(see index for correct answer)

- a. General game playing
- b. Compromise
- c. Beer distribution game
- d. Game semantics

Guidance: level 1

:: Evaluation ::

_________ is the practice of being honest and showing a consistent and uncompromising adherence to strong moral and ethical principles and values.In ethics, _________ is regarded as the honesty and truthfulness or accuracy of one`s actions. _________ can stand in opposition to hypocrisy, in that judging with the standards of _________ involves regarding internal consistency as a virtue, and suggests that parties holding within themselves apparently conflicting values should account for the discrepancy or alter their beliefs. The word _________ evolved from the Latin adjective integer, meaning whole or complete. In this context, _________ is the inner sense of "wholeness" deriving from qualities such as honesty and consistency of character. As such, one may judge that others "have _________ " to the extent that they act according to the values, beliefs and principles they claim to hold.

Exam Probability: **Low**

48. *Answer choices:*

(see index for correct answer)

- a. Integrity
- b. Joint Committee on Standards for Educational Evaluation
- c. Evaluation approaches
- d. Common Criteria Testing Laboratory

Guidance: level 1

:: ::

An _________ is the production of goods or related services within an economy. The major source of revenue of a group or company is the indicator of its relevant _________. When a large group has multiple sources of revenue generation, it is considered to be working in different industries. Manufacturing _________ became a key sector of production and labour in European and North American countries during the Industrial Revolution, upsetting previous mercantile and feudal economies. This came through many successive rapid advances in technology, such as the production of steel and coal.

Exam Probability: **High**

49. *Answer choices:*

(see index for correct answer)

- a. process perspective
- b. hierarchical
- c. functional perspective
- d. Industry

Guidance: level 1

:: Workplace ::

__________ is asystematic determination of a subject`s merit, worth and significance, using criteria governed by a set of standards. It can assist an organization, program, design, project or any other intervention or initiative to assess any aim, realisable concept/proposal, or any alternative, to help in decision-making; or to ascertain the degree of achievement or value in regard to the aim and objectives and results of any such action that has been completed. The primary purpose of __________, in addition to gaining insight into prior or existing initiatives, is to enable reflection and assist in the identification of future change.

Exam Probability: **High**

50. *Answer choices:*

(see index for correct answer)

- a. Work etiquette
- b. Workplace spirituality
- c. Feminisation of the workplace
- d. Workplace wellness

Guidance: level 1

:: Planning ::

__________ is a high level plan to achieve one or more goals under conditions of uncertainty. In the sense of the "art of the general," which included several subsets of skills including tactics, siegecraft, logistics etc., the term came into use in the 6th century C.E. in East Roman terminology, and was translated into Western vernacular languages only in the 18th century. From then until the 20th century, the word "__________" came to denote "a comprehensive way to try to pursue political ends, including the threat or actual use of force, in a dialectic of wills" in a military conflict, in which both adversaries interact.

Exam Probability: **Medium**

51. *Answer choices:*

(see index for correct answer)

- a. Default effect
- b. Strategy
- c. Concept driven strategy
- d. Commercial area

Guidance: level 1

:: Production and manufacturing ::

__________ is a set of techniques and tools for process improvement. Though as a shortened form it may be found written as 6S, it should not be confused with the methodology known as 6S .

Exam Probability: **Low**

52. *Answer choices:*

(see index for correct answer)

- a. Safety Network International e.V.
- b. Transfer cars
- c. Capacity planning
- d. Six Sigma

Guidance: level 1

:: Human resource management ::

An organizational chart is a diagram that shows the structure of an organization and the relationships and relative ranks of its parts and positions/jobs. The term is also used for similar diagrams, for example ones showing the different elements of a field of knowledge or a group of languages.

Exam Probability: **Medium**

53. *Answer choices:*

(see index for correct answer)

- a. Organization chart
- b. Professional employer organization
- c. E-HRM
- d. Simultaneous recruiting of new graduates

Guidance: level 1

:: Human resource management ::

_________ is the corporate management term for the act of reorganizing the legal, ownership, operational, or other structures of a company for the purpose of making it more profitable, or better organized for its present needs. Other reasons for _________ include a change of ownership or ownership structure, demerger, or a response to a crisis or major change in the business such as bankruptcy, repositioning, or buyout. _________ may also be described as corporate _________ , debt _________ and financial _________ .

Exam Probability: **High**

54. *Answer choices:*

(see index for correct answer)

- a. Behavioral Competencies
- b. Restructuring
- c. Reward management
- d. Focal Point Review

Guidance: level 1

:: Statistical terminology ::

_________ is the ability to avoid wasting materials, energy, efforts, money, and time in doing something or in producing a desired result. In a more general sense, it is the ability to do things well, successfully, and without waste. In more mathematical or scientific terms, it is a measure of the extent to which input is well used for an intended task or function . It often specifically comprises the capability of a specific application of effort to produce a specific outcome with a minimum amount or quantity of waste, expense, or unnecessary effort. _________ refers to very different inputs and outputs in different fields and industries.

Exam Probability: **Medium**

55. *Answer choices:*

(see index for correct answer)

- a. Univariate
- b. Observable variable
- c. Efficiency
- d. Studentization

Guidance: level 1

:: ::

_________ involves decision making. It can include judging the merits of multiple options and selecting one or more of them. One can make a _________ between imagined options or between real options followed by the corresponding action. For example, a traveler might choose a route for a journey based on the preference of arriving at a given destination as soon as possible. The preferred route can then follow from information such as the length of each of the possible routes, traffic conditions, etc. The arrival at a _________ can include more complex motivators such as cognition, instinct, and feeling.

Exam Probability: **High**

56. *Answer choices:*

(see index for correct answer)

- a. personal values
- b. Choice
- c. deep-level diversity
- d. Character

Guidance: level 1

:: Project management ::

Some scenarios associate "this kind of planning" with learning "life skills". _________ s are necessary, or at least useful, in situations where individuals need to know what time they must be at a specific location to receive a specific service, and where people need to accomplish a set of goals within a set time period.

Exam Probability: **High**

57. *Answer choices:*

(see index for correct answer)

- a. Advanced Integrated Practice
- b. Executive sponsor
- c. Level of Effort
- d. Schedule

Guidance: level 1

:: Human resource management ::

_________ are the people who make up the workforce of an organization, business sector, or economy. "Human capital" is sometimes used synonymously with " _________ ", although human capital typically refers to a narrower effect . Likewise, other terms sometimes used include manpower, talent, labor, personnel, or simply people.

Exam Probability: **Medium**

58. *Answer choices:*

(see index for correct answer)

- a. Lego Serious Play
- b. Turnover
- c. Job analysis
- d. Human resources

Guidance: level 1

:: Business terms ::

A _________ is a short statement of why an organization exists, what its overall goal is, identifying the goal of its operations: what kind of product or service it provides, its primary customers or market, and its geographical region of operation. It may include a short statement of such fundamental matters as the organization`s values or philosophies, a business`s main competitive advantages, or a desired future state—the "vision".

Exam Probability: **Medium**

59. *Answer choices:*

(see index for correct answer)

- a. front office
- b. year-to-date
- c. Mission statement
- d. strategic plan

Guidance: level 1

Business law

Corporate law (also known as business law) is the body of law governing the rights, relations, and conduct of persons, companies, organizations and businesses. It refers to the legal practice relating to, or the theory of corporations. Corporate law often describes the law relating to matters which derive directly from the life-cycle of a corporation. It thus encompasses the formation, funding, governance, and death of a corporation.

:: ::

A _________ loan or, simply, _________ is used either by purchasers of real property to raise funds to buy real estate, or alternatively by existing property owners to raise funds for any purpose, while putting a lien on the property being _________d. The loan is "secured" on the borrower`s property through a process known as _________ origination. This means that a legal mechanism is put into place which allows the lender to take possession and sell the secured property to pay off the loan in the event the borrower defaults on the loan or otherwise fails to abide by its terms. The word _________ is derived from a Law French term used in Britain in the Middle Ages meaning "death pledge" and refers to the pledge ending when either the obligation is fulfilled or the property is taken through foreclosure. A _________ can also be described as "a borrower giving consideration in the form of a collateral for a benefit ".

Exam Probability: **Medium**

1. *Answer choices:*

(see index for correct answer)

- a. empathy
- b. hierarchical perspective
- c. Sarbanes-Oxley act of 2002
- d. Mortgage

Guidance: level 1

:: Contract law ::

A __________, unlike a void contract, is a valid contract which may be either affirmed or rejected at the option of one of the parties. At most, one party to the contract is bound. The unbound party may repudiate the contract, at which time the contract becomes void.

Exam Probability: **High**

2. *Answer choices:*

(see index for correct answer)

- a. Time is of the essence
- b. Four corners
- c. Good faith
- d. Voidable contract

Guidance: level 1

:: Contract law ::

Coercion is the practice of forcing another party to act in an involuntary manner by use of threats or force. It involves a set of various types of forceful actions that violate the free will of an individual to induce a desired response, for example: a bully demanding lunch money from a student or the student gets beaten. These actions may include extortion, blackmail, torture, threats to induce favors, or even sexual assault. In law, coercion is codified as a __________ crime. Such actions are used as leverage, to force the victim to act in a way contrary to their own interests. Coercion may involve the actual infliction of physical pain/injury or psychological harm in order to enhance the credibility of a threat. The threat of further harm may lead to the cooperation or obedience of the person being coerced.

Exam Probability: **Low**

3. *Answer choices:*

(see index for correct answer)

- a. Prenuptial agreement
- b. Mirror image rule
- c. Duress
- d. Cost-plus-incentive fee

Guidance: level 1

:: ::

_________ Motor Company is an American multinational automaker that has its main headquarter in Dearborn, Michigan, a suburb of Detroit. It was founded by Henry _________ and incorporated on June 16, 1903. The company sells automobiles and commercial vehicles under the _________ brand and most luxury cars under the Lincoln brand. _________ also owns Brazilian SUV manufacturer Troller, an 8% stake in Aston Martin of the United Kingdom and a 32% stake in Jiangling Motors. It also has joint-ventures in China , Taiwan , Thailand , Turkey , and Russia . The company is listed on the New York Stock Exchange and is controlled by the _________ family; they have minority ownership but the majority of the voting power.

Exam Probability: **Medium**

4. *Answer choices:*

(see index for correct answer)

- a. Ford
- b. levels of analysis
- c. empathy
- d. deep-level diversity

Guidance: level 1

:: Business law ::

An _________ is a clause in a contract that requires the parties to resolve their disputes through an arbitration process. Although such a clause may or may not specify that arbitration occur within a specific jurisdiction, it always binds the parties to a type of resolution outside the courts, and is therefore considered a kind of forum selection clause.

Exam Probability: **Low**

5. *Answer choices:*

(see index for correct answer)

- a. Limited liability
- b. Arbitration clause
- c. Enhanced use lease
- d. Lease

Guidance: level 1

:: ::

A _________ is a sworn body of people convened to render an impartial verdict officially submitted to them by a court, or to set a penalty or judgment. Modern juries tend to be found in courts to ascertain the guilt or lack thereof in a crime. In Anglophone jurisdictions, the verdict may be guilty or not guilty . The old institution of grand juries still exists in some places, particularly the United States, to investigate whether enough evidence of a crime exists to bring someone to trial.

Exam Probability: **High**

6. *Answer choices:*

(see index for correct answer)

- a. cultural
- b. open system
- c. surface-level diversity
- d. imperative

Guidance: level 1

:: ::

_________ , often abbreviated cert. in the United States, is a process for seeking judicial review and a writ issued by a court that agrees to review. A _________ is issued by a superior court, directing an inferior court, tribunal, or other public authority to send the record of a proceeding for review.

Exam Probability: **Low**

7. *Answer choices:*

(see index for correct answer)

- a. open system
- b. cultural
- c. empathy
- d. Certiorari

Guidance: level 1

:: Progressive Era in the United States ::

The Clayton Antitrust Act of 1914 , was a part of United States antitrust law with the goal of adding further substance to the U.S. antitrust law regime; the _________ sought to prevent anticompetitive practices in their incipiency. That regime started with the Sherman Antitrust Act of 1890, the first Federal law outlawing practices considered harmful to consumers . The _________ specified particular prohibited conduct, the three-level enforcement scheme, the exemptions, and the remedial measures.

Exam Probability: **High**

8. *Answer choices:*
(see index for correct answer)

- a. pragmatism
- b. Clayton Act
- c. Mann Act

Guidance: level 1

:: Sureties ::

In finance, a _________ , _________ bond or guaranty involves a promise by one party to assume responsibility for the debt obligation of a borrower if that borrower defaults. The person or company providing the promise is also known as a " _________ " or as a "guarantor".

Exam Probability: **Low**

9. *Answer choices:*
(see index for correct answer)

- a. Surety
- b. Aval
- c. Peace bond
- d. Parole bond

Guidance: level 1

:: Project management ::

A _________ is a source or supply from which a benefit is produced and it has some utility. _________ s can broadly be classified upon their availability—they are classified into renewable and non-renewable _________ s.Examples of non renewable _________ s are coal ,crude oil natural gas nuclear energy etc. Examples of renewable _________ s are air,water,wind,solar energy etc. They can also be classified as actual and potential on the basis of level of development and use, on the basis of origin they can be classified as biotic and abiotic, and on the basis of their distribution, as ubiquitous and localized . An item becomes a _________ with time and developing technology. Typically, _________ s are materials, energy, services, staff, knowledge, or other assets that are transformed to produce benefit and in the process may be consumed or made unavailable. Benefits of _________ utilization may include increased wealth, proper functioning of a system, or enhanced well-being. From a human perspective a natural _________ is anything obtained from the environment to satisfy human needs and wants. From a broader biological or ecological perspective a _________ satisfies the needs of a living organism .

Exam Probability: **Medium**

10. *Answer choices:*

(see index for correct answer)

- a. Resource
- b. Gantt chart
- c. Student syndrome
- d. Project team

Guidance: level 1

:: Negotiable instrument law ::

In the United States, The Preservation of Consumers' Claims and Defenses [_________ Rule], formally known as the "Trade Regulation Rule Concerning Preservation of Consumers` Claims and Defenses," protects consumers when merchants sell a consumer`s credit contracts to other lenders. Specifically, it preserves consumers` right to assert the same legal claims and defenses against anyone who purchases the credit contract, as they would have against the seller who originally provided the credit. [16 Code of Federal Regulations Part 433]

Exam Probability: **High**

11. *Answer choices:*
(see index for correct answer)

- a. Blank endorsement
- b. Holder in due course
- c. Expedited Funds Availability Act
- d. Real defense

Guidance: level 1

:: Information technology audit ::

__________ is the act of using a computer to take or alter electronic data, or to gain unlawful use of a computer or system. In the United States, __________ is specifically proscribed by the __________ and Abuse Act, which criminalizes computer-related acts under federal jurisdiction. Types of __________ include.

Exam Probability: **High**

12. *Answer choices:*
(see index for correct answer)

- a. Computer fraud
- b. Code audit
- c. Computer forensics
- d. Information technology audit

Guidance: level 1

:: ::

__________ is a process under which executive or legislative actions are subject to review by the judiciary. A court with authority for __________ may invalidate laws, acts and governmental actions that are incompatible with a higher authority: an executive decision may be invalidated for being unlawful or a statute may be invalidated for violating the terms of a constitution. __________ is one of the checks and balances in the separation of powers: the power of the judiciary to supervise the legislative and executive branches when the latter exceed their authority. The doctrine varies between jurisdictions, so the procedure and scope of __________ may differ between and within countries.

Exam Probability: **High**

13. *Answer choices:*

(see index for correct answer)

- a. open system
- b. co-culture
- c. deep-level diversity
- d. Judicial review

Guidance: level 1

:: Competition law ::

In competition law, a __________ is a market in which a particular product or service is sold. It is the intersection of a relevant product market and a relevant geographic market. The European Commission defines a __________ and its product and geographic components as follows.

Exam Probability: **Low**

14. *Answer choices:*

(see index for correct answer)

- a. Relevant market
- b. Centre for Competition Policy
- c. European Union Microsoft competition case
- d. History of competition law

Guidance: level 1

:: Abuse of the legal system ::

__________ occurs when a person is restricted in their personal movement within any area without justification or consent. Actual physical restraint is not necessary for __________ to occur. A __________ claim may be made based upon private acts, or upon wrongful governmental detention. For detention by the police, proof of __________ provides a basis to obtain a writ of habeas corpus.

Exam Probability: **Medium**

15. *Answer choices:*

(see index for correct answer)

- a. False arrest

- b. Obstruction of Justice
- c. False imprisonment

Guidance: level 1

:: Advertising ::

In law, __________ is speech or writing on behalf of a business with the intent of earning revenue or a profit. It is economic in nature and usually attempts to persuade consumers to purchase the business`s product or service. The Supreme Court of the United States defines __________ as speech that "proposes a commercial transaction".

Exam Probability: **Low**

16. *Answer choices:*

(see index for correct answer)

- a. Commercial speech
- b. Fear mongering
- c. Ad-ID
- d. Effective frequency

Guidance: level 1

:: Contract law ::

In the law of contracts, the __________ , also referred to as an unequivocal and absolute acceptance requirement, states that an offer must be accepted exactly with no modifications. The offeror is the master of one`s own offer. An attempt to accept the offer on different terms instead creates a counter-offer, and this constitutes a rejection of the original offer.

Exam Probability: **Low**

17. *Answer choices:*

(see index for correct answer)

- a. Parol evidence rule
- b. Quantum meruit
- c. Mirror image rule
- d. Pre-existing duty rule

Guidance: level 1

:: Business law ::

__________ is where a person`s financial liability is limited to a fixed sum, most commonly the value of a person`s investment in a company or partnership. If a company with __________ is sued, then the claimants are suing the company, not its owners or investors. A shareholder in a limited company is not personally liable for any of the debts of the company, other than for the amount already invested in the company and for any unpaid amount on the shares in the company, if any. The same is true for the members of a __________ partnership and the limited partners in a limited partnership. By contrast, sole proprietors and partners in general partnerships are each liable for all the debts of the business .

Exam Probability: **Low**

18. *Answer choices:*

(see index for correct answer)

- a. Limited liability
- b. Ordinary resolution
- c. Lease
- d. Limited partnership

Guidance: level 1

:: Real property law ::

__________, sometimes colloquially described as ‘squatter`s rights’, is a legal principle under which a person who does not have legal title to a piece of property—usually land —acquires legal ownership based on continuous possession or occupation of the land without the permission of its legal owner.

Exam Probability: **Medium**

19. *Answer choices:*

(see index for correct answer)

- a. 72-hour clause
- b. Adverse possession
- c. Solar easement
- d. Thomond deeds

Guidance: level 1

:: Real property law ::

A __________ is any legal instrument in writing which passes, affirms or confirms an interest, right, or property and that is signed, attested, delivered, and in some jurisdictions, sealed. It is commonly associated with transferring title to property. The __________ has a greater presumption of validity and is less rebuttable than an instrument signed by the party to the __________. A __________ can be unilateral or bilateral. __________s include conveyances, commissions, licenses, patents, diplomas, and conditionally powers of attorney if executed as __________s. The __________ is the modern descendant of the medieval charter, and delivery is thought to symbolically replace the ancient ceremony of livery of seisin.

Exam Probability: **Medium**

20. *Answer choices:*

(see index for correct answer)

- a. Deed
- b. Straw deed
- c. Public land
- d. Avenage

Guidance: level 1

:: Legal terms ::

__________ is the set of laws that governs how members of a society are to behave. It is contrasted with procedural law, which is the set of procedures for making, administering, and enforcing __________. __________ defines rights and responsibilities in civil law, and crimes and punishments in criminal law. It may be codified in statutes or exist through precedent in common law.

Exam Probability: **High**

21. *Answer choices:*

(see index for correct answer)

- a. Family purpose doctrine
- b. Natural person
- c. Community standards
- d. Substantive law

Guidance: level 1

:: Contract law ::

An _________, or simply option, is defined as "a promise which meets the requirements for the formation of a contract and limits the promisor`s power to revoke an offer."

Exam Probability: **Low**

22. *Answer choices:*

(see index for correct answer)

- a. Fixed-price contract
- b. Franchisor
- c. Void contract
- d. Option contract

Guidance: level 1

:: Criminal law ::

_________ is the body of law that relates to crime. It proscribes conduct perceived as threatening, harmful, or otherwise endangering to the property, health, safety, and moral welfare of people inclusive of one`s self. Most _________ is established by statute, which is to say that the laws are enacted by a legislature. _________ includes the punishment and rehabilitation of people who violate such laws. _________ varies according to jurisdiction, and differs from civil law, where emphasis is more on dispute resolution and victim compensation, rather than on punishment or rehabilitation. Criminal procedure is a formalized official activity that authenticates the fact of commission of a crime and authorizes punitive or rehabilitative treatment of the offender.

Exam Probability: **High**

23. *Answer choices:*

(see index for correct answer)

- a. Self-incrimination
- b. Criminal law
- c. Mala prohibita
- d. Mala in se

Guidance: level 1

:: ::

A __________ is any person who contracts to acquire an asset in return for some form of consideration.

Exam Probability: **Low**

24. *Answer choices:*

(see index for correct answer)

- a. process perspective
- b. interpersonal communication
- c. corporate values
- d. Buyer

Guidance: level 1

:: Employment discrimination ::

__________ is a form of discrimination based on race, gender, religion, national origin, physical or mental disability, age, sexual orientation, and gender identity by employers. Earnings differentials or occupational differentiation—where differences in pay come from differences in qualifications or responsibilities—should not be confused with __________ . Discrimination can be intended and involve disparate treatment of a group or be unintended, yet create disparate impact for a group.

Exam Probability: **Medium**

25. *Answer choices:*

(see index for correct answer)

- a. MacBride Principles
- b. Employment discrimination
- c. Marriage bars
- d. Employment discrimination law in the European Union

Guidance: level 1

:: ::

The __________ of 1933, also known as the 1933 Act, the __________, the Truth in __________, the Federal __________, and the `33 Act, was enacted by the United States Congress on May 27, 1933, during the Great Depression, after the stock market crash of 1929. Legislated pursuant to the Interstate Commerce Clause of the Constitution, it requires every offer or sale of securities that uses the means and instrumentalities of interstate commerce to be registered with the SEC pursuant to the 1933 Act, unless an exemption from registration exists under the law. The term "means and instrumentalities of interstate commerce" is extremely broad and it is virtually impossible to avoid the operation of the statute by attempting to offer or sell a security without using an "instrumentality" of interstate commerce. Any use of a telephone, for example, or the mails would probably be enough to subject the transaction to the statute.

Exam Probability: **Medium**

26. *Answer choices:*

(see index for correct answer)

- a. co-culture
- b. corporate values
- c. deep-level diversity
- d. Securities Act

Guidance: level 1

:: Legal procedure ::

An __________ is generally the first occasion that the trier of fact has to hear from a lawyer in a trial, aside possibly from questioning during voir dire. The __________ is generally constructed to serve as a "road map" for the fact-finder. This is especially essential, in many jury trials, since jurors know nothing at all about the case before the trial, . Though such statements may be dramatic and vivid, they must be limited to the evidence reasonably expected to be presented during the trial. Attorneys generally conclude __________s with a reminder that at the conclusion of evidence, the attorney will return to ask the fact-finder to find in his or her client`s favor.

Exam Probability: **Medium**

27. *Answer choices:*
(see index for correct answer)

- a. Procedural law
- b. civil procedure
- c. appellate
- d. Closing argument

Guidance: level 1

:: Treaties ::

A __________ is an agreement under international law entered into by actors in international law, namely sovereign states and international organizations. A __________ may also be known as an agreement, protocol, covenant, convention, pact, or exchange of letters, among other terms. Regardless of terminology, all of these forms of agreements are, under international law, equally considered treaties and the rules are the same.

Exam Probability: **High**

28. *Answer choices:*
(see index for correct answer)

- a. Reservation
- b. Treaty
- c. Multilateral treaty
- d. Quasi alliance

Guidance: level 1

:: ::

An __________ is a written sworn statement of fact voluntarily made by an affiant or deponent under an oath or affirmation administered by a person authorized to do so by law. Such statement is witnessed as to the authenticity of the affiant`s signature by a taker of oaths, such as a notary public or commissioner of oaths. An __________ is a type of verified statement or showing, or in other words, it contains a verification, meaning it is under oath or penalty of perjury, and this serves as evidence to its veracity and is required for court proceedings.

Exam Probability: **Medium**

29. *Answer choices:*
(see index for correct answer)

- a. cultural
- b. corporate values
- c. hierarchical perspective
- d. personal values

Guidance: level 1

:: Real property law ::

__________ is the judicial process whereby a will is "proved" in a court of law and accepted as a valid public document that is the true last testament of the deceased, or whereby the estate is settled according to the laws of intestacy in the state of residence [or real property] of the deceased at time of death in the absence of a legal will.

Exam Probability: **Low**

30. *Answer choices:*
(see index for correct answer)

- a. Lis pendens
- b. Grant deed
- c. Real Estate Settlement Procedures Act
- d. Probate

Guidance: level 1

:: Intention ::

__________ is the mental element of a person`s intention to commit a crime; or knowledge that one`s action or lack of action would cause a crime to be committed. It is a necessary element of many crimes.

Exam Probability: **Medium**

31. *Answer choices:*
(see index for correct answer)

- a. Mens rea
- b. Letter of Intent

Guidance: level 1

:: ::

__________ , also referred to as orthostasis, is a human position in which the body is held in an upright position and supported only by the feet.

Exam Probability: **Medium**

32. *Answer choices:*

(see index for correct answer)

- a. interpersonal communication
- b. hierarchical
- c. Standing
- d. Sarbanes-Oxley act of 2002

Guidance: level 1

:: ::

A __________ is an organization, usually a group of people or a company, authorized to act as a single entity and recognized as such in law. Early incorporated entities were established by charter . Most jurisdictions now allow the creation of new __________ s through registration.

Exam Probability: **Low**

33. *Answer choices:*

(see index for correct answer)

- a. functional perspective
- b. Sarbanes-Oxley act of 2002
- c. cultural
- d. Corporation

Guidance: level 1

:: Euthenics ::

_________ is an ethical framework and suggests that an entity, be it an organization or individual, has an obligation to act for the benefit of society at large. _________ is a duty every individual has to perform so as to maintain a balance between the economy and the ecosystems. A trade-off may exist between economic development, in the material sense, and the welfare of the society and environment, though this has been challenged by many reports over the past decade. _________ means sustaining the equilibrium between the two. It pertains not only to business organizations but also to everyone whose any action impacts the environment. This responsibility can be passive, by avoiding engaging in socially harmful acts, or active, by performing activities that directly advance social goals. _________ must be intergenerational since the actions of one generation have consequences on those following.

Exam Probability: **High**

34. *Answer choices:*

(see index for correct answer)

- a. Euthenics
- b. Home economics
- c. Minnie Cumnock Blodgett
- d. Family and consumer science

Guidance: level 1

:: Contract law ::

In contract law, a _________ is a promise which is not a condition of the contract or an innominate term: it is a term "not going to the root of the contract", and which only entitles the innocent party to damages if it is breached: i.e. the _________ is not true or the defaulting party does not perform the contract in accordance with the terms of the _________ . A _________ is not guarantee. It is a mere promise. It may be enforced if it is breached by an award for the legal remedy of damages.

Exam Probability: **Low**

35. *Answer choices:*

(see index for correct answer)

- a. Non-repudiation
- b. Last shot
- c. Warranty tolling

- d. Oral contract

Guidance: level 1

:: Debt ::

__________ is the trust which allows one party to provide money or resources to another party wherein the second party does not reimburse the first party immediately , but promises either to repay or return those resources at a later date. In other words, __________ is a method of making reciprocity formal, legally enforceable, and extensible to a large group of unrelated people.

Exam Probability: **High**

36. *Answer choices:*

(see index for correct answer)

- a. Student debt
- b. Financial assistance
- c. Debt wall
- d. Paid outside closing

Guidance: level 1

:: Debt ::

A __________ is a party that has a claim on the services of a second party. It is a person or institution to whom money is owed. The first party, in general, has provided some property or service to the second party under the assumption that the second party will return an equivalent property and service. The second party is frequently called a debtor or borrower. The first party is called the __________ , which is the lender of property, service, or money.

Exam Probability: **Low**

37. *Answer choices:*

(see index for correct answer)

- a. Recourse debt
- b. Medical debt
- c. Consumer debt
- d. Floating charge

Guidance: level 1

:: ::

A federation is a political entity characterized by a union of partially self-governing provinces, states, or other regions under a central __________. In a federation, the self-governing status of the component states, as well as the division of power between them and the central government, is typically constitutionally entrenched and may not be altered by a unilateral decision of either party, the states or the federal political body. Alternatively, federation is a form of government in which sovereign power is formally divided between a central authority and a number of constituent regions so that each region retains some degree of control over its internal affairs. It is often argued that federal states where the central government has the constitutional authority to suspend a constituent state`s government by invoking gross mismanagement or civil unrest, or to adopt national legislation that overrides or infringe on the constituent states` powers by invoking the central government`s constitutional authority to ensure "peace and good government" or to implement obligations contracted under an international treaty, are not truly federal states.

Exam Probability: **Low**

38. *Answer choices:*

(see index for correct answer)

- a. cultural
- b. Federal government
- c. Character
- d. open system

Guidance: level 1

:: ::

Competition arises whenever at least two parties strive for a goal which cannot be shared: where one`s gain is the other`s loss .

Exam Probability: **High**

39. *Answer choices:*

(see index for correct answer)

- a. hierarchical perspective
- b. deep-level diversity
- c. Competitor
- d. similarity-attraction theory

Guidance: level 1

:: ::

_________ is a concept of English common law and is a necessity for simple contracts but not for special contracts . The concept has been adopted by other common law jurisdictions, including the US.

Exam Probability: **Medium**

40. *Answer choices:*

(see index for correct answer)

- a. surface-level diversity
- b. Consideration
- c. corporate values
- d. similarity-attraction theory

Guidance: level 1

:: Business models ::

A _________ is "an autonomous association of persons united voluntarily to meet their common economic, social, and cultural needs and aspirations through a jointly-owned and democratically-controlled enterprise". _________ s may include.

Exam Probability: **Low**

41. *Answer choices:*

(see index for correct answer)

- a. Defensive patent aggregation
- b. Cooperative
- c. Low-cost carrier
- d. Paid To Click

Guidance: level 1

:: Business law ::

The term is used to designate a range of diverse, if often kindred, concepts. These have historically been addressed in a number of discrete disciplines, notably mathematics, physics, chemistry, ethics, aesthetics, ontology, and theology.

Exam Probability: **Medium**

42. *Answer choices:*

(see index for correct answer)

- a. Wrongful trading
- b. Bulk transfer
- c. Registered agent
- d. Perfection

Guidance: level 1

:: Personal property law ::

Bailment describes a legal relationship in common law where physical possession of personal property, or a chattel, is transferred from one person to another person who subsequently has possession of the property. It arises when a person gives property to someone else for safekeeping, and is a cause of action independent of contract or tort.

Exam Probability: **Low**

43. *Answer choices:*

(see index for correct answer)

- a. bailment
- b. Bailee

Guidance: level 1

:: Contract law ::

Offer and acceptance analysis is a traditional approach in contract law. The offer and acceptance formula, developed in the 19th century, identifies a moment of formation when the parties are of one mind. This classical approach to contract formation has been modified by developments in the law of estoppel, misleading conduct, misrepresentation and unjust enrichment.

Exam Probability: **Medium**

44. *Answer choices:*

(see index for correct answer)

- a. Piggy-back
- b. Per minas
- c. Offeror
- d. Liquidated damages

Guidance: level 1

:: ::

Business is the activity of making one`s living or making money by producing or buying and selling products . Simply put, it is "any activity or enterprise entered into for profit. It does not mean it is a company, a corporation, partnership, or have any such formal organization, but it can range from a street peddler to General Motors."

Exam Probability: **High**

45. *Answer choices:*

(see index for correct answer)

- a. empathy
- b. corporate values
- c. open system
- d. Firm

Guidance: level 1

:: Contract law ::

__________ is an equitable remedy in the law of contract, whereby a court issues an order requiring a party to perform a specific act, such as to complete performance of the contract. It is typically available in the sale of land, but otherwise is not generally available if damages are an appropriate alternative. __________ is almost never available for contracts of personal service, although performance may also be ensured through the threat of proceedings for contempt of court.

Exam Probability: **Medium**

46. *Answer choices:*

(see index for correct answer)

- a. Publishing contract
- b. Culpa in contrahendo
- c. Extinguishment
- d. Interlineation

Guidance: level 1

:: ::

__________ is property that is movable. In common law systems, __________ may also be called chattels or personalty. In civil law systems, __________ is often called movable property or movables – any property that can be moved from one location to another.

Exam Probability: **Low**

47. *Answer choices:*

(see index for correct answer)

- a. Personal property
- b. corporate values
- c. hierarchical perspective
- d. Sarbanes-Oxley act of 2002

Guidance: level 1

:: ::

__________ s and acquisitions are transactions in which the ownership of companies, other business organizations, or their operating units are transferred or consolidated with other entities. As an aspect of strategic management, M&A can allow enterprises to grow or downsize, and change the nature of their business or competitive position.

Exam Probability: **Low**

48. *Answer choices:*

(see index for correct answer)

- a. Merger
- b. co-culture
- c. surface-level diversity
- d. interpersonal communication

Guidance: level 1

:: ::

__________ is widespread, interconnected digital technology. The term entered the popular culture from science fiction and the arts but is now used by technology strategists, security professionals, government, military and industry leaders and entrepreneurs to describe the domain of the global technology environment. Others consider __________ to be just a notional environment in which communication over computer networks occurs. The word became popular in the 1990s when the uses of the Internet, networking, and digital communication were all growing dramatically and the term " __________ " was able to represent the many new ideas and phenomena that were emerging. It has been called the largest unregulated and uncontrolled domain in the history of mankind, and is also unique because it is a domain created by people vice the traditional physical domains.

Exam Probability: **Medium**

49. *Answer choices:*

(see index for correct answer)

- a. personal values
- b. imperative
- c. deep-level diversity
- d. Cyberspace

Guidance: level 1

:: ::

A __________ , in common law jurisdictions, is a civil wrong that causes a claimant to suffer loss or harm resulting in legal liability for the person who commits the __________ ious act. It can include the intentional infliction of emotional distress, negligence, financial losses, injuries, invasion of privacy, and many other things.

Exam Probability: **Low**

50. *Answer choices:*

(see index for correct answer)

- a. imperative
- b. Tort
- c. deep-level diversity
- d. information systems assessment

Guidance: level 1

:: Psychometrics ::

__________ is a dynamic, structured, interactive process where a neutral third party assists disputing parties in resolving conflict through the use of specialized communication and negotiation techniques. All participants in __________ are encouraged to actively participate in the process. __________ is a "party-centered" process in that it is focused primarily upon the needs, rights, and interests of the parties. The mediator uses a wide variety of techniques to guide the process in a constructive direction and to help the parties find their optimal solution. A mediator is facilitative in that she/he manages the interaction between parties and facilitates open communication. __________ is also evaluative in that the mediator analyzes issues and relevant norms , while refraining from providing prescriptive advice to the parties .

Exam Probability: **Medium**

51. *Answer choices:*

(see index for correct answer)

- a. Differential item functioning
- b. Repeatability
- c. SESAMO
- d. William H. Tucker

Guidance: level 1

:: Monopoly (economics) ::

A _________ is a form of intellectual property that gives its owner the legal right to exclude others from making, using, selling, and importing an invention for a limited period of years, in exchange for publishing an enabling public disclosure of the invention. In most countries _________ rights fall under civil law and the _________ holder needs to sue someone infringing the _________ in order to enforce his or her rights. In some industries _________ s are an essential form of competitive advantage; in others they are irrelevant.

Exam Probability: **High**

52. *Answer choices:*

(see index for correct answer)

- a. Herfindahl index
- b. Public utility
- c. Patent
- d. Average cost pricing

Guidance: level 1

:: Statutory law ::

_________ is a principal's approval of an act of its agent that lacked the authority to bind the principal legally. _________ defines the international act in which a state indicates its consent to be bound to a treaty if the parties intended to show their consent by such an act. In the case of bilateral treaties, _________ is usually accomplished by exchanging the requisite instruments, and in the case of multilateral treaties, the usual procedure is for the depositary to collect the _________ s of all states, keeping all parties informed of the situation.

Exam Probability: **Low**

53. *Answer choices:*

(see index for correct answer)

- a. Statute of repose
- b. Ratification

- c. statute law
- d. Statutory law

Guidance: level 1

:: ::

__________ is the production of products for use or sale using labour and machines, tools, chemical and biological processing, or formulation. The term may refer to a range of human activity, from handicraft to high tech, but is most commonly applied to industrial design, in which raw materials are transformed into finished goods on a large scale. Such finished goods may be sold to other manufacturers for the production of other, more complex products, such as aircraft, household appliances, furniture, sports equipment or automobiles, or sold to wholesalers, who in turn sell them to retailers, who then sell them to end users and consumers.

Exam Probability: **Low**

54. *Answer choices:*

(see index for correct answer)

- a. Manufacturing
- b. hierarchical
- c. similarity-attraction theory
- d. levels of analysis

Guidance: level 1

:: Insolvency ::

__________ is a legal process through which people or other entities who cannot repay debts to creditors may seek relief from some or all of their debts. In most jurisdictions, __________ is imposed by a court order, often initiated by the debtor.

Exam Probability: **High**

55. *Answer choices:*

(see index for correct answer)

- a. Personal Insolvency Arrangement
- b. Debt consolidation
- c. George Samuel Ford

- d. Liquidator

Guidance: level 1

:: ::

In general, _________ is a form of dishonesty or criminal activity undertaken by a person or organization entrusted with a position of authority, often to acquire illicit benefit. _________ may include many activities including bribery and embezzlement, though it may also involve practices that are legal in many countries. Political _________ occurs when an office-holder or other governmental employee acts in an official capacity for personal gain. _________ is most commonplace in kleptocracies, oligarchies, narco-states and mafia states.

Exam Probability: **Medium**

56. *Answer choices:*

(see index for correct answer)

- a. co-culture
- b. Corruption
- c. functional perspective
- d. information systems assessment

Guidance: level 1

:: ::

In legal terminology, a _________ is any formal legal document that sets out the facts and legal reasons that the filing party or parties believes are sufficient to support a claim against the party or parties against whom the claim is brought that entitles the plaintiff to a remedy . For example, the Federal Rules of Civil Procedure that govern civil litigation in United States courts provide that a civil action is commenced with the filing or service of a pleading called a _________ . Civil court rules in states that have incorporated the Federal Rules of Civil Procedure use the same term for the same pleading.

Exam Probability: **Low**

57. *Answer choices:*

(see index for correct answer)

- a. hierarchical perspective
- b. Complaint
- c. imperative
- d. personal values

Guidance: level 1

:: Debt ::

__________ , in finance and economics, is payment from a borrower or deposit-taking financial institution to a lender or depositor of an amount above repayment of the principal sum , at a particular rate. It is distinct from a fee which the borrower may pay the lender or some third party. It is also distinct from dividend which is paid by a company to its shareholders from its profit or reserve, but not at a particular rate decided beforehand, rather on a pro rata basis as a share in the reward gained by risk taking entrepreneurs when the revenue earned exceeds the total costs.

Exam Probability: **High**

58. *Answer choices:*

(see index for correct answer)

- a. Sum certain
- b. Interest
- c. Extendible bond
- d. Debit note

Guidance: level 1

:: International trade ::

A __________ is a document issued by a carrier to acknowledge receipt of cargo for shipment. Although the term historically related only to carriage by sea, a __________ may today be used for any type of carriage of goods.

Exam Probability: **Medium**

59. *Answer choices:*

(see index for correct answer)

- a. Import
- b. Bill of lading
- c. Terms of trade
- d. Common external tariff

Guidance: level 1

Finance

Finance is a field that is concerned with the allocation (investment) of assets and liabilities over space and time, often under conditions of risk or uncertainty. Finance can also be defined as the science of money management. Participants in the market aim to price assets based on their risk level, fundamental value, and their expected rate of return. Finance can be split into three sub-categories: public finance, corporate finance and personal finance.

:: Credit cards ::

A __________ is a payment card issued to users to enable the cardholder to pay a merchant for goods and services based on the cardholder's promise to the card issuer to pay them for the amounts plus the other agreed charges. The card issuer creates a revolving account and grants a line of credit to the cardholder, from which the cardholder can borrow money for payment to a merchant or as a cash advance.

Exam Probability: **Medium**

1. *Answer choices:*

(see index for correct answer)

- a. China UnionPay
- b. Cashplus
- c. Rail travel card
- d. Wireless identity theft

Guidance: level 1

:: Income taxes ::

An _________ is a tax imposed on individuals or entities that varies with respective income or profits . _________ generally is computed as the product of a tax rate times taxable income. Taxation rates may vary by type or characteristics of the taxpayer.

Exam Probability: **Low**

2. *Answer choices:*

(see index for correct answer)

- a. Hall income tax
- b. Income Tax Assessment Act 1997
- c. Negative income tax
- d. Income tax

Guidance: level 1

:: Marketing ::

A _________ is an overall experience of a customer that distinguishes an organization or product from its rivals in the eyes of the customer. _________ s are used in business, marketing, and advertising. Name _________ s are sometimes distinguished from generic or store _________ s.

Exam Probability: **Low**

3. *Answer choices:*

(see index for correct answer)

- a. Brand
- b. Earned media
- c. NauticExpo
- d. Audience development

Guidance: level 1

:: ::

__________ is the collection of techniques, skills, methods, and processes used in the production of goods or services or in the accomplishment of objectives, such as scientific investigation. __________ can be the knowledge of techniques, processes, and the like, or it can be embedded in machines to allow for operation without detailed knowledge of their workings. Systems applying __________ by taking an input, changing it according to the system`s use, and then producing an outcome are referred to as __________ systems or technological systems.

Exam Probability: **High**

4. *Answer choices:*

(see index for correct answer)

- a. open system
- b. Technology
- c. Sarbanes-Oxley act of 2002
- d. imperative

Guidance: level 1

:: Asset ::

In financial accounting, an __________ is any resource owned by the business. Anything tangible or intangible that can be owned or controlled to produce value and that is held by a company to produce positive economic value is an __________. Simply stated, __________ s represent value of ownership that can be converted into cash . The balance sheet of a firm records the monetary value of the __________ s owned by that firm. It covers money and other valuables belonging to an individual or to a business.

Exam Probability: **Medium**

5. *Answer choices:*

(see index for correct answer)

- a. Current asset
- b. Asset

Guidance: level 1

:: Costs ::

In economics, _________ is the total economic cost of production and is made up of variable cost, which varies according to the quantity of a good produced and includes inputs such as labour and raw materials, plus fixed cost, which is independent of the quantity of a good produced and includes inputs that cannot be varied in the short term: fixed costs such as buildings and machinery, including sunk costs if any. Since cost is measured per unit of time, it is a flow variable.

Exam Probability: **High**

6. *Answer choices:*

(see index for correct answer)

- a. Repugnancy costs
- b. Cost of products sold
- c. Total cost
- d. Cost overrun

Guidance: level 1

:: Financial markets ::

A _________ is a market in which people trade financial securities and derivatives such as futures and options at low transaction costs. Securities include stocks and bonds, and precious metals.

Exam Probability: **Medium**

7. *Answer choices:*

(see index for correct answer)

- a. Financial market
- b. Capital market
- c. Municipal bond arbitrage
- d. Volatility arbitrage

Guidance: level 1

:: Notes (finance) ::

A _________ , sometimes referred to as a note payable, is a legal instrument , in which one party promises in writing to pay a determinate sum of money to the other , either at a fixed or determinable future time or on demand of the payee, under specific terms.

Exam Probability: **Medium**

8. *Answer choices:*

(see index for correct answer)

- a. note payable
- b. Note issuance facility
- c. Circular note
- d. Surplus note

Guidance: level 1

:: ::

_________ is the concept of one topic being connected to another topic in a way that makes it useful to consider the second topic when considering the first. The concept of _________ is studied in many different fields, including cognitive sciences, logic, and library and information science. Most fundamentally, however, it is studied in epistemology . Different theories of knowledge have different implications for what is considered relevant and these fundamental views have implications for all other fields as well.

Exam Probability: **Low**

9. *Answer choices:*

(see index for correct answer)

- a. open system
- b. levels of analysis
- c. process perspective
- d. hierarchical perspective

Guidance: level 1

:: Separation of investment and commercial banking ::

A __________ is a type of bank that provides services such as accepting deposits, making business loans, and offering basic investment products that is operated as a business for profit.

Exam Probability: **Low**

10. *Answer choices:*

(see index for correct answer)

- a. Independent Commission on Banking
- b. GLBA
- c. Commercial bank
- d. Bank Holding Company Act

Guidance: level 1

:: ::

An __________ is a contingent motivator. Traditional __________ s are extrinsic motivators which reward actions to yield a desired outcome. The effectiveness of traditional __________ s has changed as the needs of Western society have evolved. While the traditional __________ model is effective when there is a defined procedure and goal for a task, Western society started to require a higher volume of critical thinkers, so the traditional model became less effective. Institutions are now following a trend in implementing strategies that rely on intrinsic motivations rather than the extrinsic motivations that the traditional __________ s foster.

Exam Probability: **Low**

11. *Answer choices:*

(see index for correct answer)

- a. hierarchical
- b. personal values
- c. Incentive
- d. information systems assessment

Guidance: level 1

:: ::

__________ is the production of products for use or sale using labour and machines, tools, chemical and biological processing, or formulation. The term may refer to a range of human activity, from handicraft to high tech, but is most commonly applied to industrial design, in which raw materials are transformed into finished goods on a large scale. Such finished goods may be sold to other manufacturers for the production of other, more complex products, such as aircraft, household appliances, furniture, sports equipment or automobiles, or sold to wholesalers, who in turn sell them to retailers, who then sell them to end users and consumers.

Exam Probability: **Low**

12. *Answer choices:*

(see index for correct answer)

- a. functional perspective
- b. imperative
- c. corporate values
- d. Manufacturing

Guidance: level 1

:: Inventory ::

__________ is the amount of inventory a company has in stock at the end of its fiscal year. It is closely related with __________ cost, which is the amount of money spent to get these goods in stock. It should be calculated at the lower of cost or market.

Exam Probability: **High**

13. *Answer choices:*

(see index for correct answer)

- a. Inventory control problem
- b. Order fulfillment
- c. New old stock
- d. LIFO

Guidance: level 1

:: Leasing ::

A finance lease is a type of lease in which a finance company is typically the legal owner of the asset for the duration of the lease, while the lessee not only has operating control over the asset, but also has a some share of the economic risks and returns from the change in the valuation of the underlying asset.

Exam Probability: **Medium**

14. *Answer choices:*

(see index for correct answer)

- a. Synthetic lease
- b. Farmout agreement

Guidance: level 1

:: Bonds (finance) ::

A __________ is a fund established by an economic entity by setting aside revenue over a period of time to fund a future capital expense, or repayment of a long-term debt.

Exam Probability: **High**

15. *Answer choices:*

(see index for correct answer)

- a. Sinking fund
- b. Global Country of World Peace
- c. Bond market index
- d. Current yield

Guidance: level 1

:: Mutualism (movement) ::

A __________ is a professionally managed investment fund that pools money from many investors to purchase securities. These investors may be retail or institutional in nature.

Exam Probability: **High**

16. *Answer choices:*

(see index for correct answer)

- a. Benefit society
- b. Mutual fund
- c. ICA Group
- d. History of the cooperative movement

Guidance: level 1

:: Business economics ::

__________ is one of the constituents of a leasing calculus or operation. It describes the future value of a good in terms of absolute value in monetary terms and it is sometimes abbreviated into a percentage of the initial price when the item was new.

Exam Probability: **Low**

17. *Answer choices:*

(see index for correct answer)

- a. Residual value
- b. Tradespace
- c. Corporate ecosystem
- d. Vendor finance

Guidance: level 1

:: Accounting in the United States ::

__________ is the title of qualified accountants in numerous countries in the English-speaking world. In the United States, the CPA is a license to provide accounting services to the public. It is awarded by each of the 50 states for practice in that state. Additionally, almost every state has passed mobility laws to allow CPAs from other states to practice in their state. State licensing requirements vary, but the minimum standard requirements include passing the Uniform __________ Examination, 150 semester units of college education, and one year of accounting related experience.

Exam Probability: **High**

18. *Answer choices:*

(see index for correct answer)

- a. International Qualification Examination
- b. Cotton Plantation Record and Account Book
- c. Variable interest entity
- d. Revolving fund

Guidance: level 1

:: Legal terms ::

__________ s may be governments, corporations or investment trusts. __________ s are legally responsible for the obligations of the issue and for reporting financial conditions, material developments and any other operational activities as required by the regulations of their jurisdictions.

Exam Probability: **Low**

19. *Answer choices:*

(see index for correct answer)

- a. Colour of right
- b. Condonation
- c. Issuer
- d. Perjury

Guidance: level 1

:: Financial accounting ::

__________ is a financial metric which represents operating liquidity available to a business, organisation or other entity, including governmental entities. Along with fixed assets such as plant and equipment, __________ is considered a part of operating capital. Gross __________ is equal to current assets. __________ is calculated as current assets minus current liabilities. If current assets are less than current liabilities, an entity has a __________ deficiency, also called a __________ deficit.

Exam Probability: **High**

20. *Answer choices:*

(see index for correct answer)

- a. Asset recovery
- b. Working capital
- c. Mark-to-market accounting
- d. SEC filing

Guidance: level 1

:: ::

__________ focuses on ratios, equities and debts. It is useful for portfolio management,distribution of dividend,capital raising,hedging and looking after fluctuations in foreign currency and product cycles.Financial managers are the people who will do research and based on the research, decide what sort of capital to obtain in order to fund the company`s assets as well as maximizing the value of the firm for all the stakeholders. It also refers to the efficient and effective management of money in such a manner as to accomplish the objectives of the organization. It is the specialized function directly associated with the top management. The significance of this function is not seen in the `Line` but also in the capacity of the `Staff` in overall of a company. It has been defined differently by different experts in the field.

Exam Probability: **Medium**

21. *Answer choices:*

(see index for correct answer)

- a. cultural
- b. Financial management
- c. interpersonal communication
- d. levels of analysis

Guidance: level 1

:: ::

_________ is the quantity of three-dimensional space enclosed by a closed surface, for example, the space that a substance or shape occupies or contains. _________ is often quantified numerically using the SI derived unit, the cubic metre. The _________ of a container is generally understood to be the capacity of the container; i. e., the amount of fluid that the container could hold, rather than the amount of space the container itself displaces.Three dimensional mathematical shapes are also assigned _________ s. _________ s of some simple shapes, such as regular, straight-edged, and circular shapes can be easily calculated using arithmetic formulas. _________ s of complicated shapes can be calculated with integral calculus if a formula exists for the shape`s boundary. One-dimensional figures and two-dimensional shapes are assigned zero _________ in the three-dimensional space.

Exam Probability: **Medium**

22. *Answer choices:*

(see index for correct answer)

- a. Volume
- b. deep-level diversity
- c. Character
- d. imperative

Guidance: level 1

:: Subprime mortgage crisis ::

The _________ Group, Inc., is an American multinational investment bank and financial services company headquartered in New York City. It offers services in investment management, securities, asset management, prime brokerage, and securities underwriting.

Exam Probability: **Low**

23. *Answer choices:*

(see index for correct answer)

- a. Cramdown
- b. Regulatory responses to the subprime crisis
- c. Foreclosure rescue
- d. Goldman Sachs

Guidance: level 1

:: Margin policy ::

In finance, a __________ is a standardized forward contract, a legal agreement to buy or sell something at a predetermined price at a specified time in the future, between parties not known to each other. The asset transacted is usually a commodity or financial instrument. The predetermined price the parties agree to buy and sell the asset for is known as the forward price. The specified time in the future—which is when delivery and payment occur—is known as the delivery date. Because it is a function of an underlying asset, a __________ is a derivative product.

Exam Probability: **Medium**

24. *Answer choices:*

(see index for correct answer)

- a. Futures contract
- b. Margin account

Guidance: level 1

:: Social security ::

__________ is "any government system that provides monetary assistance to people with an inadequate or no income." In the United States, this is usually called welfare or a social safety net, especially when talking about Canada and European countries.

Exam Probability: **High**

25. *Answer choices:*

(see index for correct answer)

- a. Baby bonus
- b. Shidu
- c. Social insurance
- d. Social security

Guidance: level 1

:: Economics terminology ::

A corporation`s share capital or _________ is the portion of a corporation`s equity that has been obtained by the issue of shares in the corporation to a shareholder, usually for cash. "Share capital" may also denote the number and types of shares that compose a corporation`s share structure.

Exam Probability: **High**

26. *Answer choices:*
(see index for correct answer)

- a. Physical capital
- b. External costs
- c. Capital cost
- d. Capital stock

Guidance: level 1

:: ::

_________ refers to a business or organization attempting to acquire goods or services to accomplish its goals. Although there are several organizations that attempt to set standards in the _________ process, processes can vary greatly between organizations. Typically the word " _________ " is not used interchangeably with the word "procurement", since procurement typically includes expediting, supplier quality, and transportation and logistics in addition to _________ .

Exam Probability: **Medium**

27. *Answer choices:*
(see index for correct answer)

- a. Purchasing
- b. Sarbanes-Oxley act of 2002
- c. cultural
- d. deep-level diversity

Guidance: level 1

:: Decision theory ::

Within economics the concept of _________ is used to model worth or value, but its usage has evolved significantly over time. The term was introduced initially as a measure of pleasure or satisfaction within the theory of utilitarianism by moral philosophers such as Jeremy Bentham and John Stuart Mill. But the term has been adapted and reapplied within neoclassical economics, which dominates modern economic theory, as a _________ function that represents a consumer`s preference ordering over a choice set. As such, it is devoid of its original interpretation as a measurement of the pleasure or satisfaction obtained by the consumer from that choice.

Exam Probability: **Low**

28. *Answer choices:*

(see index for correct answer)

- a. Utility
- b. ERulemaking
- c. Choice architecture
- d. Psychological pricing

Guidance: level 1

:: Financial markets ::

The _________ , also called the aftermarket and follow on public offering is the financial market in which previously issued financial instruments such as stock, bonds, options, and futures are bought and sold. Another frequent usage of " _________ " is to refer to loans which are sold by a mortgage bank to investors such as Fannie Mae and Freddie Mac.

Exam Probability: **Medium**

29. *Answer choices:*

(see index for correct answer)

- a. Arbitrage
- b. Real-time economy
- c. Secondary market
- d. Market impact

Guidance: level 1

:: Business law ::

__________ is where a person's financial liability is limited to a fixed sum, most commonly the value of a person's investment in a company or partnership. If a company with __________ is sued, then the claimants are suing the company, not its owners or investors. A shareholder in a limited company is not personally liable for any of the debts of the company, other than for the amount already invested in the company and for any unpaid amount on the shares in the company, if any. The same is true for the members of a __________ partnership and the limited partners in a limited partnership. By contrast, sole proprietors and partners in general partnerships are each liable for all the debts of the business .

Exam Probability: **Low**

30. *Answer choices:*

(see index for correct answer)

- a. Complex structured finance transactions
- b. Sole proprietorship
- c. Limited liability
- d. Board of directors

Guidance: level 1

:: Free accounting software ::

A __________ is the principal book or computer file for recording and totaling economic transactions measured in terms of a monetary unit of account by account type, with debits and credits in separate columns and a beginning monetary balance and ending monetary balance for each account.

Exam Probability: **Low**

31. *Answer choices:*

(see index for correct answer)

- a. JFin
- b. Ofuz
- c. LedgerSMB
- d. Grisbi

Guidance: level 1

:: Marketing ::

_________ is a financial mechanism in which a debtor obtains the right to delay payments to a creditor, for a defined period of time, in exchange for a charge or fee. Essentially, the party that owes money in the present purchases the right to delay the payment until some future date. The discount, or charge, is the difference between the original amount owed in the present and the amount that has to be paid in the future to settle the debt.

Exam Probability: **High**

32. *Answer choices:*

(see index for correct answer)

- a. Cultural consumer
- b. Price
- c. Discounting
- d. Experiential marketing

Guidance: level 1

:: Monopoly (economics) ::

A _________ is a form of intellectual property that gives its owner the legal right to exclude others from making, using, selling, and importing an invention for a limited period of years, in exchange for publishing an enabling public disclosure of the invention. In most countries _________ rights fall under civil law and the _________ holder needs to sue someone infringing the _________ in order to enforce his or her rights. In some industries _________ s are an essential form of competitive advantage; in others they are irrelevant.

Exam Probability: **Low**

33. *Answer choices:*

(see index for correct answer)

- a. Practice of law
- b. Patent
- c. Concentration ratio
- d. Trust

Guidance: level 1

:: Financial ratios ::

The _________ or dividend-price ratio of a share is the dividend per share, divided by the price per share. It is also a company`s total annual dividend payments divided by its market capitalization, assuming the number of shares is constant. It is often expressed as a percentage.

Exam Probability: **High**

34. *Answer choices:*

(see index for correct answer)

- a. Yield gap
- b. Dividend yield
- c. Debt service ratio
- d. Total revenue share

Guidance: level 1

:: ::

A _________ is a fund into which a sum of money is added during an employee`s employment years, and from which payments are drawn to support the person`s retirement from work in the form of periodic payments. A _________ may be a "defined benefit plan" where a fixed sum is paid regularly to a person, or a "defined contribution plan" under which a fixed sum is invested and then becomes available at retirement age. _________ s should not be confused with severance pay; the former is usually paid in regular installments for life after retirement, while the latter is typically paid as a fixed amount after involuntary termination of employment prior to retirement.

Exam Probability: **Low**

35. *Answer choices:*

(see index for correct answer)

- a. interpersonal communication
- b. Pension
- c. process perspective
- d. Character

Guidance: level 1

:: Fixed income analysis ::

The __________ , book yield or redemption yield of a bond or other fixed-interest security, such as gilts, is the internal rate of return earned by an investor who buys the bond today at the market price, assuming that the bond is held until maturity, and that all coupon and principal payments are made on schedule. __________ is the discount rate at which the sum of all future cash flows from the bond is equal to the current price of the bond. The YTM is often given in terms of Annual Percentage Rate , but more often market convention is followed. In a number of major markets the convention is to quote annualized yields with semi-annual compounding ; thus, for example, an annual effective yield of 10.25% would be quoted as 10.00%, because 1.05 × 1.05 = 1.1025 and 2 × 5 = 10.

Exam Probability: **Low**

36. *Answer choices:*

(see index for correct answer)

- a. Embedded option
- b. Market yield
- c. Option Adjusted Spread
- d. Bond equivalent yield

Guidance: level 1

:: Generally Accepted Accounting Principles ::

The __________ principle is a cornerstone of accrual accounting together with the matching principle. They both determine the accounting period in which revenues and expenses are recognized. According to the principle, revenues are recognized when they are realized or realizable, and are earned , no matter when cash is received. In cash accounting – in contrast – revenues are recognized when cash is received no matter when goods or services are sold.

Exam Probability: **High**

37. *Answer choices:*

(see index for correct answer)

- a. Gross profit
- b. Petty cash
- c. Revenue recognition
- d. Financial position of the United States

Guidance: level 1

:: Accounting terminology ::

_________ or capital expense is the money a company spends to buy, maintain, or improve its fixed assets, such as buildings, vehicles, equipment, or land. It is considered a _________ when the asset is newly purchased or when money is used towards extending the useful life of an existing asset, such as repairing the roof.

Exam Probability: **High**

38. *Answer choices:*
(see index for correct answer)

- a. Account
- b. Accounts payable
- c. Chart of accounts
- d. Cash flow management

Guidance: level 1

:: ::

An _________ is an asset that lacks physical substance. It is defined in opposition to physical assets such as machinery and buildings. An _________ is usually very hard to evaluate. Patents, copyrights, franchises, goodwill, trademarks, and trade names. The general interpretation also includes software and other intangible computer based assets are all examples of _________ s. _________ s generally—though not necessarily—suffer from typical market failures of non-rivalry and non-excludability.

Exam Probability: **Low**

39. *Answer choices:*
(see index for correct answer)

- a. empathy
- b. process perspective
- c. Intangible asset
- d. personal values

Guidance: level 1

:: Banking ::

_________ refers to a broad area of finance involving the collection, handling, and usage of cash. It involves assessing market liquidity, cash flow, and investments.

Exam Probability: **Low**

40. *Answer choices:*
(see index for correct answer)

- a. Clap note
- b. Cash management
- c. Fiscal agent
- d. Overnight market

Guidance: level 1

:: Generally Accepted Accounting Principles ::

In accounting, an economic item`s _________ is the original nominal monetary value of that item. _________ accounting involves reporting assets and liabilities at their _________ s, which are not updated for changes in the items` values. Consequently, the amounts reported for these balance sheet items often differ from their current economic or market values.

Exam Probability: **Low**

41. *Answer choices:*
(see index for correct answer)

- a. Net profit
- b. Historical cost
- c. Profit
- d. Consolidation

Guidance: level 1

:: ::

A _________ , in the word`s original meaning, is a sheet of paper on which one performs work. They come in many forms, most commonly associated with children`s school work assignments, tax forms, and accounting or other business environments. Software is increasingly taking over the paper-based _________ .

Exam Probability: **Medium**

42. *Answer choices:*

(see index for correct answer)

- a. co-culture
- b. levels of analysis
- c. imperative
- d. hierarchical perspective

Guidance: level 1

:: Finance ::

__________ is a field that is concerned with the allocation of assets and liabilities over space and time, often under conditions of risk or uncertainty. __________ can also be defined as the art of money management. Participants in the market aim to price assets based on their risk level, fundamental value, and their expected rate of return. __________ can be split into three sub-categories: public __________, corporate __________ and personal __________.

Exam Probability: **Medium**

43. *Answer choices:*

(see index for correct answer)

- a. Retention ratio
- b. Finance
- c. Tax haven
- d. Multilateral trading facility

Guidance: level 1

:: Loans ::

In corporate finance, a _________ is a medium- to long-term debt instrument used by large companies to borrow money, at a fixed rate of interest. The legal term " _________ " originally referred to a document that either creates a debt or acknowledges it, but in some countries the term is now used interchangeably with bond, loan stock or note. A _________ is thus like a certificate of loan or a loan bond evidencing the fact that the company is liable to pay a specified amount with interest and although the money raised by the _________ s becomes a part of the company's capital structure, it does not become share capital. Senior _________ s get paid before subordinate _________ s, and there are varying rates of risk and payoff for these categories.

Exam Probability: **Medium**

44. *Answer choices:*

(see index for correct answer)

- a. Debenture
- b. Loan origination
- c. Student loan
- d. BankBazaar

Guidance: level 1

:: Commerce ::

A _________ , manufacturing plant or a production plant is an industrial site, usually consisting of buildings and machinery, or more commonly a complex having several buildings, where workers manufacture goods or operate machines processing one product into another.

Exam Probability: **Low**

45. *Answer choices:*

(see index for correct answer)

- a. Straw purchase
- b. Agio
- c. Fixed price
- d. Factory

Guidance: level 1

:: Pharmaceutical industry ::

A __________ is a document in which data collected for a clinical trial is first recorded. This data is usually later entered in the case report form. The International Conference on Harmonisation of Technical Requirements for Registration of Pharmaceuticals for Human Use guidelines define __________ s as "original documents, data, and records." __________ s contain source data, which is defined as "all information in original records and certified copies of original records of clinical findings, observations, or other activities in a clinical trial necessary for the reconstruction and evaluation of the trial."

Exam Probability: **High**

46. *Answer choices:*

(see index for correct answer)

- a. Pharmaceutical sales representative
- b. Norwegian Medicines Agency
- c. Pre-clinical development
- d. Drug discovery

Guidance: level 1

:: Elementary geometry ::

The __________ is the front of an animal`s head that features three of the head`s sense organs, the eyes, nose, and mouth, and through which animals express many of their emotions. The __________ is crucial for human identity, and damage such as scarring or developmental deformities affects the psyche adversely.

Exam Probability: **Low**

47. *Answer choices:*

(see index for correct answer)

- a. Vertical translation
- b. Central angle
- c. Face
- d. Locus

Guidance: level 1

:: Debt ::

A _________ is a monetary amount owed to a creditor that is unlikely to be paid and, or which the creditor is not willing to take action to collect for various reasons, often due to the debtor not having the money to pay, for example due to a company going into liquidation or insolvency. There are various technical definitions of what constitutes a _________ , depending on accounting conventions, regulatory treatment and the institution provisioning. In the USA, bank loans with more than ninety days` arrears become "problem loans". Accounting sources advise that the full amount of a _________ be written off to the profit and loss account or a provision for _________ s as soon as it is foreseen.

Exam Probability: **Medium**

48. *Answer choices:*

(see index for correct answer)

- a. Debt-lag
- b. Debt crisis
- c. Bad debt
- d. Floating charge

Guidance: level 1

:: ::

A _________ is the period used by governments for accounting and budget purposes, which varies between countries. It is also used for financial reporting by business and other organizations. Laws in many jurisdictions require company financial reports to be prepared and published on an annual basis, but generally do not require the reporting period to align with the calendar year . Taxation laws generally require accounting records to be maintained and taxes calculated on an annual basis, which usually corresponds to the _________ used for government purposes. The calculation of tax on an annual basis is especially relevant for direct taxation, such as income tax. Many annual government fees—such as Council rates, licence fees, etc.—are also levied on a _________ basis, while others are charged on an anniversary basis.

Exam Probability: **High**

49. *Answer choices:*

(see index for correct answer)

- a. Sarbanes-Oxley act of 2002
- b. interpersonal communication
- c. Fiscal year
- d. personal values

Guidance: level 1

:: Market research ::

__________ , an acronym for Information through Disguised Experimentation is an annual market research fair conducted by the students of IIM-Lucknow. Students create games and use various other simulated environments to capture consumers' subconscious thoughts. This innovative method of market research removes the sensitization effect that might bias peoples answers to questions. This ensures that the most truthful answers are captured to research questions. The games are designed in such a way that the observers can elicit all the required information just by observing and noting down the behaviour and the responses of the participants.

Exam Probability: **High**

50. *Answer choices:*

(see index for correct answer)

- a. Viral Marketing Research
- b. INDEX
- c. Preference regression
- d. Firmographics

Guidance: level 1

:: Manufacturing ::

__________ s are goods that have completed the manufacturing process but have not yet been sold or distributed to the end user.

Exam Probability: **Low**

51. *Answer choices:*

(see index for correct answer)

- a. Build to stock
- b. Finished good
- c. Glass production
- d. Lean manufacturing

Guidance: level 1

:: Human resource management ::

__________ is the corporate management term for the act of reorganizing the legal, ownership, operational, or other structures of a company for the purpose of making it more profitable, or better organized for its present needs. Other reasons for __________ include a change of ownership or ownership structure, demerger, or a response to a crisis or major change in the business such as bankruptcy, repositioning, or buyout. __________ may also be described as corporate __________, debt __________ and financial __________.

Exam Probability: **Low**

52. *Answer choices:*

(see index for correct answer)

- a. Fresh tracks
- b. Applicant tracking system
- c. Restructuring
- d. Open-book management

Guidance: level 1

:: Management accounting ::

__________ is a managerial accounting cost concept. Under this method, manufacturing overhead is incurred in the period that a product is produced. This addresses the issue of absorption costing that allows income to rise as production rises. Under an absorption cost method, management can push forward costs to the next period when products are sold. This artificially inflates profits in the period of production by incurring less cost than would be incurred under a __________ system. __________ is generally not used for external reporting purposes. Under the Tax Reform Act of 1986, income statements must use absorption costing to comply with GAAP.

Exam Probability: **High**

53. *Answer choices:*

(see index for correct answer)

- a. Corporate travel management
- b. Variable cost

- c. Variable Costing
- d. Direct material usage variance

Guidance: level 1

:: Currency ::

A __________ , in the most specific sense is money in any form when in use or circulation as a medium of exchange, especially circulating banknotes and coins. A more general definition is that a __________ is a system of money in common use, especially for people in a nation. Under this definition, US dollars , pounds sterling , Australian dollars , European euros , Russian rubles and Indian Rupees are examples of currencies. These various currencies are recognized as stores of value and are traded between nations in foreign exchange markets, which determine the relative values of the different currencies. Currencies in this sense are defined by governments, and each type has limited boundaries of acceptance.

Exam Probability: **Medium**

54. *Answer choices:*

(see index for correct answer)

- a. Fiat money
- b. Remonetisation
- c. Currency
- d. Monetary sovereignty

Guidance: level 1

:: ::

__________ is a costing method that identifies activities in an organization and assigns the cost of each activity to all products and services according to the actual consumption by each. This model assigns more indirect costs into direct costs compared to conventional costing.

Exam Probability: **Low**

55. *Answer choices:*

(see index for correct answer)

- a. similarity-attraction theory
- b. corporate values

- c. Activity-based costing
- d. hierarchical perspective

Guidance: level 1

:: ::

__________ is the process of making predictions of the future based on past and present data and most commonly by analysis of trends. A commonplace example might be estimation of some variable of interest at some specified future date. Prediction is a similar, but more general term. Both might refer to formal statistical methods employing time series, cross-sectional or longitudinal data, or alternatively to less formal judgmental methods. Usage can differ between areas of application: for example, in hydrology the terms "forecast" and " __________ " are sometimes reserved for estimates of values at certain specific future times, while the term "prediction" is used for more general estimates, such as the number of times floods will occur over a long period.

Exam Probability: **Medium**

56. *Answer choices:*

(see index for correct answer)

- a. surface-level diversity
- b. levels of analysis
- c. Forecasting
- d. similarity-attraction theory

Guidance: level 1

:: Marketing terminology ::

__________ in capital budgeting refers to the period of time required to recoup the funds expended in an investment, or to reach the break-even point. For example, a $1000 investment made at the start of year 1 which returned $500 at the end of year 1 and year 2 respectively would have a two-year __________ . __________ is usually expressed in years. Starting from investment year by calculating Net Cash Flow for each year: Net Cash Flow Year 1 = Cash Inflow Year 1 - Cash Outflow Year 1. Then Cumulative Cash Flow = Accumulate by year until Cumulative Cash Flow is a positive number: that year is the payback year.

Exam Probability: **Low**

57. *Answer choices:*

(see index for correct answer)

- a. Factory-to-consumer
- b. Payback period
- c. Low-end market
- d. Category performance ratio

Guidance: level 1

:: Management accounting ::

In _________ or managerial accounting, managers use the provisions of accounting information in order to better inform themselves before they decide matters within their organizations, which aids their management and performance of control functions.

Exam Probability: **Low**

58. *Answer choices:*

(see index for correct answer)

- a. Management accounting
- b. Semi-variable cost
- c. Job costing
- d. Bridge life-cycle cost analysis

Guidance: level 1

:: Consumer theory ::

A _________ is a technical term in psychology, economics and philosophy usually used in relation to choosing between alternatives. For example, someone prefers A over B if they would rather choose A than B.

Exam Probability: **Low**

59. *Answer choices:*

(see index for correct answer)

- a. Preference
- b. Demand set
- c. Quality bias
- d. Demand vacuum

Guidance: level 1

Human resource management

Human resource (HR) management is the strategic approach to the effective management of organization workers so that they help the business gain a competitive advantage. It is designed to maximize employee performance in service of an employer's strategic objectives. HR is primarily concerned with the management of people within organizations, focusing on policies and on systems. HR departments are responsible for overseeing employee-benefits design, employee recruitment, training and development, performance appraisal, and rewarding (e.g., managing pay and benefit systems). HR also concerns itself with organizational change and industrial relations, that is, the balancing of organizational practices with requirements arising from collective bargaining and from governmental laws.

:: Cognitive biases ::

In personality psychology, _________ is the degree to which people believe that they have control over the outcome of events in their lives, as opposed to external forces beyond their control. Understanding of the concept was developed by Julian B. Rotter in 1954, and has since become an aspect of personality studies. A person's "locus" is conceptualized as internal or external .

Exam Probability: **High**

1. *Answer choices:*

(see index for correct answer)

- a. Positive illusions
- b. Moral credential
- c. Familiarity heuristic
- d. Locus of control

Guidance: level 1

:: Human resource management ::

__________ or work sharing is an employment arrangement where typically two people are retained on a part-time or reduced-time basis to perform a job normally fulfilled by one person working full-time. Since all positions are shared thus leads to a net reduction in per-employee income. The people sharing the job work as a team to complete the job task and are equally responsible for the job workload. Compensation is apportioned between the workers. Working hours, pay and holidays are divided equally. The pay as you go system helps make deductions for national insurance and superannuations are made as a straightforward percentage.

Exam Probability: **Medium**

2. *Answer choices:*

(see index for correct answer)

- a. The war for talent
- b. Induction training
- c. Job sharing
- d. SLT Human Capital Solutions

Guidance: level 1

:: Recruitment ::

__________ is a tool companies and organizations use as a way to communicate the good and the bad characteristics of the job during the hiring process of new employees, or as a tool to reestablish job specificity for existing employees. __________ s should provide the individuals with a well-rounded description that details what obligations the individual can expect to perform while working for that specific company. Descriptions may include, but are not limited to, work environment, expectations, and Company policies .

Exam Probability: **Medium**

3. *Answer choices:*

(see index for correct answer)

- a. Realistic job preview
- b. Social recruiting
- c. Acquisourcing
- d. Talent community

Guidance: level 1

:: Human resource management ::

__________ is a family of procedures to identify the content of a job in terms of activities involved and attributes or job requirements needed to perform the activities. __________ provides information of organizations which helps to determine which employees are best fit for specific jobs. Through __________, the analyst needs to understand what the important tasks of the job are, how they are carried out, and the necessary human qualities needed to complete the job successfully.

Exam Probability: **Low**

4. *Answer choices:*

(see index for correct answer)

- a. Administrative services organization
- b. Enterprise architecture
- c. Competency-based management
- d. Job analysis

Guidance: level 1

:: Employment compensation ::

__________, merit increase or pay for performance, is performance-related pay, most frequently in the context of educational reform or government civil service reform . It provides bonuses for workers who perform their jobs effectively, according to easily measurable criteria. In the United States, policy makers are divided on whether __________ should be offered to public school teachers, and other public employees, as is commonly the case in the United Kingdom.

Exam Probability: **Low**

5. *Answer choices:*

(see index for correct answer)

- a. Thirteenth salary
- b. Merit pay
- c. Total Reward
- d. Commission

Guidance: level 1

:: Asset ::

In financial accounting, an _________ is any resource owned by the business. Anything tangible or intangible that can be owned or controlled to produce value and that is held by a company to produce positive economic value is an _________ . Simply stated, _________ s represent value of ownership that can be converted into cash . The balance sheet of a firm records the monetary value of the _________ s owned by that firm. It covers money and other valuables belonging to an individual or to a business.

Exam Probability: **High**

6. *Answer choices:*

(see index for correct answer)

- a. Fixed asset
- b. Current asset

Guidance: level 1

:: Labor rights ::

The _________ is the concept that people have a human _________ , or engage in productive employment, and may not be prevented from doing so. The _________ is enshrined in the Universal Declaration of Human Rights and recognized in international human rights law through its inclusion in the International Covenant on Economic, Social and Cultural Rights, where the _________ emphasizes economic, social and cultural development.

Exam Probability: **High**

7. *Answer choices:*

(see index for correct answer)

- a. China Labor Watch
- b. Right to work
- c. The Hyatt 100
- d. Kate Mullany House

Guidance: level 1

:: Training ::

__________ refers to practicing newly acquired skills beyond the point of initial mastery. The term is also often used to refer to the pedagogical theory that this form of practice leads to automaticity or other beneficial consequences.

Exam Probability: **Low**

8. *Answer choices:*

(see index for correct answer)

- a. Hypoventilation training
- b. Trainee
- c. Enforcement
- d. Boardcast

Guidance: level 1

:: Management ::

The __________ is a strategy performance management tool – a semi-standard structured report, that can be used by managers to keep track of the execution of activities by the staff within their control and to monitor the consequences arising from these actions.

Exam Probability: **Low**

9. *Answer choices:*

(see index for correct answer)

- a. Personal offshoring
- b. Overtime rate
- c. Balanced scorecard
- d. Narcissistic leadership

Guidance: level 1

:: Management education ::

_________ refers to simulation games that are used as an educational tool for teaching business. _________ s may be carried out for various business training such as: general management, finance, organizational behaviour, human resources, etc. Often, the term "business simulation" is used with the same meaning.

Exam Probability: **Medium**

10. *Answer choices:*

(see index for correct answer)

- a. Training simulation
- b. MBA degree
- c. Business game
- d. System Design and Management

Guidance: level 1

:: Television terminology ::

Distance education or long- _________ is the education of students who may not always be physically present at a school. Traditionally, this usually involved correspondence courses wherein the student corresponded with the school via post. Today it involves online education. Courses that are conducted are either hybrid, blended or 100% _________ . Massive open online courses , offering large-scale interactive participation and open access through the World Wide Web or other network technologies, are recent developments in distance education. A number of other terms are used roughly synonymously with distance education.

Exam Probability: **Medium**

11. *Answer choices:*

(see index for correct answer)

- a. Distance learning
- b. Satellite television
- c. nonprofit
- d. multiplexing

Guidance: level 1

:: Offshoring ::

A __________ is the temporary suspension or permanent termination of employment of an employee or, more commonly, a group of employees for business reasons, such as personnel management or downsizing an organization. Originally, __________ referred exclusively to a temporary interruption in work, or employment but this has evolved to a permanent elimination of a position in both British and US English, requiring the addition of "temporary" to specify the original meaning of the word. A __________ is not to be confused with wrongful termination. Laid off workers or displaced workers are workers who have lost or left their jobs because their employer has closed or moved, there was insufficient work for them to do, or their position or shift was abolished . Downsizing in a company is defined to involve the reduction of employees in a workforce. Downsizing in companies became a popular practice in the 1980s and early 1990s as it was seen as a way to deliver better shareholder value as it helps to reduce the costs of employers . Indeed, recent research on downsizing in the U.S., UK, and Japan suggests that downsizing is being regarded by management as one of the preferred routes to help declining organizations, cutting unnecessary costs, and improve organizational performance. Usually a __________ occurs as a cost cutting measure.

Exam Probability: **Low**

12. *Answer choices:*

(see index for correct answer)

- a. Body shopping
- b. Offshoring Research Network
- c. Layoff
- d. Sourcing advisory

Guidance: level 1

:: Labour relations ::

A __________, also known as a post-entry closed shop, is a form of a union security clause. Under this, the employer agrees to either only hire labor union members or to require that any new employees who are not already union members become members within a certain amount of time. Use of the __________ varies widely from nation to nation, depending on the level of protection given trade unions in general.

Exam Probability: **High**

13. *Answer choices:*
(see index for correct answer)

- a. Review Body
- b. Union representative
- c. Union shop
- d. Picketing

Guidance: level 1

:: Organizational theory ::

_________ is the process of creating, retaining, and transferring knowledge within an organization. An organization improves over time as it gains experience. From this experience, it is able to create knowledge. This knowledge is broad, covering any topic that could better an organization. Examples may include ways to increase production efficiency or to develop beneficial investor relations. Knowledge is created at four different units: individual, group, organizational, and inter organizational.

Exam Probability: **Medium**

14. *Answer choices:*
(see index for correct answer)

- a. Organizational learning
- b. Team leader
- c. Exit-Voice-Loyalty-Neglect Model
- d. Team Service Management

Guidance: level 1

:: Labour relations ::

An _________ is a place of employment at which one is not required to join or financially support a union as a condition of hiring or continued employment. _________ is also known as a merit shop.

Exam Probability: **Medium**

15. *Answer choices:*
(see index for correct answer)

- a. Broad left
- b. Union representative

- c. Open shop
- d. Impasse

Guidance: level 1

:: Validity (statistics) ::

__________ is the extent to which a test accurately measures what it is supposed to measure. In the fields of psychological testing and educational testing, "validity refers to the degree to which evidence and theory support the interpretations of test scores entailed by proposed uses of tests". Although classical models divided the concept into various "validities" , the currently dominant view is that validity is a single unitary construct.

Exam Probability: **Medium**

16. *Answer choices:*
(see index for correct answer)

- a. Criterion validity
- b. External validity
- c. Predictive validity
- d. Test validity

Guidance: level 1

:: Learning methods ::

__________ is an approach to problem solving. It involves taking action and reflecting upon the results. This helps improve the problem-solving process as well as simplify the solutions developed by the team.

Exam Probability: **Low**

17. *Answer choices:*
(see index for correct answer)

- a. Audience response system
- b. Double-loop learning
- c. double loop learning
- d. Action learning

Guidance: level 1

:: Validity (statistics) ::

In psychometrics, _________ refers to the extent to which a measure represents all facets of a given construct. For example, a depression scale may lack _________ if it only assesses the affective dimension of depression but fails to take into account the behavioral dimension. An element of subjectivity exists in relation to determining _________, which requires a degree of agreement about what a particular personality trait such as extraversion represents. A disagreement about a personality trait will prevent the gain of a high _________.

Exam Probability: **High**

18. *Answer choices:*

(see index for correct answer)

- a. Convergent validity
- b. Content validity
- c. Statistical conclusion validity
- d. Internal validity

Guidance: level 1

:: Labor ::

_________ s are workers whose main capital is knowledge. Examples include programmers, physicians, pharmacists, architects, engineers, scientists, design thinkers, public accountants, lawyers, and academics, and any other white-collar workers, whose line of work requires the one to "think for a living".

Exam Probability: **Medium**

19. *Answer choices:*

(see index for correct answer)

- a. Knowledge worker
- b. Day labor
- c. Surplus labour
- d. Eurosclerosis

Guidance: level 1

:: Social psychology ::

_________ is a type of nonverbal communication in which physical behaviors, as opposed to words, are used to express or convey information. Such behavior includes facial expressions, body posture, gestures, eye movement, touch and the use of space. _________ exists in both animals and humans, but this article focuses on interpretations of human _________ . It is also known as kinesics.

Exam Probability: **High**

20. *Answer choices:*

(see index for correct answer)

- a. social loafing
- b. Body language
- c. co-optation
- d. Impression formation

Guidance: level 1

:: Human resource management ::

_________ is the strategic approach to the effective management of people in an organization so that they help the business to gain a competitive advantage. It is designed to maximize employee performance in service of an employer`s strategic objectives. HR is primarily concerned with the management of people within organizations, focusing on policies and on systems. HR departments are responsible for overseeing employee-benefits design, employee recruitment, training and development, performance appraisal, and Reward management . HR also concerns itself with organizational change and industrial relations, that is, the balancing of organizational practices with requirements arising from collective bargaining and from governmental laws.

Exam Probability: **Medium**

21. *Answer choices:*

(see index for correct answer)

- a. Reward management
- b. Human resource management
- c. Focal Point Review
- d. Adecco Group North America

Guidance: level 1

:: ::

A __________ , covering letter, motivation letter, motivational letter or a letter of motivation is a letter of introduction attached to, or accompanying another document such as a résumé or curriculum vitae.

Exam Probability: **High**

22. *Answer choices:*

(see index for correct answer)

- a. functional perspective
- b. Cover letter
- c. interpersonal communication
- d. process perspective

Guidance: level 1

:: Employment compensation ::

A __________ , also known as a flexible spending arrangement, is one of a number of tax-advantaged financial accounts, resulting in payroll tax savings. Before the Patient Protection and Affordable Care Act, one significant disadvantage to using an FSA was that funds not used by the end of the plan year were forfeited to the employer, known as the "use it or lose it" rule. Under the terms of the Affordable Care Act, a plan may permit an employee to carry over up to $500 into the following year without losing the funds.

Exam Probability: **Medium**

23. *Answer choices:*

(see index for correct answer)

- a. Pay scale
- b. Sliding wage scale
- c. Flexible spending account
- d. Thirteenth salary

Guidance: level 1

:: Business law ::

__________ or employment relations is the multidisciplinary academic field that studies the employment relationship; that is, the complex interrelations between employers and employees, labor/trade unions, employer organizations and the state.

Exam Probability: **Low**

24. *Answer choices:*

(see index for correct answer)

- a. Ordinary course of business
- b. License
- c. Sole proprietorship
- d. Industrial relations

Guidance: level 1

:: Information systems ::

__________ is the process of creating, sharing, using and managing the knowledge and information of an organisation. It refers to a multidisciplinary approach to achieving organisational objectives by making the best use of knowledge.

Exam Probability: **Low**

25. *Answer choices:*

(see index for correct answer)

- a. Information systems
- b. Expert systems for mortgages
- c. Knowledge management
- d. Earthquake Early Warning

Guidance: level 1

:: Training ::

__________ is the process of ensuring compliance with laws, regulations, rules, standards, or social norms. By enforcing laws and regulations, governments attempt to effectuate successful implementation of policies.

Exam Probability: **Medium**

26. *Answer choices:*

(see index for correct answer)

- a. Personal trainer
- b. Enforcement
- c. Overlearning
- d. Training camp

Guidance: level 1

:: Outsourcing ::

_________ is the practice of sourcing from the global market for goods and services across geopolitical boundaries. _________ often aims to exploit global efficiencies in the delivery of a product or service. These efficiencies include low cost skilled labor, low cost raw material and other economic factors like tax breaks and low trade tariffs. A large number of Information Technology projects and Services, including IS Applications and Mobile Apps and database services are outsourced globally to countries like Pakistan and India for more economical pricing.

Exam Probability: **High**

27. *Answer choices:*

(see index for correct answer)

- a. Affiliated Computer Services
- b. Global sourcing
- c. Service review
- d. Infosys

Guidance: level 1

:: Employment compensation ::

A _________ is pay and benefits employees receive when they leave employment at a company unwillfully. In addition to their remaining regular pay, it may include some of the following.

Exam Probability: **Medium**

28. *Answer choices:*

(see index for correct answer)

- a. Employee benefit
- b. Stock appreciation right
- c. Maximum wage
- d. Severance package

Guidance: level 1

:: Employment of foreign-born ::

__________ refers to the international labor pool of workers, including those employed by multinational companies and connected through a global system of networking and production, immigrant workers, transient migrant workers, telecommuting workers, those in export-oriented employment, contingent work or other precarious employment. As of 2012, the global labor pool consisted of approximately 3 billion workers, around 200 million unemployed.

Exam Probability: **Low**

29. *Answer choices:*

(see index for correct answer)

- a. Foreign born
- b. Global workforce
- c. L-2 visa
- d. Reverse brain drain

Guidance: level 1

:: ::

An __________ is a process where candidates are examined to determine their suitability for specific types of employment, especially management or military command. The candidates` personality and aptitudes are determined by techniques including interviews, group exercises, presentations, examinations and psychometric testing.

Exam Probability: **Medium**

30. *Answer choices:*

(see index for correct answer)

- a. interpersonal communication
- b. imperative
- c. empathy
- d. levels of analysis

Guidance: level 1

:: Management education ::

__________ is the implementation of government policy and also an academic discipline that studies this implementation and prepares civil servants for working in the public service. As a "field of inquiry with a diverse scope" whose fundamental goal is to "advance management and policies so that government can function". Some of the various definitions which have been offered for the term are: "the management of public programs"; the "translation of politics into the reality that citizens see every day"; and "the study of government decision making, the analysis of the policies themselves, the various inputs that have produced them, and the inputs necessary to produce alternative policies."

Exam Probability: **High**

31. *Answer choices:*

(see index for correct answer)

- a. Training simulation
- b. Doctor of Commerce
- c. Public administration
- d. Association for Business Communication

Guidance: level 1

:: ::

A trade union is an association of workers forming a legal unit or legal personhood, usually called a "bargaining unit", which acts as bargaining agent and legal representative for a unit of employees in all matters of law or right arising from or in the administration of a collective agreement. Labour unions typically fund the formal organisation, head office, and legal team functions of the labour union through regular fees or union dues. The delegate staff of the labour union representation in the workforce are made up of workplace volunteers who are appointed by members in democratic elections.

Exam Probability: **Medium**

32. *Answer choices:*

(see index for correct answer)

- a. Labor union
- b. levels of analysis
- c. information systems assessment
- d. Sarbanes-Oxley act of 2002

Guidance: level 1

:: Recruitment ::

The __________ is an American nonprofit professional association established in 1956 in Bethlehem, Pennsylvania, for college career services, recruiting practitioners, and others who wish to hire the college educated.

Exam Probability: **High**

33. *Answer choices:*

(see index for correct answer)

- a. National Association of Colleges and Employers
- b. Acqui-hiring
- c. Recruitment process insourcing
- d. Staff Selection Commission

Guidance: level 1

:: Personnel economics ::

In labor economics, the __________ hypothesis argues that wages, at least in some markets, form in a way that is not market-clearing. Specifically, it points to the incentive for managers to pay their employees more than the market-clearing wage in order to increase their productivity or efficiency, or reduce costs associated with turnover, in industries where the costs of replacing labor are high. This increased labor productivity and/or decreased costs pay for the higher wages.

Exam Probability: **High**

34. *Answer choices:*

(see index for correct answer)

- a. Personnel economics
- b. Luxury tax
- c. Efficiency wage

Guidance: level 1

:: Occupational safety and health law ::

The _________ of 1970 is a US labor law governing the federal law of occupational health and safety in the private sector and federal government in the United States. It was enacted by Congress in 1970 and was signed by President Richard Nixon on December 29, 1970. Its main goal is to ensure that employers provide employees with an environment free from recognized hazards, such as exposure to toxic chemicals, excessive noise levels, mechanical dangers, heat or cold stress, or unsanitary conditions. The Act created the Occupational Safety and Health Administration and the National Institute for Occupational Safety and Health .

Exam Probability: **High**

35. *Answer choices:*

(see index for correct answer)

- a. Factories Act 1961
- b. Occupational Safety and Health Act 1994
- c. Mines and Collieries Act 1842
- d. Factory and Workshop Act 1895

Guidance: level 1

:: Business law ::

A _________ is an arrangement where parties, known as partners, agree to cooperate to advance their mutual interests. The partners in a _________ may be individuals, businesses, interest-based organizations, schools, governments or combinations. Organizations may partner to increase the likelihood of each achieving their mission and to amplify their reach. A _________ may result in issuing and holding equity or may be only governed by a contract.

Exam Probability: **High**

36. *Answer choices:*

(see index for correct answer)

- a. Consularization
- b. Trusted Computing
- c. Independent contractor
- d. Partnership

Guidance: level 1

:: Developmental psychology ::

_________ behavior refers to behavior that enables a person to get along in his or her environment with greatest success and least conflict with others. This is a term used in the areas of psychology and special education. _________ behavior relates to every day skills or tasks that the average person is able to complete, similar to the term life skills.

Exam Probability: **Medium**

37. *Answer choices:*

(see index for correct answer)

- a. Adaptive
- b. Cognitive development

Guidance: level 1

:: Legal terms ::

_________, a form of alternative dispute resolution , is a way to resolve disputes outside the courts. The dispute will be decided by one or more persons , which renders the " _________ award". An _________ award is legally binding on both sides and enforceable in the courts.

Exam Probability: **High**

38. *Answer choices:*

(see index for correct answer)

- a. Concurring opinion
- b. IRAC
- c. Arbitrariness
- d. Arbitration

Guidance: level 1

:: Power (social and political) ::

_________ is a form of reverence gained by a leader who has strong interpersonal relationship skills. _________ , as an aspect of personal power, becomes particularly important as organizational leadership becomes increasingly about collaboration and influence, rather than command and control.

Exam Probability: **Medium**

39. *Answer choices:*

(see index for correct answer)

- a. Expert power
- b. need for power
- c. Hard power

Guidance: level 1

:: Human resource management ::

_________ involves improving the effectiveness of organizations and the individuals and teams within them. Training may be viewed as related to immediate changes in organizational effectiveness via organized instruction, while development is related to the progress of longer-term organizational and employee goals. While _________ technically have differing definitions, the two are oftentimes used interchangeably and/or together. _________ has historically been a topic within applied psychology but has within the last two decades become closely associated with human resources management, talent management, human resources development, instructional design, human factors, and knowledge management.

Exam Probability: **Medium**

40. *Answer choices:*

(see index for correct answer)

- a. Senior management
- b. Professional employer organization
- c. Training and development
- d. Joint Personnel Administration

Guidance: level 1

:: Organizational behavior ::

_________ is the act of matching attitudes, beliefs, and behaviors to group norms or politics. Norms are implicit, specific rules, shared by a group of individuals, that guide their interactions with others. People often choose to conform to society rather than to pursue personal desires because it is often easier to follow the path others have made already, rather than creating a new one. This tendency to conform occurs in small groups and/or society as a whole, and may result from subtle unconscious influences , or direct and overt social pressure. _________ can occur in the presence of others, or when an individual is alone. For example, people tend to follow social norms when eating or watching television, even when alone.

Exam Probability: **Low**

41. *Answer choices:*
(see index for correct answer)

- a. Organizational commitment
- b. Boreout
- c. Conformity
- d. History of contingency theories of leadership

Guidance: level 1

:: Organizational behavior ::

In organizational behavior and industrial and organizational psychology, _________ is an individual`s psychological attachment to the organization. The basis behind many of these studies was to find ways to improve how workers feel about their jobs so that these workers would become more committed to their organizations. _________ predicts work variables such as turnover, organizational citizenship behavior, and job performance. Some of the factors such as role stress, empowerment, job insecurity and employability, and distribution of leadership have been shown to be connected to a worker`s sense of _________ .

Exam Probability: **Medium**

42. *Answer choices:*
(see index for correct answer)

- a. Burnout
- b. Group behaviour
- c. Organizational storytelling

- d. Organizational commitment

Guidance: level 1

:: Human resource management ::

_________ is a continual process used to align the needs and priorities of the organization with those of its workforce to ensure it can meet its legislative, regulatory, service and production requirements and organizational objectives. _________ enables evidence based workforce development strategies.

Exam Probability: **Low**

43. *Answer choices:*

(see index for correct answer)

- a. Employee silence
- b. E-HRM
- c. Workforce planning
- d. Inclusive business

Guidance: level 1

:: Business law ::

An _________ is a natural person, business, or corporation that provides goods or services to another entity under terms specified in a contract or within a verbal agreement. Unlike an employee, an _________ does not work regularly for an employer but works as and when required, during which time they may be subject to law of agency. _________ s are usually paid on a freelance basis. Contractors often work through a limited company or franchise, which they themselves own, or may work through an umbrella company.

Exam Probability: **Low**

44. *Answer choices:*

(see index for correct answer)

- a. Hundi
- b. Statutory authority
- c. Limited liability
- d. Independent contractor

Guidance: level 1

:: Leadership ::

__________ is a theory of leadership where a leader works with teams to identify needed change, creating a vision to guide the change through inspiration, and executing the change in tandem with committed members of a group; it is an integral part of the Full Range Leadership Model. __________ serves to enhance the motivation, morale, and job performance of followers through a variety of mechanisms; these include connecting the follower`s sense of identity and self to a project and to the collective identity of the organization; being a role model for followers in order to inspire them and to raise their interest in the project; challenging followers to take greater ownership for their work, and understanding the strengths and weaknesses of followers, allowing the leader to align followers with tasks that enhance their performance.

Exam Probability: **Low**

45. *Answer choices:*

(see index for correct answer)

- a. Transformational leadership
- b. Coro
- c. Outstanding leadership theory
- d. Agentic leadership

Guidance: level 1

:: Workplace ::

__________ or occupational violence refers to violence, usually in the form of physical abuse or threat, that creates a risk to the health and safety of an employee or multiple employees. The National Institute for Occupational Safety and Health defines worker on worker, personal relationship, customer/client, and criminal intent all as categories of violence in the workplace. These four categories are further broken down into three levels: Level one displays early warning signs of violence, Level two is slightly more violent, and level three is significantly violent. Many workplaces have initiated programs and protocols to protect their workers as the Occupational Health Act of 1970 states that employers must provide an environment in which employees are free of harm or harmful conditions.

Exam Probability: **Low**

46. *Answer choices:*

(see index for correct answer)

- a. Workplace incivility
- b. Workplace violence
- c. Work etiquette
- d. Workplace deviance

Guidance: level 1

:: Life skills ::

_________ , emotional leadership , emotional quotient and _________ quotient , is the capability of individuals to recognize their own emotions and those of others, discern between different feelings and label them appropriately, use emotional information to guide thinking and behavior, and manage and/or adjust emotions to adapt to environments or achieve one's goal.

Exam Probability: **High**

47. *Answer choices:*

(see index for correct answer)

- a. Emotional intelligence
- b. coping mechanism
- c. Social intelligence
- d. emotion work

Guidance: level 1

:: Validity (statistics) ::

_________ is a type of evidence that can be gathered to defend the use of a test for predicting other outcomes. It is a parameter used in sociology, psychology, and other psychometric or behavioral sciences. _________ is demonstrated when a test correlates well with a measure that has previously been validated. The two measures may be for the same construct, but more often used for different, but presumably related, constructs.

Exam Probability: **Low**

48. *Answer choices:*

(see index for correct answer)

- a. Face validity
- b. Verification and validation
- c. Concurrent validity
- d. Validation

Guidance: level 1

:: Workplace ::

A __________ , also referred to as a performance review, performance evaluation, development discussion, or employee appraisal is a method by which the job performance of an employee is documented and evaluated. __________ s are a part of career development and consist of regular reviews of employee performance within organizations.

Exam Probability: **Low**

49. *Answer choices:*

(see index for correct answer)

- a. Workplace conflict
- b. labour turnover
- c. Staff turnover
- d. Workplace health surveillance

Guidance: level 1

:: Organizational structure ::

An __________ defines how activities such as task allocation, coordination, and supervision are directed toward the achievement of organizational aims.

Exam Probability: **Low**

50. *Answer choices:*

(see index for correct answer)

- a. Unorganisation
- b. The Starfish and the Spider
- c. Blessed Unrest
- d. Organizational structure

Guidance: level 1

:: Labor ::

The workforce or labour force is the labour pool in employment. It is generally used to describe those working for a single company or industry, but can also apply to a geographic region like a city, state, or country. Within a company, its value can be labelled as its "Workforce in Place". The workforce of a country includes both the employed and the unemployed. The labour force participation rate, LFPR , is the ratio between the labour force and the overall size of their cohort . The term generally excludes the employers or management, and can imply those involved in manual labour. It may also mean all those who are available for work.

Exam Probability: **Low**

51. *Answer choices:*

(see index for correct answer)

- a. Distributed workforce
- b. Occupational safety and health
- c. Labor force
- d. Wage compression

Guidance: level 1

:: ::

Refresher/ __________ is the process of learning a new or the same old skill or trade for the same group of personnel. Refresher/ __________ is required to be provided on regular basis to avoid personnel obsolescence due to technological changes & the individuals memory capacity. This short term instruction course shall serve to re-acquaint personnel with skills previously learnt or to bring one`s knowledge or skills up-to-date so that skills stay sharp. This kind of training could be provided annually or more frequently as maybe required, based on the importance of consistency of the task of which the skill is involved. Examples of refreshers are cGMP, GDP, HSE trainings. __________ shall also be conducted for an employee, when the employee is rated as ‘not qualified’ for a skill or knowledge, as determined based on the assessment of answers in the training questionnaire of the employee.

Exam Probability: **High**

52. *Answer choices:*

(see index for correct answer)

- a. imperative
- b. Retraining
- c. similarity-attraction theory
- d. levels of analysis

Guidance: level 1

:: ::

__________ medicine is an approach to medical practice intended to optimize decision-making by emphasizing the use of evidence from well-designed and well-conducted research. Although all medicine based on science has some degree of empirical support, EBM goes further, classifying evidence by its epistemologic strength and requiring that only the strongest types can yield strong recommendations; weaker types can yield only weak recommendations. The term was originally used to describe an approach to teaching the practice of medicine and improving decisions by individual physicians about individual patients. Use of the term rapidly expanded to include a previously described approach that emphasized the use of evidence in the design of guidelines and policies that apply to groups of patients and populations . It has subsequently spread to describe an approach to decision-making that is used at virtually every level of health care as well as other fields .

Exam Probability: **High**

53. *Answer choices:*
(see index for correct answer)

- a. corporate values
- b. hierarchical
- c. Sarbanes-Oxley act of 2002
- d. Evidence-based

Guidance: level 1

:: Employment compensation ::

__________ refers to various incentive plans introduced by businesses that provide direct or indirect payments to employees that depend on company`s profitability in addition to employees` regular salary and bonuses. In publicly traded companies these plans typically amount to allocation of shares to employees. One of the earliest pioneers of __________ was Englishman Theodore Cooke Taylor, who is known to have introduced the practice in his woollen mills during the late 1800s .

Exam Probability: **High**

54. *Answer choices:*

(see index for correct answer)

- a. Fringe benefits tax
- b. Employee assistance program
- c. Employees%27 Compensation Appeals Board
- d. Profit sharing

Guidance: level 1

:: Human resource management ::

An __________ is a diagram that shows the structure of an organization and the relationships and relative ranks of its parts and positions/jobs. The term is also used for similar diagrams, for example ones showing the different elements of a field of knowledge or a group of languages.

Exam Probability: **Medium**

55. *Answer choices:*

(see index for correct answer)

- a. Job description management
- b. Organizational chart
- c. The Giving of Orders
- d. Open plan

Guidance: level 1

:: ::

In educational development, __________ provides a person, often a student, focus for selecting a career or subject to undertake in the future. Often educational institutions provide career counsellors to assist students with their educational development.

Exam Probability: **Medium**

56. *Answer choices:*

(see index for correct answer)

- a. hierarchical
- b. Sarbanes-Oxley act of 2002
- c. deep-level diversity
- d. Career development

Guidance: level 1

:: ::

A __________ is monetary compensation paid by an employer to an employee in exchange for work done. Payment may be calculated as a fixed amount for each task completed , or at an hourly or daily rate , or based on an easily measured quantity of work done.

Exam Probability: **Medium**

57. *Answer choices:*

(see index for correct answer)

- a. empathy
- b. imperative
- c. similarity-attraction theory
- d. Wage

Guidance: level 1

:: ::

_________ was the plaintiff in the American employment discrimination case Ledbetter v. Goodyear Tire & Rubber Co. Congress passed a fair pay act in her name, the _________ Fair Pay Act of 2009. She has since become a women`s equality activist, public speaker, and author. In 2011, Ledbetter was inducted into the National Women`s Hall of Fame.

Exam Probability: **Low**

58. *Answer choices:*
(see index for correct answer)

- a. interpersonal communication
- b. cultural
- c. Lilly Ledbetter
- d. surface-level diversity

Guidance: level 1

:: Industrial agreements ::

_________ is a process of negotiation between employers and a group of employees aimed at agreements to regulate working salaries, working conditions, benefits, and other aspects of workers` compensation and rights for workers. The interests of the employees are commonly presented by representatives of a trade union to which the employees belong. The collective agreements reached by these negotiations usually set out wage scales, working hours, training, health and safety, overtime, grievance mechanisms, and rights to participate in workplace or company affairs.

Exam Probability: **High**

59. *Answer choices:*
(see index for correct answer)

- a. Australian Industrial Relations Commission
- b. Pattern bargaining
- c. Ex parte H.V. McKay
- d. Collective bargaining

Guidance: level 1

Information systems

Information systems (IS) are formal, sociotechnical, organizational systems designed to collect, process, store, and distribute information. In a sociotechnical perspective Information Systems are composed by four components: technology, process, people and organizational structure.

:: Data privacy ::

The _________ is an information security standard for organizations that handle branded credit cards from the major card schemes.

Exam Probability: **Low**

1. *Answer choices:*

(see index for correct answer)

- a. Unclick
- b. De-identification
- c. Payment Card Industry Data Security Standard
- d. Federal Data Protection and Information Commissioner

Guidance: level 1

:: ::

A database is an organized collection of data, generally stored and accessed electronically from a computer system. Where databases are more complex they are often developed using formal design and modeling techniques.

Exam Probability: **Low**

2. *Answer choices:*

(see index for correct answer)

- a. Database management system
- b. imperative
- c. process perspective
- d. information systems assessment

Guidance: level 1

:: Data management ::

" __________ " is a field that treats ways to analyze, systematically extract information from, or otherwise deal with data sets that are too large or complex to be dealt with by traditional data-processing application software. Data with many cases offer greater statistical power, while data with higher complexity may lead to a higher false discovery rate. __________ challenges include capturing data, data storage, data analysis, search, sharing, transfer, visualization, querying, updating, information privacy and data source. __________ was originally associated with three key concepts: volume, variety, and velocity. Other concepts later attributed with __________ are veracity and value.

Exam Probability: **High**

3. *Answer choices:*

(see index for correct answer)

- a. Electronic lab notebook
- b. Serializability
- c. Navigational database
- d. Modular concurrency control

Guidance: level 1

:: Data ::

__________ is a branch of mathematics working with data collection, organization, analysis, interpretation and presentation. In applying __________ to, for example, a scientific, industrial, or social problem, it is conventional to begin with a statistical population or a statistical model process to be studied. Populations can be diverse topics such as "all people living in a country" or "every atom composing a crystal". __________ deals with every aspect of data, including the planning of data collection in terms of the design of surveys and experiments.See glossary of probability and __________ .

Exam Probability: **High**

4. *Answer choices:*
(see index for correct answer)

- a. DataSplice
- b. QUADRIGRAM
- c. Statistics
- d. Data redundancy

Guidance: level 1

:: Teams ::

A __________ usually refers to a group of individuals who work together from different geographic locations and rely on communication technology such as email, FAX, and video or voice conferencing services in order to collaborate. The term can also refer to groups or teams that work together asynchronously or across organizational levels. Powell, Piccoli and Ives define __________ s as "groups of geographically, organizationally and/or time dispersed workers brought together by information and telecommunication technologies to accomplish one or more organizational tasks." According to Ale Ebrahim et. al. , __________ s can also be defined as "small temporary groups of geographically, organizationally and/or time dispersed knowledge workers who coordinate their work predominantly with electronic information and communication technologies in order to accomplish one or more organization tasks."

Exam Probability: **High**

5. *Answer choices:*
(see index for correct answer)

- a. team composition
- b. Team-building

Guidance: level 1

:: E-commerce ::

Electronic governance or e-governance is the application of information and communication technology for delivering government services, exchange of information, communication transactions, integration of various stand-alone systems and services between government-to-citizen , _________ , government-to-government , government-to-employees as well as back-office processes and interactions within the entire government framework. Through e-governance, government services are made available to citizens in a convenient, efficient, and transparent manner. The three main target groups that can be distinguished in governance concepts are government, citizens, andbusinesses/interest groups. In e-governance, there are no distinct boundaries.

Exam Probability: **Medium**

6. *Answer choices:*

(see index for correct answer)

- a. Loquo
- b. Inter-protocol exploitation
- c. Virtual goods
- d. Online Revolution

Guidance: level 1

:: Critical thinking ::

In psychology, _________ is regarded as the cognitive process resulting in the selection of a belief or a course of action among several alternative possibilities. Every _________ process produces a final choice, which may or may not prompt action.

Exam Probability: **Medium**

7. *Answer choices:*

(see index for correct answer)

- a. Explanation
- b. Argument by example
- c. Informal logic
- d. Decidophobia

Guidance: level 1

:: Systems theory ::

A __________ is a group of interacting or interrelated entities that form a unified whole. A __________ is delineated by its spatial and temporal boundaries, surrounded and influenced by its environment, described by its structure and purpose and expressed in its functioning.

Exam Probability: **High**

8. *Answer choices:*

(see index for correct answer)

- a. Viable System Model
- b. equifinality
- c. transient state
- d. Black box

Guidance: level 1

:: Reputation management ::

__________ refers to the influencing and controlling of an individual's or group's reputation. Originally a public relations term, the growth of the internet and social media, along with __________ companies, have made search results a core part of an individual's or group's reputation. Online __________ , sometimes abbreviated as ORM, focuses on the management of product and service search website results. Ethical grey areas include mug shot removal sites, astroturfing customer review sites, censoring negative complaints, and using search engine optimization tactics to influence results.

Exam Probability: **Medium**

9. *Answer choices:*

(see index for correct answer)

- a. Reputation management
- b. Distrust
- c. EigenTrust

- d. Sybil attack

Guidance: level 1

:: Production economics ::

__________ is a way of producing goods and services that relies on self-organizing communities of individuals. In such communities, the labor of a large number of people is coordinated towards a shared outcome.

Exam Probability: **Low**

10. *Answer choices:*

(see index for correct answer)

- a. Average fixed cost
- b. Value and Capital
- c. Cost-of-production theory of value
- d. Peer production

Guidance: level 1

:: E-commerce ::

Customer to customer markets provide an innovative way to allow customers to interact with each other. Traditional markets require business to customer relationships, in which a customer goes to the business in order to purchase a product or service. In customer to customer markets, the business facilitates an environment where customers can sell goods or services to each other. Other types of markets include business to business and business to customer .

Exam Probability: **High**

11. *Answer choices:*

(see index for correct answer)

- a. MOL AccessPortal
- b. Webjet
- c. Consumer-to-consumer
- d. Bill2phone

Guidance: level 1

:: Production economics ::

In microeconomics, _________ are the cost advantages that enterprises obtain due to their scale of operation , with cost per unit of output decreasing with increasing scale.

Exam Probability: **High**

12. *Answer choices:*

(see index for correct answer)

- a. Post-Fordism
- b. Hicks-neutral technical change
- c. Marginal cost
- d. Total factor productivity

Guidance: level 1

:: Consumer behaviour ::

_________ is the ratio of users who click on a specific link to the number of total users who view a page, email, or advertisement. It is commonly used to measure the success of an online advertising campaign for a particular website as well as the effectiveness of email campaigns.

Exam Probability: **Medium**

13. *Answer choices:*

(see index for correct answer)

- a. Customer delight
- b. Customer engagement
- c. Click-through rate
- d. Conspicuous expression

Guidance: level 1

:: ::

_________ is a brand name associated with the development of the _________ web browser. It is now owned by Verizon Media, a subsidiary of Verizon. The brand belonged to the _________ Communications Corporation , an independent American computer services company, whose headquarters were in Mountain View, California, and later Dulles, Virginia. The browser was once dominant but lost to Internet Explorer and other competitors after the so-called first browser war, its market share falling from more than 90 percent in the mid-1990s to less than 1 percent in 2006.

Exam Probability: **Medium**

14. *Answer choices:*
(see index for correct answer)

- a. open system
- b. Netscape
- c. corporate values
- d. process perspective

Guidance: level 1

:: ::

The _________ , commonly known as the Web, is an information system where documents and other web resources are identified by Uniform Resource Locators , which may be interlinked by hypertext, and are accessible over the Internet. The resources of the WWW may be accessed by users by a software application called a web browser.

Exam Probability: **Medium**

15. *Answer choices:*
(see index for correct answer)

- a. empathy
- b. similarity-attraction theory
- c. open system
- d. functional perspective

Guidance: level 1

:: Metadata ::

__________ s usage can be discovered by inspection of software applications or application data files through a process of manual or automated Application Discovery and Understanding. Once __________ s are discovered they can be registered in a metadata registry.

Exam Probability: **High**

16. *Answer choices:*

(see index for correct answer)

- a. Transclusion
- b. Data element
- c. Learning Resource Metadata Initiative
- d. Image Cytometry Standard

Guidance: level 1

:: Data ::

In computer main memory, auxiliary storage and computer buses, __________ is the existence of data that is additional to the actual data and permits correction of errors in stored or transmitted data. The additional data can simply be a complete copy of the actual data, or only select pieces of data that allow detection of errors and reconstruction of lost or damaged data up to a certain level.

Exam Probability: **Medium**

17. *Answer choices:*

(see index for correct answer)

- a. Data redundancy
- b. Dummy data
- c. Data citation
- d. Serial concatenated convolutional codes

Guidance: level 1

:: Data collection ::

__________ is the application of data mining techniques to discover patterns from the World Wide Web. As the name proposes, this is information gathered by mining the web. It makes utilization of automated apparatuses to reveal and extricate data from servers and web2 reports, and it permits organizations to get to both organized and unstructured information from browser activities, server logs, website and link structure, page content and different sources.

Exam Probability: **Medium**

18. *Answer choices:*

(see index for correct answer)

- a. Field recording
- b. PowerLab
- c. Five Eyes
- d. Data scraping

Guidance: level 1

:: Internet marketing ::

__________ is the measurement, collection, analysis and reporting of web data for purposes of understanding and optimizing web usage. However, __________ is not just a process for measuring web traffic but can be used as a tool for business and market research, and to assess and improve the effectiveness of a website. __________ applications can also help companies measure the results of traditional print or broadcast advertising campaigns. It helps one to estimate how traffic to a website changes after the launch of a new advertising campaign. __________ provides information about the number of visitors to a website and the number of page views. It helps gauge traffic and popularity trends which is useful for market research.

Exam Probability: **High**

19. *Answer choices:*

(see index for correct answer)

- a. Squeeze page
- b. Web analytics
- c. Crown Partners
- d. Microsoft pubCenter

Guidance: level 1

:: Data security ::

__________ are safeguards or countermeasures to avoid, detect, counteract, or minimize security risks to physical property, information, computer systems, or other assets.

Exam Probability: **Medium**

20. *Answer choices:*

(see index for correct answer)

- a. Active hard-drive protection
- b. Gutmann method
- c. Security controls
- d. Cracking of wireless networks

Guidance: level 1

:: Management ::

The __________ is a strategy performance management tool – a semi-standard structured report, that can be used by managers to keep track of the execution of activities by the staff within their control and to monitor the consequences arising from these actions.

Exam Probability: **Medium**

21. *Answer choices:*

(see index for correct answer)

- a. Balanced scorecard
- b. Industrial democracy
- c. Line management
- d. Submission management

Guidance: level 1

:: ::

__________ is a set of values of subjects with respect to qualitative or quantitative variables.

Exam Probability: **Medium**

22. *Answer choices:*

(see index for correct answer)

- a. hierarchical
- b. cultural
- c. interpersonal communication
- d. Data

Guidance: level 1

:: Security compliance ::

__________ refers to the inability to withstand the effects of a hostile environment. A window of __________ is a time frame within which defensive measures are diminished, compromised or lacking.

Exam Probability: **Medium**

23. *Answer choices:*

(see index for correct answer)

- a. North American Electric Reliability Corporation
- b. Nikto Web Scanner
- c. Vulnerability
- d. Threat

Guidance: level 1

:: E-commerce ::

Electronic governance or e-governance is the application of information and communication technology for delivering government services, exchange of information, communication transactions, integration of various stand-alone systems and services between __________ , government-to-business , government-to-government , government-to-employees as well as back-office processes and interactions within the entire government framework. Through e-governance, government services are made available to citizens in a convenient, efficient, and transparent manner. The three main target groups that can be distinguished in governance concepts are government, citizens, andbusinesses/interest groups. In e-governance, there are no distinct boundaries.

Exam Probability: **Low**

24. *Answer choices:*
(see index for correct answer)

- a. ChannelAdvisor
- b. Gazaro
- c. FastSpring
- d. Government-to-citizen

Guidance: level 1

:: Data privacy ::

_________ is the relationship between the collection and dissemination of data, technology, the public expectation of privacy, legal and political issues surrounding them. It is also known as data privacy or data protection.

Exam Probability: **Medium**

25. *Answer choices:*
(see index for correct answer)

- a. Swedish Data Inspection Board
- b. Information privacy
- c. BarWatch
- d. Unclick

Guidance: level 1

:: Information technology management ::

The term _________ is used to refer to periods when a system is unavailable. _________ or outage duration refers to a period of time that a system fails to provide or perform its primary function. Reliability, availability, recovery, and unavailability are related concepts.The unavailability is the proportion of a time-span that a system is unavailable or offline.This is usually a result of the system failing to function because of an unplanned event, or because of routine maintenance .

Exam Probability: **Low**

26. *Answer choices:*
(see index for correct answer)

- a. Information Services Procurement Library
- b. IT risk

- c. Downtime
- d. Infra Corporation

Guidance: level 1

:: Enterprise architecture ::

Enterprise software, also known as _________ software , is computer software used to satisfy the needs of an organization rather than individual users. Such organizations include businesses, schools, interest-based user groups, clubs, charities, and governments. Enterprise software is an integral part of a information system.

Exam Probability: **Medium**

27. *Answer choices:*

(see index for correct answer)

- a. Enterprise application
- b. Enterprise architecture management
- c. Mobile enterprise application platform
- d. Dynamic enterprise

Guidance: level 1

:: Telecommunications engineering ::

A _________ is a computer processor that incorporates the functions of a central processing unit on a single integrated circuit , or at most a few integrated circuits. The _________ is a multipurpose, clock driven, register based, digital integrated circuit that accepts binary data as input, processes it according to instructions stored in its memory and provides results as output. _________ s contain both combinational logic and sequential digital logic. _________ s operate on numbers and symbols represented in the binary number system.

Exam Probability: **High**

28. *Answer choices:*

(see index for correct answer)

- a. Computer network
- b. network architecture

Guidance: level 1

:: Data quality ::

__________ or data cleaning is the process of detecting and correcting corrupt or inaccurate records from a record set, table, or database and refers to identifying incomplete, incorrect, inaccurate or irrelevant parts of the data and then replacing, modifying, or deleting the dirty or coarse data. __________ may be performed interactively with data wrangling tools, or as batch processing through scripting.

Exam Probability: **Medium**

29. *Answer choices:*

(see index for correct answer)

- a. Data Quality Firewall
- b. Information quality
- c. Database preservation
- d. Data cleansing

Guidance: level 1

:: Information systems ::

__________ s are information systems that are developed in response to corporate business initiative. They are intended to give competitive advantage to the organization. They may deliver a product or service that is at a lower cost, that is differentiated, that focuses on a particular market segment, or is innovative.

Exam Probability: **High**

30. *Answer choices:*

(see index for correct answer)

- a. Transport standards organisations
- b. System of record
- c. Strategic information system
- d. Electronic markets

Guidance: level 1

:: Telecommunication theory ::

In reliability theory and reliability engineering, the term _________ has the following meanings.

Exam Probability: **High**

31. *Answer choices:*

(see index for correct answer)

- a. Digital signal processing
- b. Asynchronous operation
- c. Modal bandwidth
- d. Reflection loss

Guidance: level 1

:: ::

A _________ is a discussion or informational website published on the World Wide Web consisting of discrete, often informal diary-style text entries . Posts are typically displayed in reverse chronological order, so that the most recent post appears first, at the top of the web page. Until 2009, _________ s were usually the work of a single individual, occasionally of a small group, and often covered a single subject or topic. In the 2010s, "multi-author _________ s" emerged, featuring the writing of multiple authors and sometimes professionally edited. MABs from newspapers, other media outlets, universities, think tanks, advocacy groups, and similar institutions account for an increasing quantity of _________ traffic. The rise of Twitter and other "micro _________ ging" systems helps integrate MABs and single-author _________ s into the news media. _________ can also be used as a verb, meaning to maintain or add content to a _________ .

Exam Probability: **Medium**

32. *Answer choices:*

(see index for correct answer)

- a. Sarbanes-Oxley act of 2002
- b. empathy
- c. co-culture
- d. Blog

Guidance: level 1

:: ::

A __________ is a computer file which stores data to be used by a computer application or system, including input and output data. A __________ usually does not contain instructions or code to be executed .

Exam Probability: **High**

33. *Answer choices:*

(see index for correct answer)

- a. levels of analysis
- b. cultural
- c. personal values
- d. Data file

Guidance: level 1

:: Transaction processing ::

Transaction processing is information processing in computer science that is divided into individual, indivisible operations called transactions. Each transaction must succeed or fail as a complete unit; it can never be only partially complete.

Exam Probability: **High**

34. *Answer choices:*

(see index for correct answer)

- a. Straight-through processing
- b. Tandem Computers
- c. Pseudoconversational transaction
- d. Memory semantics

Guidance: level 1

:: ::

A __________ is a control panel usually located directly ahead of a vehicle`s driver, displaying instrumentation and controls for the vehicle`s operation.

Exam Probability: **Medium**

35. *Answer choices:*

(see index for correct answer)

- a. Sarbanes-Oxley act of 2002
- b. information systems assessment
- c. surface-level diversity
- d. Character

Guidance: level 1

:: Big data ::

_________ is the discovery, interpretation, and communication of meaningful patterns in data; and the process of applying those patterns towards effective decision making. In other words, _________ can be understood as the connective tissue between data and effective decision making, within an organization. Especially valuable in areas rich with recorded information, _________ relies on the simultaneous application of statistics, computer programming and operations research to quantify performance.

Exam Probability: **Medium**

36. *Answer choices:*

(see index for correct answer)

- a. Flytxt
- b. Analytics
- c. Continuuity
- d. Attivio

Guidance: level 1

:: Knowledge representation ::

__________ is the system in which users apply public tags to online items, typically to make those items easier for themselves or others to find later. Over time, this can give rise to a classification system based on those tags and how often they are applied or searched for, in contrast to a taxonomic classification designed by the owners of the content and specified when it is published. This practice is also known as collaborative tagging, social classification, social indexing, and social tagging. __________ was originally "the result of personal free tagging of information [...] for one`s own retrieval", but online sharing and interaction expanded it into collaborative forms. Social tagging is the application of tags in an open online environment where the tags of other users are available to others. Collaborative tagging is tagging performed by a group of users. This type of __________ is commonly used in cooperative and collaborative projects such as research, content repositories, and social bookmarking.

Exam Probability: **Low**

37. *Answer choices:*

(see index for correct answer)

- a. Enactive interfaces
- b. Folksonomy
- c. Darwin Core Archive
- d. Pretext

Guidance: level 1

:: Policy ::

A __________ is a statement or a legal document that discloses some or all of the ways a party gathers, uses, discloses, and manages a customer or client`s data. It fulfills a legal requirement to protect a customer or client`s privacy. Personal information can be anything that can be used to identify an individual, not limited to the person`s name, address, date of birth, marital status, contact information, ID issue, and expiry date, financial records, credit information, medical history, where one travels, and intentions to acquire goods and services. In the case of a business it is often a statement that declares a party`s policy on how it collects, stores, and releases personal information it collects. It informs the client what specific information is collected, and whether it is kept confidential, shared with partners, or sold to other firms or enterprises. Privacy policies typically represent a broader, more generalized treatment, as opposed to data use statements, which tend to be more detailed and specific.

Exam Probability: **Low**

38. *Answer choices:*
(see index for correct answer)

- a. Privacy policy
- b. Institute of International and European Affairs
- c. Policy Monitoring
- d. Multifunctionality in agriculture

Guidance: level 1

:: Business models ::

__________, a portmanteau of the words "free" and "premium", is a pricing strategy by which a product or service is provided free of charge, but money is charged for additional features, services, or virtual or physical goods. The business model has been in use by the software industry since the 1980s as a licensing scheme. A subset of this model used by the video game industry is called free-to-play.

Exam Probability: **Low**

39. *Answer choices:*
(see index for correct answer)

- a. Strategy map
- b. Artel

- c. Co-operative Wholesale Society
- d. The India Way

Guidance: level 1

:: Data modeling languages ::

An entity–relationship model describes interrelated things of interest in a specific domain of knowledge. A basic ER model is composed of entity types and specifies relationships that can exist between entities .

Exam Probability: **Low**

40. *Answer choices:*

(see index for correct answer)

- a. TREX
- b. Text Encoding Initiative
- c. Standard Generalized Markup Language
- d. Binary Format Description language

Guidance: level 1

:: Global Positioning System ::

A _________ is a mechanism for determining the location of an object in space. Technologies for this task exist ranging from worldwide coverage with meter accuracy to workspace coverage with sub-millimetre accuracy.

Exam Probability: **High**

41. *Answer choices:*

(see index for correct answer)

- a. Positioning system
- b. UNAVCO
- c. VZ Navigator
- d. StarFire

Guidance: level 1

:: ::

A __________ is a research instrument consisting of a series of questions for the purpose of gathering information from respondents. The __________ was invented by the Statistical Society of London in 1838.

Exam Probability: **Medium**

42. *Answer choices:*

(see index for correct answer)

- a. Character
- b. co-culture
- c. functional perspective
- d. Questionnaire

Guidance: level 1

:: ::

__________ are electronic transfer of money from one bank account to another, either within a single financial institution or across multiple institutions, via computer-based systems, without the direct intervention of bank staff.

Exam Probability: **High**

43. *Answer choices:*

(see index for correct answer)

- a. Character
- b. interpersonal communication
- c. functional perspective
- d. deep-level diversity

Guidance: level 1

:: ::

A __________ is a telecommunications network that extends over a large geographical distance for the primary purpose of computer networking. __________ s are often established with leased telecommunication circuits.

Exam Probability: **Low**

44. *Answer choices:*
(see index for correct answer)

- a. levels of analysis
- b. Character
- c. open system
- d. hierarchical

Guidance: level 1

:: Help desk ::

Data center management is the collection of tasks performed by those responsible for managing ongoing operation of a data center This includes Business service management and planning for the future.

Exam Probability: **High**

45. *Answer choices:*
(see index for correct answer)

- a. Technical support
- b. HEAT
- c. Help desk
- d. KnowledgeBase Manager Pro

Guidance: level 1

:: ::

__________, Inc. was a company that provided human resource management systems , Financial Management Solutions , supply chain management , customer relationship management , and enterprise performance management software, as well as software for manufacturing, and student administration to large corporations, governments, and organizations. It existed as an independent corporation until its acquisition by Oracle Corporation in 2005. The __________ name and product line are now marketed by Oracle.

Exam Probability: **Low**

46. *Answer choices:*
(see index for correct answer)

- a. empathy
- b. open system

* c. PeopleSoft
* d. hierarchical perspective

Guidance: level 1

:: ::

A __________ or data centre is a building, dedicated space within a building, or a group of buildings used to house computer systems and associated components, such as telecommunications and storage systems.

Exam Probability: **Medium**

47. *Answer choices:*

(see index for correct answer)

* a. deep-level diversity
* b. functional perspective
* c. empathy
* d. Data center

Guidance: level 1

:: Payment systems ::

A __________ is any system used to settle financial transactions through the transfer of monetary value. This includes the institutions, instruments, people, rules, procedures, standards, and technologies that make it exchange possible. A common type of __________ is called an operational network that links bank accounts and provides for monetary exchange using bank deposits. Some __________ s also include credit mechanisms, which are essentially a different aspect of payment.

Exam Probability: **Medium**

48. *Answer choices:*

(see index for correct answer)

* a. E-toll
* b. Invoicera
* c. Certified Payment-Card Industry Security Implementer
* d. WorldPay

Guidance: level 1

:: Survey methodology ::

A _________ is the procedure of systematically acquiring and recording information about the members of a given population. The term is used mostly in connection with national population and housing _________ es; other common _________ es include agriculture, business, and traffic _________ es. The United Nations defines the essential features of population and housing _________ es as "individual enumeration, universality within a defined territory, simultaneity and defined periodicity", and recommends that population _________ es be taken at least every 10 years. United Nations recommendations also cover _________ topics to be collected, official definitions, classifications and other useful information to co-ordinate international practice.

Exam Probability: **Low**

49. *Answer choices:*

(see index for correct answer)

- a. Census
- b. Data editing
- c. World Association for Public Opinion Research
- d. Self-report study

Guidance: level 1

:: Data management ::

_________ represents the business objects that contain the most valuable, agreed upon information shared across an organization. It can cover relatively static reference data, transactional, unstructured, analytical, hierarchical and metadata. It is the primary focus of the information technology discipline of _________ management .

Exam Probability: **Low**

50. *Answer choices:*

(see index for correct answer)

- a. Master data
- b. Document capture software
- c. Data archaeology
- d. Electronic lab notebook

Guidance: level 1

:: Network architecture ::

An __________ is a controlled private network that allows access to partners, vendors and suppliers or an authorized set of customers – normally to a subset of the information accessible from an organization`s intranet. An __________ is similar to a DMZ in that it provides access to needed services for authorized parties, without granting access to an organization`s entire network. An __________ is a private network organization.

Exam Probability: **Medium**

51. *Answer choices:*

(see index for correct answer)

- a. Internetworking
- b. Extranet

Guidance: level 1

:: Information systems ::

__________ is a process used in the life cycle area of the dynamic systems development method to collect business requirements while developing new information systems for a company. "The JAD process also includes approaches for enhancing user participation, expediting development, and improving the quality of specifications." It consists of a workshop where "knowledge workers and IT specialists meet, sometimes for several days, to define and review the business requirements for the system." The attendees include high level management officials who will ensure the product provides the needed reports and information at the end. This acts as "a management process which allows Corporate Information Services departments to work more effectively with users in a shorter time frame".

Exam Probability: **Low**

52. *Answer choices:*

(see index for correct answer)

- a. Website Meta Language
- b. Payroll automation
- c. Joint application design

- d. Expert system

Guidance: level 1

:: E-commerce ::

The phrase _________ was originally coined in 1997 by Kevin Duffey at the launch of the Global _________ Forum, to mean "the delivery of electronic commerce capabilities directly into the consumer's hand, anywhere, via wireless technology." Many choose to think of _________ as meaning "a retail outlet in your customer's pocket."

Exam Probability: **Low**

53. *Answer choices:*
(see index for correct answer)

- a. Mobile commerce
- b. Friend-to-friend
- c. Inventory Information Approval System
- d. Mobile commerce service provider

Guidance: level 1

:: Multi-agent systems ::

A _________ is a number of Internet-connected devices, each of which is running one or more bots. _________ s can be used to perform distributed denial-of-service attack , steal data, send spam, and allows the attacker to access the device and its connection. The owner can control the _________ using command and control software. The word " _________ " is a combination of the words "robot" and "network". The term is usually used with a negative or malicious connotation.

Exam Probability: **Low**

54. *Answer choices:*
(see index for correct answer)

- a. Net-SNMP
- b. Botnet
- c. 2APL
- d. Xymon

Guidance: level 1

:: ::

__________ is software designed to provide a platform for other software. Examples of __________ include operating systems like macOS, Ubuntu and Microsoft Windows, computational science software, game engines, industrial automation, and software as a service applications.

Exam Probability: **Medium**

55. *Answer choices:*
(see index for correct answer)

- a. open system
- b. similarity-attraction theory
- c. Sarbanes-Oxley act of 2002
- d. System software

Guidance: level 1

:: Human–computer interaction ::

__________ is a database query language for relational databases. It was devised by Moshé M. Zloof at IBM Research during the mid-1970s, in parallel to the development of SQL. It is the first graphical query language, using visual tables where the user would enter commands, example elements and conditions. Many graphical front-ends for databases use the ideas from QBE today. Originally limited only for the purpose of retrieving data, QBE was later extended to allow other operations, such as inserts, deletes and updates, as well as creation of temporary tables.

Exam Probability: **High**

56. *Answer choices:*
(see index for correct answer)

- a. Affordance
- b. Query by Example
- c. The Magical Number Seven, Plus or Minus Two
- d. Reading path

Guidance: level 1

:: Information technology management ::

In information technology to _________ means to move from one place to another, information to detailed data by focusing in on something. In a GUI-environment, "drilling-down" may involve clicking on some representation in order to reveal more detail.

Exam Probability: **Medium**

57. *Answer choices:*

(see index for correct answer)

- a. E-Booking
- b. Automic
- c. Contract management
- d. CatDV

Guidance: level 1

:: Network management ::

_________ is the process of administering and managing computer networks. Services provided by this discipline include fault analysis, performance management, provisioning of networks and maintaining the quality of service. Software that enables network administrators to perform their functions is called _________ software.

Exam Probability: **Low**

58. *Answer choices:*

(see index for correct answer)

- a. IP Virtual Server
- b. Network management
- c. WS-Management
- d. Element Management

Guidance: level 1

:: E-commerce ::

__________ , and its now-deprecated predecessor, Secure Sockets Layer , are cryptographic protocols designed to provide communications security over a computer network. Several versions of the protocols find widespread use in applications such as web browsing, email, instant messaging, and voice over IP . Websites can use TLS to secure all communications between their servers and web browsers.

Exam Probability: **Low**

59. *Answer choices:*

(see index for correct answer)

- a. Yemeksepeti
- b. Transport Layer Security
- c. Seja online
- d. Affiliate marketing

Guidance: level 1

Marketing

Marketing is the study and management of exchange relationships. Marketing is the business process of creating relationships with and satisfying customers. With its focus on the customer, marketing is one of the premier components of business management.
Marketing is defined by the American Marketing Association as "the activity, set of institutions, and processes for creating, communicating, delivering, and exchanging offerings that have value for customers, clients, partners, and society at large."

:: ::

__________ consists of using generic or ad hoc methods in an orderly manner to find solutions to problems. Some of the problem-solving techniques developed and used in philosophy, artificial intelligence, computer science, engineering, mathematics, or medicine are related to mental problem-solving techniques studied in psychology.

Exam Probability: **High**

1. *Answer choices:*

(see index for correct answer)

- a. Problem Solving
- b. levels of analysis
- c. information systems assessment
- d. hierarchical

Guidance: level 1

:: ::

__________ is the means to see, hear, or become aware of something or someone through our fundamental senses. The term __________ derives from the Latin word perceptio, and is the organization, identification, and interpretation of sensory information in order to represent and understand the presented information, or the environment.

Exam Probability: **High**

2. *Answer choices:*

(see index for correct answer)

- a. Perception
- b. cultural
- c. open system
- d. Sarbanes-Oxley act of 2002

Guidance: level 1

:: ::

A __________ is a graphic mark, emblem, or symbol used to aid and promote public identification and recognition. It may be of an abstract or figurative design or include the text of the name it represents as in a wordmark.

Exam Probability: **Low**

3. *Answer choices:*

(see index for correct answer)

- a. similarity-attraction theory
- b. hierarchical
- c. Logo
- d. interpersonal communication

Guidance: level 1

:: Monopoly (economics) ::

A __________ is a form of intellectual property that gives its owner the legal right to exclude others from making, using, selling, and importing an invention for a limited period of years, in exchange for publishing an enabling public disclosure of the invention. In most countries __________ rights fall under civil law and the __________ holder needs to sue someone infringing the __________ in order to enforce his or her rights. In some industries __________ s are an essential form of competitive advantage; in others they are irrelevant.

Exam Probability: **Low**

4. *Answer choices:*

(see index for correct answer)

- a. Special 301 Report
- b. Practice of law
- c. Patent
- d. Privatization

Guidance: level 1

:: Business ::

The seller, or the provider of the goods or services, completes a sale in response to an acquisition, appropriation, requisition or a direct interaction with the buyer at the point of sale. There is a passing of title of the item, and the settlement of a price, in which agreement is reached on a price for which transfer of ownership of the item will occur. The seller, not the purchaser typically executes the sale and it may be completed prior to the obligation of payment. In the case of indirect interaction, a person who sells goods or service on behalf of the owner is known as a __________ man or __________ woman or __________ person, but this often refers to someone selling goods in a store/shop, in which case other terms are also common, including __________ clerk, shop assistant, and retail clerk.

Exam Probability: **Medium**

5. *Answer choices:*

(see index for correct answer)

- a. Sales
- b. Service recovery
- c. Number

- d. Price-based selling

Guidance: level 1

:: International trade ::

In finance, an _________ is the rate at which one currency will be exchanged for another. It is also regarded as the value of one country's currency in relation to another currency. For example, an interbank _________ of 114 Japanese yen to the United States dollar means that ¥114 will be exchanged for each US$1 or that US$1 will be exchanged for each ¥114. In this case it is said that the price of a dollar in relation to yen is ¥114, or equivalently that the price of a yen in relation to dollars is $1/114.

Exam Probability: **Low**

6. *Answer choices:*

(see index for correct answer)

- a. International Organisation of Employers
- b. Exchange rate
- c. Internationalization
- d. Outward Processing Arrangement

Guidance: level 1

:: Management accounting ::

In economics, _________ s, indirect costs or overheads are business expenses that are not dependent on the level of goods or services produced by the business. They tend to be time-related, such as interest or rents being paid per month, and are often referred to as overhead costs. This is in contrast to variable costs, which are volume-related and unknown at the beginning of the accounting year. For a simple example, such as a bakery, the monthly rent for the baking facilities, and the monthly payments for the security system and basic phone line are _________ s, as they do not change according to how much bread the bakery produces and sells. On the other hand, the wage costs of the bakery are variable, as the bakery will have to hire more workers if the production of bread increases. Economists reckon _________ as a entry barrier for new entrepreneurs.

Exam Probability: **Low**

7. *Answer choices:*

(see index for correct answer)

- a. Environmental full-cost accounting
- b. Variance
- c. activity based costing
- d. Fixed cost

Guidance: level 1

:: Communication design ::

An _________ is a series of advertisement messages that share a single idea and theme which make up an integrated marketing communication . An IMC is a platform in which a group of people can group their ideas, beliefs, and concepts into one large media base. _________ s utilize diverse media channels over a particular time frame and target identified audiences.

Exam Probability: **High**

8. *Answer choices:*

(see index for correct answer)

- a. Nissa Quanstrom
- b. Stuart Bailey
- c. Advertising campaign
- d. Penguin Composition Rules

Guidance: level 1

:: ::

In financial markets, a share is a unit used as mutual funds, limited partnerships, and real estate investment trusts. The owner of _________ in the corporation/company is a shareholder of the corporation. A share is an indivisible unit of capital, expressing the ownership relationship between the company and the shareholder. The denominated value of a share is its face value, and the total of the face value of issued _________ represent the capital of a company, which may not reflect the market value of those _________ .

Exam Probability: **Medium**

9. *Answer choices:*

(see index for correct answer)

- a. functional perspective
- b. similarity-attraction theory
- c. Shares
- d. levels of analysis

Guidance: level 1

:: ::

A _________ is any person who contracts to acquire an asset in return for some form of consideration.

Exam Probability: **High**

10. *Answer choices:*

(see index for correct answer)

- a. hierarchical
- b. Buyer
- c. Sarbanes-Oxley act of 2002
- d. personal values

Guidance: level 1

:: ::

Bloomberg Businessweek is an American weekly business magazine published since 2009 by Bloomberg L.P. Businessweek, founded in 1929, aimed to provide information and interpretation about events in the business world. The magazine is headquartered in New York City. Megan Murphy served as editor from November 2016; she stepped down from the role in January 2018 and Joel Weber was appointed in her place.The magazine is published 47 times a year.

Exam Probability: **Low**

11. *Answer choices:*

(see index for correct answer)

- a. Character
- b. Business Week
- c. interpersonal communication
- d. deep-level diversity

Guidance: level 1

:: Business ::

In commerce, _________ is the product of an interaction between an organization and a customer over the duration of their relationship.This interaction is made up of three parts: the customer journey, the brand touchpoints the customer interacts with, and the environments the _________ s during their experience. A good _________ means that the individual`s experience during all points of contact matches the individual`s expectations. Gartner asserts the importance of managing the customer`s experience.

Exam Probability: **High**

12. *Answer choices:*

(see index for correct answer)

- a. Customer experience
- b. Religion and business
- c. Values scales
- d. NEWSCYCLE Solutions

Guidance: level 1

:: ::

In marketing jargon, product lining is offering several related products for sale individually. Unlike product bundling, where several products are combined into one group, which is then offered for sale as a units, product lining involves offering the products for sale separately. A line can comprise related products of various sizes, types, colors, qualities, or prices. Line depth refers to the number of subcategories a category has. Line consistency refers to how closely related the products that make up the line are. Line vulnerability refers to the percentage of sales or profits that are derived from only a few products in the line.

Exam Probability: **High**

13. *Answer choices:*

(see index for correct answer)

- a. interpersonal communication
- b. Character
- c. Product line
- d. open system

Guidance: level 1

:: Reputation management ::

A _________ is an astronomical object consisting of a luminous spheroid of plasma held together by its own gravity. The nearest _________ to Earth is the Sun. Many other _________ s are visible to the naked eye from Earth during the night, appearing as a multitude of fixed luminous points in the sky due to their immense distance from Earth. Historically, the most prominent _________ s were grouped into constellations and asterisms, the brightest of which gained proper names. Astronomers have assembled _________ catalogues that identify the known _________ s and provide standardized stellar designations. However, most of the estimated 300 sextillion _________ s in the Universe are invisible to the naked eye from Earth, including all _________ s outside our galaxy, the Milky Way.

Exam Probability: **Medium**

14. *Answer choices:*

(see index for correct answer)

- a. ClaimID
- b. Slashdot
- c. Reputation management
- d. Star

Guidance: level 1

:: ::

A _________ is an organization, usually a group of people or a company, authorized to act as a single entity and recognized as such in law. Early incorporated entities were established by charter . Most jurisdictions now allow the creation of new _________ s through registration.

Exam Probability: **Medium**

15. *Answer choices:*

(see index for correct answer)

- a. functional perspective
- b. imperative
- c. hierarchical

- d. Corporation

Guidance: level 1

:: Production and manufacturing ::

_________ consists of organization-wide efforts to "install and make permanent climate where employees continuously improve their ability to provide on demand products and services that customers will find of particular value." "Total" emphasizes that departments in addition to production are obligated to improve their operations; "management" emphasizes that executives are obligated to actively manage quality through funding, training, staffing, and goal setting. While there is no widely agreed-upon approach, TQM efforts typically draw heavily on the previously developed tools and techniques of quality control. TQM enjoyed widespread attention during the late 1980s and early 1990s before being overshadowed by ISO 9000, Lean manufacturing, and Six Sigma.

Exam Probability: **High**

16. *Answer choices:*

(see index for correct answer)

- a. Bill of resources
- b. Safety Network International e.V.
- c. Craft production
- d. Feeder line

Guidance: level 1

:: Stock market ::

_________ is freedom from, or resilience against, potential harm caused by others. Beneficiaries of _________ may be of persons and social groups, objects and institutions, ecosystems or any other entity or phenomenon vulnerable to unwanted change by its environment.

Exam Probability: **High**

17. *Answer choices:*

(see index for correct answer)

- a. Witching hour
- b. Security
- c. Depositary receipt

- d. Paper valuation

Guidance: level 1

:: Auctioneering ::

An _________ is a process of buying and selling goods or services by offering them up for bid, taking bids, and then selling the item to the highest bidder. The open ascending price _________ is arguably the most common form of _________ in use today. Participants bid openly against one another, with each subsequent bid required to be higher than the previous bid. An _________ eer may announce prices, bidders may call out their bids themselves , or bids may be submitted electronically with the highest current bid publicly displayed. In a Dutch _________ , the _________ eer begins with a high asking price for some quantity of like items; the price is lowered until a participant is willing to accept the _________ eer`s price for some quantity of the goods in the lot or until the seller`s reserve price is met. While _________ s are most associated in the public imagination with the sale of antiques, paintings, rare collectibles and expensive wines, _________ s are also used for commodities, livestock, radio spectrum and used cars. In economic theory, an _________ may refer to any mechanism or set of trading rules for exchange.

Exam Probability: **Low**

18. *Answer choices:*

(see index for correct answer)

- a. Auction chant
- b. Auction
- c. Calcutta auction
- d. AntiqueWeek

Guidance: level 1

:: Summary statistics ::

_________ is the number of occurrences of a repeating event per unit of time. It is also referred to as temporal _________ , which emphasizes the contrast to spatial _________ and angular _________ . The period is the duration of time of one cycle in a repeating event, so the period is the reciprocal of the _________ . For example: if a newborn baby's heart beats at a _________ of 120 times a minute, its period—the time interval between beats—is half a second . _________ is an important parameter used in science and engineering to specify the rate of oscillatory and vibratory phenomena, such as mechanical vibrations, audio signals , radio waves, and light.

Exam Probability: **Medium**

19. *Answer choices:*

(see index for correct answer)

- a. Quartile
- b. Higher-order statistics
- c. Frequency
- d. Generalized entropy index

Guidance: level 1

:: Marketing ::

A _________ is something that is necessary for an organism to live a healthy life. _________ s are distinguished from wants in that, in the case of a _________ , a deficiency causes a clear adverse outcome: a dysfunction or death. In other words, a _________ is something required for a safe, stable and healthy life while a want is a desire, wish or aspiration. When _________ s or wants are backed by purchasing power, they have the potential to become economic demands.

Exam Probability: **High**

20. *Answer choices:*

(see index for correct answer)

- a. Cola Wars
- b. Need
- c. Green marketing
- d. Market sector

Guidance: level 1

:: ::

_________ is a concept of English common law and is a necessity for simple contracts but not for special contracts . The concept has been adopted by other common law jurisdictions, including the US.

Exam Probability: **Medium**

21. *Answer choices:*

(see index for correct answer)

- a. deep-level diversity
- b. Character
- c. Sarbanes-Oxley act of 2002
- d. Consideration

Guidance: level 1

:: Monopoly (economics) ::

A _________ exists when a specific person or enterprise is the only supplier of a particular commodity. This contrasts with a monopsony which relates to a single entity`s control of a market to purchase a good or service, and with oligopoly which consists of a few sellers dominating a market. Monopolies are thus characterized by a lack of economic competition to produce the good or service, a lack of viable substitute goods, and the possibility of a high _________ price well above the seller`s marginal cost that leads to a high _________ profit. The verb monopolise or monopolize refers to the process by which a company gains the ability to raise prices or exclude competitors. In economics, a _________ is a single seller. In law, a _________ is a business entity that has significant market power, that is, the power to charge overly high prices. Although monopolies may be big businesses, size is not a characteristic of a _________ . A small business may still have the power to raise prices in a small industry .

Exam Probability: **High**

22. *Answer choices:*

(see index for correct answer)

- a. Government monopoly
- b. Government-granted monopoly
- c. Monopoly
- d. Privatization

Guidance: level 1

:: ::

A __________ is a research instrument consisting of a series of questions for the purpose of gathering information from respondents. The __________ was invented by the Statistical Society of London in 1838.

Exam Probability: **Low**

23. *Answer choices:*

(see index for correct answer)

- a. Questionnaire
- b. co-culture
- c. empathy
- d. functional perspective

Guidance: level 1

:: Data management ::

__________ is a form of intellectual property that grants the creator of an original creative work an exclusive legal right to determine whether and under what conditions this original work may be copied and used by others, usually for a limited term of years. The exclusive rights are not absolute but limited by limitations and exceptions to __________ law, including fair use. A major limitation on __________ on ideas is that __________ protects only the original expression of ideas, and not the underlying ideas themselves.

Exam Probability: **High**

24. *Answer choices:*

(see index for correct answer)

- a. Flat file database
- b. Hybrid array
- c. Semantic translation
- d. BBC Archives

Guidance: level 1

:: Television commercials ::

_________ is a characteristic that distinguishes physical entities that have biological processes, such as signaling and self-sustaining processes, from those that do not, either because such functions have ceased , or because they never had such functions and are classified as inanimate. Various forms of _________ exist, such as plants, animals, fungi, protists, archaea, and bacteria. The criteria can at times be ambiguous and may or may not define viruses, viroids, or potential synthetic _________ as "living". Biology is the science concerned with the study of _________ .

Exam Probability: **Low**

25. *Answer choices:*
(see index for correct answer)

- a. Life
- b. Go On Lad
- c. Bo Knows
- d. ZADZADZ

Guidance: level 1

:: Pricing ::

_________ is unwanted sound judged to be unpleasant, loud or disruptive to hearing. From a physics standpoint, _________ is indistinguishable from sound, as both are vibrations through a medium, such as air or water. The difference arises when the brain receives and perceives a sound.

Exam Probability: **High**

26. *Answer choices:*
(see index for correct answer)

- a. Local exchange trading system
- b. Noise
- c. Value meal
- d. Base period price

Guidance: level 1

:: Promotion and marketing communications ::

__________ is one of the elements of the promotional mix. . __________ uses both media and non-media marketing communications for a pre-determined, limited time to increase consumer demand, stimulate market demand or improve product availability. Examples include contests, coupons, freebies, loss leaders, point of purchase displays, premiums, prizes, product samples, and rebates.

Exam Probability: **Medium**

27. *Answer choices:*

(see index for correct answer)

- a. Air Miles
- b. Radio advertisement
- c. direct-mail
- d. Video news release

Guidance: level 1

:: Social psychology ::

__________ s is a qualitative methodology used to describe consumers on psychological attributes. __________ s have been applied to the study of personality, values, opinions, attitudes, interests, and lifestyles. While __________ s are often equated with lifestyle research, it has been argued that __________ s should apply to the study of cognitive attributes such as attitudes, interests, opinions, and beliefs while lifestyle should apply to the study of overt behavior . Because this area of research focuses on activities, interests, and opinions, __________ factors are sometimes abbreviated to `AIO variables`.

Exam Probability: **High**

28. *Answer choices:*

(see index for correct answer)

- a. externalization
- b. Mind control
- c. Psychographic
- d. Personal space

Guidance: level 1

:: ::

According to the philosopher Piyush Mathur , "Tangibility is the property that a phenomenon exhibits if it has and/or transports mass and/or energy and/or momentum".

Exam Probability: **High**

29. *Answer choices:*

(see index for correct answer)

- a. Tangible
- b. hierarchical perspective
- c. functional perspective
- d. personal values

Guidance: level 1

:: ::

An _________ is a systematic and independent examination of books, accounts, statutory records, documents and vouchers of an organization to ascertain how far the financial statements as well as non-financial disclosures present a true and fair view of the concern. It also attempts to ensure that the books of accounts are properly maintained by the concern as required by law. _________ ing has become such a ubiquitous phenomenon in the corporate and the public sector that academics started identifying an " _________ Society". The _________ or perceives and recognises the propositions before them for examination, obtains evidence, evaluates the same and formulates an opinion on the basis of his judgement which is communicated through their _________ ing report.

Exam Probability: **Low**

30. *Answer choices:*

(see index for correct answer)

- a. corporate values
- b. Sarbanes-Oxley act of 2002
- c. Audit
- d. process perspective

Guidance: level 1

:: ::

A __________ is an organized collection of data, generally stored and accessed electronically from a computer system. Where __________ s are more complex they are often developed using formal design and modeling techniques.

Exam Probability: **Medium**

31. *Answer choices:*

(see index for correct answer)

- a. levels of analysis
- b. Character
- c. deep-level diversity
- d. cultural

Guidance: level 1

:: Product development ::

In business and engineering, __________ covers the complete process of bringing a new product to market. A central aspect of NPD is product design, along with various business considerations. __________ is described broadly as the transformation of a market opportunity into a product available for sale. The product can be tangible or intangible , though sometimes services and other processes are distinguished from "products." NPD requires an understanding of customer needs and wants, the competitive environment, and the nature of the market.Cost, time and quality are the main variables that drive customer needs. Aiming at these three variables, innovative companies develop continuous practices and strategies to better satisfy customer requirements and to increase their own market share by a regular development of new products. There are many uncertainties and challenges which companies must face throughout the process. The use of best practices and the elimination of barriers to communication are the main concerns for the management of the NPD .

Exam Probability: **Low**

32. *Answer choices:*

(see index for correct answer)

- a. Specification tree
- b. Virtual prototyping
- c. New product development
- d. Brief

Guidance: level 1

:: Business economics ::

In economics, _________ is demand for a factor of production or intermediate good that occurs as a result of the demand for another intermediate or final good. In essence, the demand for, say, a factor of production by a firm is dependent on the demand by consumers for the product produced by the firm. The term was first introduced by Alfred Marshall in his Principles of Economics in 1890.

Exam Probability: **Low**

33. *Answer choices:*

(see index for correct answer)

- a. Staple financing
- b. Derived demand
- c. Creditor Reference
- d. Incremental operating margin

Guidance: level 1

:: Organizational structure ::

An _________ defines how activities such as task allocation, coordination, and supervision are directed toward the achievement of organizational aims.

Exam Probability: **Low**

34. *Answer choices:*

(see index for correct answer)

- a. Organization of the New York City Police Department
- b. Unorganisation
- c. The Starfish and the Spider
- d. Organizational structure

Guidance: level 1

:: Product management ::

A __________ is a professional role which is responsible for the development of products for an organization, known as the practice of product management. __________s own the business strategy behind a product , specify its functional requirements and generally manage the launch of features. They coordinate work done by many other functions and are ultimately responsible for the business success of the product.

Exam Probability: **High**

35. *Answer choices:*

(see index for correct answer)

- a. Trademark distinctiveness
- b. Obsolescence
- c. Product manager
- d. Swing tag

Guidance: level 1

:: ::

In a supply chain, a __________ , or a seller, is an enterprise that contributes goods or services. Generally, a supply chain __________ manufactures inventory/stock items and sells them to the next link in the chain. Today, these terms refer to a supplier of any good or service.

Exam Probability: **Medium**

36. *Answer choices:*

(see index for correct answer)

- a. surface-level diversity
- b. hierarchical perspective
- c. personal values
- d. Vendor

Guidance: level 1

:: Internet privacy ::

An _________ is a private network accessible only to an organization`s staff. Often, a wide range of information and services are available on an organization`s internal _________ that are unavailable to the public, unlike the Internet. A company-wide _________ can constitute an important focal point of internal communication and collaboration, and provide a single starting point to access internal and external resources. In its simplest form, an _________ is established with the technologies for local area networks and wide area networks . Many modern _________ s have search engines, user profiles, blogs, mobile apps with notifications, and events planning within their infrastructure.

Exam Probability: **Low**

37. *Answer choices:*

(see index for correct answer)

- a. Opportunistic encryption
- b. I-broker
- c. WikiScanner
- d. Intranet

Guidance: level 1

:: Library science ::

_________ refers to data which is collected by someone who is someone other than the user. Common sources of _________ for social science include censuses, information collected by government departments, organizational records and data that was originally collected for other research purposes. Primary data, by contrast, are collected by the investigator conducting the research.

Exam Probability: **Medium**

38. *Answer choices:*

(see index for correct answer)

- a. Secondary data
- b. Architectural reprography
- c. Bibliographic record
- d. History of libraries

Guidance: level 1

:: Logistics ::

_________ is generally the detailed organization and implementation of a complex operation. In a general business sense, _________ is the management of the flow of things between the point of origin and the point of consumption in order to meet requirements of customers or corporations. The resources managed in _________ may include tangible goods such as materials, equipment, and supplies, as well as food and other consumable items. The _________ of physical items usually involves the integration of information flow, materials handling, production, packaging, inventory, transportation, warehousing, and often security.

Exam Probability: **Low**

39. *Answer choices:*
(see index for correct answer)

- a. Logistics Support System
- b. Logistics
- c. Center for Transportation and Logistics Neuer Adler
- d. ISO/IEC 18000-3

Guidance: level 1

:: Problem solving ::

In other words, _________ is a situation where a group of people meet to generate new ideas and solutions around a specific domain of interest by removing inhibitions. People are able to think more freely and they suggest as many spontaneous new ideas as possible. All the ideas are noted down and those ideas are not criticized and after _________ session the ideas are evaluated.The term was popularized by Alex Faickney Osborn in the 1953 book Applied Imagination.

Exam Probability: **High**

40. *Answer choices:*
(see index for correct answer)

- a. Tar-Baby
- b. Use of force
- c. Circle time
- d. Method of focal objects

Guidance: level 1

:: ::

Employment is a relationship between two parties, usually based on a contract where work is paid for, where one party, which may be a corporation, for profit, not-for-profit organization, co-operative or other entity is the employer and the other is the employee. Employees work in return for payment, which may be in the form of an hourly wage, by piecework or an annual salary, depending on the type of work an employee does or which sector she or he is working in. Employees in some fields or sectors may receive gratuities, bonus payment or stock options. In some types of employment, employees may receive benefits in addition to payment. Benefits can include health insurance, housing, disability insurance or use of a gym. Employment is typically governed by employment laws, regulations or legal contracts.

Exam Probability: **High**

41. *Answer choices:*

(see index for correct answer)

- a. functional perspective
- b. open system
- c. surface-level diversity
- d. Personnel

Guidance: level 1

:: Consumer behaviour ::

__________ is an activity in which a customer browses the available goods or services presented by one or more retailers with the potential intent to purchase a suitable selection of them. A typology of shopper types has been developed by scholars which identifies one group of shoppers as recreational shoppers, that is, those who enjoy __________ and view it as a leisure activity.

Exam Probability: **Medium**

42. *Answer choices:*

(see index for correct answer)

- a. Customer delight

- b. Health consumerism
- c. Shopping
- d. Denomination effect

Guidance: level 1

:: Project management ::

Contemporary business and science treat as a _________ any undertaking, carried out individually or collaboratively and possibly involving research or design, that is carefully planned to achieve a particular aim.

Exam Probability: **High**

43. *Answer choices:*

(see index for correct answer)

- a. Structured data analysis
- b. Technology roadmap
- c. Project
- d. Design structure matrix

Guidance: level 1

:: Management occupations ::

_________ ship is the process of designing, launching and running a new business, which is often initially a small business. The people who create these businesses are called _________ s.

Exam Probability: **Medium**

44. *Answer choices:*

(see index for correct answer)

- a. Chief gaming officer
- b. Entrepreneur
- c. Vorstandsassistent
- d. Faculty consulting

Guidance: level 1

:: Management ::

The term _________ refers to measures designed to increase the degree of autonomy and self-determination in people and in communities in order to enable them to represent their interests in a responsible and self-determined way, acting on their own authority. It is the process of becoming stronger and more confident, especially in controlling one`s life and claiming one`s rights. _________ as action refers both to the process of self- _________ and to professional support of people, which enables them to overcome their sense of powerlessness and lack of influence, and to recognize and use their resources. To do work with power.

Exam Probability: **Low**

45. *Answer choices:*
(see index for correct answer)

- a. Advisory board
- b. Empowerment
- c. Managerial economics
- d. Swarm Development Group

Guidance: level 1

:: ::

In _________ relations and communication science, _________ s are groups of individual people, and the _________ is the totality of such groupings. This is a different concept to the sociological concept of the Öffentlichkeit or _________ sphere. The concept of a _________ has also been defined in political science, psychology, marketing, and advertising. In _________ relations and communication science, it is one of the more ambiguous concepts in the field. Although it has definitions in the theory of the field that have been formulated from the early 20th century onwards, it has suffered in more recent years from being blurred, as a result of conflation of the idea of a _________ with the notions of audience, market segment, community, constituency, and stakeholder.

Exam Probability: **Low**

46. *Answer choices:*
(see index for correct answer)

- a. hierarchical
- b. similarity-attraction theory

- c. Public
- d. open system

Guidance: level 1

:: Income ::

In business and accounting, net income is an entity's income minus cost of goods sold, expenses and taxes for an accounting period. It is computed as the residual of all revenues and gains over all expenses and losses for the period, and has also been defined as the net increase in shareholders' equity that results from a company's operations. In the context of the presentation of financial statements, the IFRS Foundation defines net income as synonymous with profit and loss. The difference between revenue and the cost of making a product or providing a service, before deducting overheads, payroll, taxation, and interest payments. This is different from operating income .

Exam Probability: **Medium**

47. *Answer choices:*

(see index for correct answer)

- a. Pay grade
- b. Windfall gain
- c. Signing bonus
- d. Imputed income

Guidance: level 1

:: Product development ::

_________ is the understanding of the dynamics of the product in order to showcase the best qualities and maximum features of the product. Marketers spend a lot of time and research in order to target their attended audience. Marketers will look into a _________ before marketing a product towards their customers.

Exam Probability: **Low**

48. *Answer choices:*

(see index for correct answer)

- a. Product concept
- b. Design brief

- c. Product line extension
- d. Design for assembly

Guidance: level 1

:: Market research ::

__________ is "the process or set of processes that links the producers, customers, and end users to the marketer through information used to identify and define marketing opportunities and problems; generate, refine, and evaluate marketing actions; monitor marketing performance; and improve understanding of marketing as a process. __________ specifies the information required to address these issues, designs the method for collecting information, manages and implements the data collection process, analyzes the results, and communicates the findings and their implications."

Exam Probability: **Low**

49. *Answer choices:*

(see index for correct answer)

- a. The Ehrenberg-Bass Institute for Marketing Science
- b. Competitive intelligence
- c. Confidence interval
- d. Market research and opinion polling in China

Guidance: level 1

:: ::

The __________ is an agreement signed by Canada, Mexico, and the United States, creating a trilateral trade bloc in North America. The agreement came into force on January 1, 1994, and superseded the 1988 Canada–United States Free Trade Agreement between the United States and Canada. The NAFTA trade bloc is one of the largest trade blocs in the world by gross domestic product.

Exam Probability: **Medium**

50. *Answer choices:*

(see index for correct answer)

- a. deep-level diversity
- b. cultural
- c. levels of analysis

- d. North American Free Trade Agreement

Guidance: level 1

:: Market research ::

__________ , an acronym for Information through Disguised Experimentation is an annual market research fair conducted by the students of IIM-Lucknow. Students create games and use various other simulated environments to capture consumers' subconscious thoughts. This innovative method of market research removes the sensitization effect that might bias peoples answers to questions. This ensures that the most truthful answers are captured to research questions. The games are designed in such a way that the observers can elicit all the required information just by observing and noting down the behaviour and the responses of the participants.

Exam Probability: **High**

51. *Answer choices:*

(see index for correct answer)

- a. Nielsen VideoScan
- b. Mendelsohn Affluent Survey
- c. Online panel
- d. Market research

Guidance: level 1

:: ::

__________ Corporation is an American multinational technology company with headquarters in Redmond, Washington. It develops, manufactures, licenses, supports and sells computer software, consumer electronics, personal computers, and related services. Its best known software products are the __________ Windows line of operating systems, the __________ Office suite, and the Internet Explorer and Edge Web browsers. Its flagship hardware products are the Xbox video game consoles and the __________ Surface lineup of touchscreen personal computers. As of 2016, it is the world`s largest software maker by revenue, and one of the world`s most valuable companies. The word " __________ " is a portmanteau of "microcomputer" and "software". __________ is ranked No. 30 in the 2018 Fortune 500 rankings of the largest United States corporations by total revenue.

Exam Probability: **Low**

52. *Answer choices:*

(see index for correct answer)

- a. hierarchical
- b. interpersonal communication
- c. Microsoft
- d. co-culture

Guidance: level 1

:: ::

__________ involves decision making. It can include judging the merits of multiple options and selecting one or more of them. One can make a __________ between imagined options or between real options followed by the corresponding action. For example, a traveler might choose a route for a journey based on the preference of arriving at a given destination as soon as possible. The preferred route can then follow from information such as the length of each of the possible routes, traffic conditions, etc. The arrival at a __________ can include more complex motivators such as cognition, instinct, and feeling.

Exam Probability: **Low**

53. *Answer choices:*

(see index for correct answer)

- a. Choice
- b. hierarchical

- c. levels of analysis
- d. Sarbanes-Oxley act of 2002

Guidance: level 1

:: Sales ::

__________ is a business discipline which is focused on the practical application of sales techniques and the management of a firm`s sales operations. It is an important business function as net sales through the sale of products and services and resulting profit drive most commercial business. These are also typically the goals and performance indicators of __________ .

Exam Probability: **Medium**

54. *Answer choices:*
(see index for correct answer)

- a. Hit rate
- b. Upselling
- c. Military surplus
- d. Sales management

Guidance: level 1

:: Debt ::

__________ is the trust which allows one party to provide money or resources to another party wherein the second party does not reimburse the first party immediately , but promises either to repay or return those resources at a later date. In other words, __________ is a method of making reciprocity formal, legally enforceable, and extensible to a large group of unrelated people.

Exam Probability: **Medium**

55. *Answer choices:*
(see index for correct answer)

- a. Credit cycle
- b. Extendible bond
- c. Credit
- d. Legal liability

Guidance: level 1

:: Management ::

In business, a _________ is the attribute that allows an organization to outperform its competitors. A _________ may include access to natural resources, such as high-grade ores or a low-cost power source, highly skilled labor, geographic location, high entry barriers, and access to new technology.

Exam Probability: **Medium**

56. *Answer choices:*

(see index for correct answer)

- a. Backsourcing
- b. Competitive advantage
- c. Behavioral risk management
- d. Project team builder

Guidance: level 1

:: Advertising ::

A _________ is a document used by creative professionals and agencies to develop creative deliverables: visual design, copy, advertising, web sites, etc. The document is usually developed by the requestor and approved by the creative team of designers, writers, and project managers. In some cases, the project`s _________ may need creative director approval before work will commence.

Exam Probability: **High**

57. *Answer choices:*

(see index for correct answer)

- a. Advertising exchange
- b. Restaurant media
- c. Category Development Index
- d. Creative brief

Guidance: level 1

:: Marketing techniques ::

The __________ or unique selling point is a marketing concept first proposed as a theory to explain a pattern in successful advertising campaigns of the early 1940s. The USP states that such campaigns made unique propositions to customers that convinced them to switch brands. The term was developed by television advertising pioneer Rosser Reeves of Ted Bates & Company. Theodore Levitt, a professor at Harvard Business School, suggested that, "Differentiation is one of the most important strategic and tactical activities in which companies must constantly engage." The term has been used to describe one`s "personal brand" in the marketplace. Today, the term is used in other fields or just casually to refer to any aspect of an object that differentiates it from similar objects.

Exam Probability: **Low**

58. *Answer choices:*

(see index for correct answer)

- a. Product life cycle
- b. Introductory rate
- c. Beauty whitewash
- d. Unique perceived benefit

Guidance: level 1

:: Market research ::

A __________ is a small, but demographically diverse group of people and whose reactions are studied especially in market research or political analysis in guided or open discussions about a new product or something else to determine the reactions that can be expected from a larger population. It is a form of qualitative research consisting of interviews in which a group of people are asked about their perceptions, opinions, beliefs, and attitudes towards a product, service, concept, advertisement, idea, or packaging. Questions are asked in an interactive group setting where participants are free to talk with other group members. During this process, the researcher either takes notes or records the vital points he or she is getting from the group. Researchers should select members of the __________ carefully for effective and authoritative responses.

Exam Probability: **Low**

59. *Answer choices:*

(see index for correct answer)

- a. DigitalMR
- b. Cambashi
- c. Virtual store research
- d. Focus group

Guidance: level 1

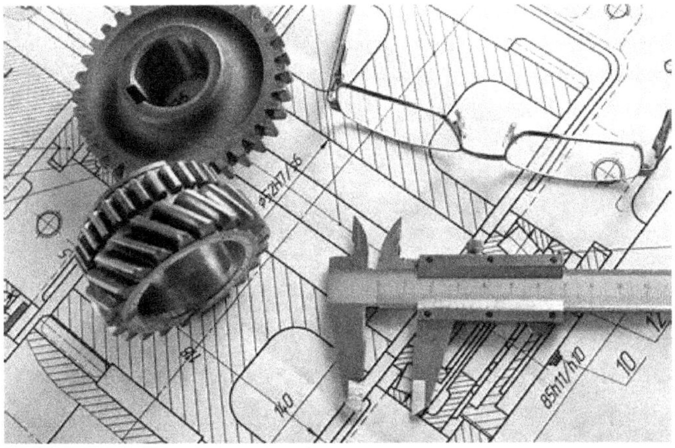

Manufacturing

Manufacturing is the production of merchandise for use or sale using labor and machines, tools, chemical and biological processing, or formulation. The term may refer to a range of human activity, from handicraft to high tech, but is most commonly applied to industrial design , in which raw materials are transformed into finished goods on a large scale. Such finished goods may be sold to other manufacturers for the production of other, more complex products, such as aircraft, household appliances, furniture, sports equipment or automobiles, or sold to wholesalers, who in turn sell them to retailers, who then sell them to end users and consumers.

:: Chemical processes ::

__________ is the understanding and application of the fundamental principles and laws of nature that allow us to transform raw material and energy into products that are useful to society, at an industrial level. By taking advantage of the driving forces of nature such as pressure, temperature and concentration gradients, as well as the law of conservation of mass, process engineers can develop methods to synthesize and purify large quantities of desired chemical products. _________ focuses on the design, operation, control, optimization and intensification of chemical, physical, and biological processes. _________ encompasses a vast range of industries, such as agriculture, automotive, biotechnical, chemical, food, material development, mining, nuclear, petrochemical, pharmaceutical, and software development. The application of systematic computer-based methods to _________ is "process systems engineering".

Exam Probability: **Medium**

1. *Answer choices:*

(see index for correct answer)

- a. Process engineering
- b. Disproportionation

- c. Water-gas shift reaction
- d. Ballotechnics

Guidance: level 1

:: Unit operations ::

__________ is the process of separating the components or substances from a liquid mixture by using selective boiling and condensation. __________ may result in essentially complete separation , or it may be a partial separation that increases the concentration of selected components in the mixture. In either case, the process exploits differences in the volatility of the mixture`s components. In industrial chemistry, __________ is a unit operation of practically universal importance, but it is a physical separation process, not a chemical reaction.

Exam Probability: **Medium**

2. *Answer choices:*

(see index for correct answer)

- a. Sedimentation coefficient
- b. Theoretical plate
- c. Settling
- d. Distillation

Guidance: level 1

:: Software testing ::

__________ 1 was the first artificial Earth satellite. The Soviet Union launched it into an elliptical low Earth orbit on 4 October 1957, orbiting for three weeks before its batteries died, then silently for two more months before falling back into the atmosphere. It was a 58 cm diameter polished metal sphere, with four external radio antennas to broadcast radio pulses. Its radio signal was easily detectable even by radio amateurs, and the 65° inclination and duration of its orbit made its flight path cover virtually the entire inhabited Earth. This surprise success precipitated the American __________ crisis and triggered the Space Race, a part of the Cold War. The launch was the beginning of a new era of political, military, technological, and scientific developments.

Exam Probability: **Low**

3. *Answer choices:*

(see index for correct answer)

- a. Code integrity
- b. Oulu University Secure Programming Group
- c. Sputnik
- d. Stream X-Machine

Guidance: level 1

:: Asset ::

In financial accounting, an _________ is any resource owned by the business. Anything tangible or intangible that can be owned or controlled to produce value and that is held by a company to produce positive economic value is an _________ . Simply stated, _________ s represent value of ownership that can be converted into cash . The balance sheet of a firm records the monetary value of the _________ s owned by that firm. It covers money and other valuables belonging to an individual or to a business.

Exam Probability: **High**

4. *Answer choices:*

(see index for correct answer)

- a. Fixed asset
- b. Asset

Guidance: level 1

:: Management ::

_________ is an iterative four-step management method used in business for the control and continuous improvement of processes and products. It is also known as the Deming circle/cycle/wheel, the Shewhart cycle, the control circle/cycle, or plan–do–study–act . Another version of this _________ cycle is O _________ . The added "O" stands for observation or as some versions say: "Observe the current condition." This emphasis on observation and current condition has currency with the literature on lean manufacturing and the Toyota Production System. The _________ cycle, with Ishikawa's changes, can be traced back to S. Mizuno of the Tokyo Institute of Technology in 1959.

Exam Probability: **Medium**

5. *Answer choices:*

(see index for correct answer)

- a. PDCA
- b. Behavioral risk management
- c. Management by exception
- d. Backsourcing

Guidance: level 1

:: Chemical reactions ::

A _________ is a process that leads to the chemical transformation of one set of chemical substances to another. Classically, _________ s encompass changes that only involve the positions of electrons in the forming and breaking of chemical bonds between atoms, with no change to the nuclei , and can often be described by a chemical equation. Nuclear chemistry is a sub-discipline of chemistry that involves the _________ s of unstable and radioactive elements where both electronic and nuclear changes can occur.

Exam Probability: **High**

6. *Answer choices:*

(see index for correct answer)

- a. Chemical reaction
- b. Collision theory
- c. Molecular promiscuity
- d. Hydrogen atom abstraction

Guidance: level 1

:: Casting (manufacturing) ::

A _________ is a regularity in the world, man-made design, or abstract ideas. As such, the elements of a _________ repeat in a predictable manner. A geometric _________ is a kind of _________ formed of geometric shapes and typically repeated like a wallpaper design.

Exam Probability: **High**

7. *Answer choices:*

(see index for correct answer)

- a. Shell molding
- b. Riser
- c. Porosity sealing
- d. Pattern

Guidance: level 1

:: Metalworking ::

A _________ is a round object with various uses. It is used in _________ games, where the play of the game follows the state of the _________ as it is hit, kicked or thrown by players. _________ s can also be used for simpler activities, such as catch or juggling. _________ s made from hard-wearing materials are used in engineering applications to provide very low friction bearings, known as _________ bearings. Black-powder weapons use stone and metal _________ s as projectiles.

Exam Probability: **High**

8. *Answer choices:*
(see index for correct answer)

- a. Semi-solid metal casting
- b. Forge
- c. Ball
- d. Indo-MIM

Guidance: level 1

:: Project management ::

Contemporary business and science treat as a _________ any undertaking, carried out individually or collaboratively and possibly involving research or design, that is carefully planned to achieve a particular aim.

Exam Probability: **Low**

9. *Answer choices:*
(see index for correct answer)

- a. Initiative
- b. Bid manager
- c. Project planning
- d. Project

Guidance: level 1

:: Management ::

__________ is the process of thinking about the activities required to achieve a desired goal. It is the first and foremost activity to achieve desired results. It involves the creation and maintenance of a plan, such as psychological aspects that require conceptual skills. There are even a couple of tests to measure someone's capability of __________ well. As such, __________ is a fundamental property of intelligent behavior. An important further meaning, often just called " __________ " is the legal context of permitted building developments.

Exam Probability: **High**

10. *Answer choices:*

(see index for correct answer)

- a. Planning
- b. Fredmund Malik
- c. Earned value management
- d. Public sector consulting

Guidance: level 1

:: Management ::

__________ is the discipline of strategically planning for, and managing, all interactions with third party organizations that supply goods and/or services to an organization in order to maximize the value of those interactions. In practice, SRM entails creating closer, more collaborative relationships with key suppliers in order to uncover and realize new value and reduce risk of failure.

Exam Probability: **High**

11. *Answer choices:*

(see index for correct answer)

- a. Supplier relationship management
- b. Relational view
- c. Complementary assets
- d. Mushroom management

Guidance: level 1

:: Project management ::

In political science, an _________ is a means by which a petition signed by a certain minimum number of registered voters can force a government to choose to either enact a law or hold a public vote in parliament in what is called indirect _________ , or under direct _________ , the proposition is immediately put to a plebiscite or referendum, in what is called a Popular initiated Referendum or citizen-initiated referendum).

Exam Probability: **Low**

12. *Answer choices:*

(see index for correct answer)

- a. Project Management South Africa
- b. Rolling Wave planning
- c. Doctor of Project Management
- d. Big Hairy Audacious Goal

Guidance: level 1

:: Project management ::

_________s can take many forms depending on the type of project being implemented and the nature of the organization. The _________ details the project deliverables and describes the major objectives. The objectives should include measurable success criteria for the project.

Exam Probability: **Low**

13. *Answer choices:*

(see index for correct answer)

- a. Theory X and Theory Y
- b. Scope statement
- c. Executive sponsor
- d. Aggregate planning

Guidance: level 1

:: Costs ::

__________ is the process used by companies to reduce their costs and increase their profits. Depending on a company's services or product, the strategies can vary. Every decision in the product development process affects cost.

Exam Probability: **Medium**

14. *Answer choices:*

(see index for correct answer)

- a. Sliding scale
- b. Further processing cost
- c. Direct labor cost
- d. Quality costs

Guidance: level 1

:: Metal heat treatments ::

__________ is a group of industrial and metalworking processes used to alter the physical, and sometimes chemical, properties of a material. The most common application is metallurgical. Heat treatments are also used in the manufacture of many other materials, such as glass. Heat treatment involves the use of heating or chilling, normally to extreme temperatures, to achieve a desired result such as hardening or softening of a material. Heat treatment techniques include annealing, case hardening, precipitation strengthening, tempering, carburizing, normalizing and quenching. It is noteworthy that while the term heat treatment applies only to processes where the heating and cooling are done for the specific purpose of altering properties intentionally, heating and cooling often occur incidentally during other manufacturing processes such as hot forming or welding.

Exam Probability: **Low**

15. *Answer choices:*

(see index for correct answer)

- a. Hardening
- b. Induction hardening
- c. Austempering
- d. Differential heat treatment

Guidance: level 1

:: ::

In a supply chain, a __________, or a seller, is an enterprise that contributes goods or services. Generally, a supply chain __________ manufactures inventory/stock items and sells them to the next link in the chain. Today, these terms refer to a supplier of any good or service.

Exam Probability: **High**

16. *Answer choices:*

(see index for correct answer)

- a. imperative
- b. empathy
- c. surface-level diversity
- d. functional perspective

Guidance: level 1

:: Production and manufacturing ::

__________ is a comprehensive and rigorous industrial process by which a previously sold, leased, used, worn or non-functional product or part is returned to a 'like-new' or 'better-than-new' condition, from both a quality and performance perspective, through a controlled, reproducible and sustainable process.

Exam Probability: **Medium**

17. *Answer choices:*

(see index for correct answer)

- a. ISO/TS 16949
- b. Economic dispatch
- c. Rolled throughput yield
- d. Variable rate feeder

Guidance: level 1

:: Production and manufacturing ::

An __________ is a manufacturing process in which parts are added as the semi-finished assembly moves from workstation to workstation where the parts are added in sequence until the final assembly is produced. By mechanically moving the parts to the assembly work and moving the semi-finished assembly from work station to work station, a finished product can be assembled faster and with less labor than by having workers carry parts to a stationary piece for assembly.

Exam Probability: **Medium**

18. *Answer choices:*

(see index for correct answer)

- a. Job shop
- b. Safety Network International e.V.
- c. Engineering validation test
- d. Assembly line

Guidance: level 1

:: Packaging materials ::

__________ is a thin material produced by pressing together moist fibres of cellulose pulp derived from wood, rags or grasses, and drying them into flexible sheets.It is a versatile material with many uses, including writing, printing, packaging, cleaning, decorating, and a number of industrial and construction processes. __________ s are essential in legal or non-legal documentation.

Exam Probability: **Medium**

19. *Answer choices:*

(see index for correct answer)

- a. Paper
- b. Velostat
- c. Aluminium foil
- d. Wrapping tissue

Guidance: level 1

:: Metals ::

A _________ is a material that, when freshly prepared, polished, or fractured, shows a lustrous appearance, and conducts electricity and heat relatively well. _________ s are typically malleable or ductile . A _________ may be a chemical element such as iron, or an alloy such as stainless steel.

Exam Probability: **Medium**

20. *Answer choices:*

(see index for correct answer)

- a. Metal
- b. Half-metal
- c. Alonizing
- d. Telluric iron

Guidance: level 1

:: Management ::

A _________ is an idea of the future or desired result that a person or a group of people envisions, plans and commits to achieve. People endeavor to reach _________ s within a finite time by setting deadlines.

Exam Probability: **Low**

21. *Answer choices:*

(see index for correct answer)

- a. Productive efficiency
- b. Goal
- c. Environmental stewardship
- d. Submission management

Guidance: level 1

:: Project management ::

A _________ is a team whose members usually belong to different groups, functions and are assigned to activities for the same project. A team can be divided into sub-teams according to need. Usually _________ s are only used for a defined period of time. They are disbanded after the project is deemed complete. Due to the nature of the specific formation and disbandment, _________ s are usually in organizations.

Exam Probability: **Low**

22. *Answer choices:*

(see index for correct answer)

- a. Sunk costs
- b. The Chicken and the Pig
- c. Project portfolio management
- d. Task management

Guidance: level 1

:: Project management ::

In general usage, a _________ is a comprehensive evaluation of an individual`s current pay and future financial state by using current known variables to predict future income, asset values and withdrawal plans. This often includes a budget which organizes an individual`s finances and sometimes includes a series of steps or specific goals for spending and saving in the future. This plan allocates future income to various types of expenses, such as rent or utilities, and also reserves some income for short-term and long-term savings. A _________ is sometimes referred to as an investment plan, but in personal finance a _________ can focus on other specific areas such as risk management, estates, college, or retirement.

Exam Probability: **Medium**

23. *Answer choices:*

(see index for correct answer)

- a. Graphical path method
- b. Financial plan
- c. Risk management plan
- d. Participatory impact pathways analysis

Guidance: level 1

:: Marketing techniques ::

A __________ is an award to be given to a person, a group of people like a sports team, or organization to recognise and reward actions or achievements. Official __________ s often involve monetary rewards as well as the fame that comes with them. Some __________ s are also associated with extravagant awarding ceremonies, such as the Academy Awards.

Exam Probability: **Medium**

24. *Answer choices:*

(see index for correct answer)

- a. Prize
- b. Self-referential marketing
- c. Channel stuffing
- d. Enterprise engagement

Guidance: level 1

:: Lean manufacturing ::

__________ is the Sino-Japanese word for "improvement". In business, __________ refers to activities that continuously improve all functions and involve all employees from the CEO to the assembly line workers. It also applies to processes, such as purchasing and logistics, that cross organizational boundaries into the supply chain. It has been applied in healthcare, psychotherapy, life-coaching, government, and banking.

Exam Probability: **Low**

25. *Answer choices:*

(see index for correct answer)

- a. Supply chain responsiveness matrix
- b. Autonomation
- c. takt
- d. Continual improvement process

Guidance: level 1

:: Auditing ::

_________ is the process of systematic examination of a quality system carried out by an internal or external _________ or or an audit team. It is an important part of an organization`s quality management system and is a key element in the ISO quality system standard, ISO 9001.

Exam Probability: **High**

26. *Answer choices:*

(see index for correct answer)

- a. Vouching
- b. Audit risk
- c. Quality audit
- d. Sales tax audit

Guidance: level 1

:: Manufacturing ::

A _________ is an object used to extend the ability of an individual to modify features of the surrounding environment. Although many animals use simple _________ s, only human beings, whose use of stone _________ s dates back hundreds of millennia, use _________ s to make other _________ s. The set of _________ s needed to perform different tasks that are part of the same activity is called gear or equipment.

Exam Probability: **Low**

27. *Answer choices:*

(see index for correct answer)

- a. Tool
- b. Production Systems Engineering
- c. Professional Electrical Apparatus Recyclers League
- d. B2MML

Guidance: level 1

:: Packaging ::

In work place, _________ or job _________ means good ranking with the hypothesized conception of requirements of a role. There are two types of job _________ s: contextual and task. Task _________ is related to cognitive ability while contextual _________ is dependent upon personality. Task _________ are behavioral roles that are recognized in job descriptions and by remuneration systems, they are directly related to organizational _________, whereas, contextual _________ are value based and additional behavioral roles that are not recognized in job descriptions and covered by compensation; they are extra roles that are indirectly related to organizational _________. Citizenship _________ like contextual _________ means a set of individual activity/contribution that supports the organizational culture.

Exam Probability: **High**

28. *Answer choices:*

(see index for correct answer)

- a. Box-sealing tape
- b. Performance
- c. Proof of purchase
- d. Cold foil printing

Guidance: level 1

:: Production and manufacturing ::

_________ was a management-led program to eliminate defects in industrial production that enjoyed brief popularity in American industry from 1964 to the early 1970s. Quality expert Philip Crosby later incorporated it into his "Absolutes of Quality Management" and it enjoyed a renaissance in the American automobile industry—as a performance goal more than as a program—in the 1990s. Although applicable to any type of enterprise, it has been primarily adopted within supply chains wherever large volumes of components are being purchased .

Exam Probability: **Medium**

29. *Answer choices:*

(see index for correct answer)

- a. Production function
- b. Accelerated aging
- c. Shop foreman
- d. Business Planning and Control System

Guidance: level 1

:: Insulators ::

A __________ is a piece of soft cloth large enough either to cover or to enfold a great portion of the user`s body, usually when sleeping or otherwise at rest, thereby trapping radiant bodily heat that otherwise would be lost through convection, and so keeping the body warm.

Exam Probability: **Low**

30. *Answer choices:*

(see index for correct answer)

- a. Pentafluoropropane
- b. Dynamic insulation
- c. Pipe insulation
- d. Malter effect

Guidance: level 1

:: Management ::

A process is a unique combination of tools, materials, methods, and people engaged in producing a measurable output; for example a manufacturing line for machine parts. All processes have inherent statistical variability which can be evaluated by statistical methods.

Exam Probability: **High**

31. *Answer choices:*

(see index for correct answer)

- a. Quick response manufacturing
- b. Kata
- c. Supervisory board
- d. Voice of the customer

Guidance: level 1

:: Sensitivity analysis ::

_________ is the study of how the uncertainty in the output of a mathematical model or system can be divided and allocated to different sources of uncertainty in its inputs. A related practice is uncertainty analysis, which has a greater focus on uncertainty quantification and propagation of uncertainty; ideally, uncertainty and _________ should be run in tandem.

Exam Probability: **Medium**

32. *Answer choices:*

(see index for correct answer)

- a. Elementary effects method
- b. Sensitivity analysis
- c. Variance-based sensitivity analysis
- d. Tornado diagram

Guidance: level 1

:: Information technology management ::

The term _________ is used to refer to periods when a system is unavailable. _________ or outage duration refers to a period of time that a system fails to provide or perform its primary function. Reliability, availability, recovery, and unavailability are related concepts.The unavailability is the proportion of a time-span that a system is unavailable or offline.This is usually a result of the system failing to function because of an unplanned event, or because of routine maintenance .

Exam Probability: **High**

33. *Answer choices:*

(see index for correct answer)

- a. Enterprise content management
- b. Downtime
- c. Performance engineering
- d. Information Technology Infrastructure Library

Guidance: level 1

:: Management ::

__________ , also known as natural process limits, are horizontal lines drawn on a statistical process control chart, usually at a distance of ±3 standard deviations of the plotted statistic from the statistic's mean.

Exam Probability: **Low**

34. *Answer choices:*
(see index for correct answer)

- a. Context analysis
- b. Place management
- c. Managerial economics
- d. Project team builder

Guidance: level 1

:: Distribution, retailing, and wholesaling ::

__________ measures the performance of a system. Certain goals are defined and the __________ gives the percentage to which those goals should be achieved. Fill rate is different from __________ .

Exam Probability: **Low**

35. *Answer choices:*
(see index for correct answer)

- a. Canal warehouse
- b. Plataforma Europa
- c. Sales variance
- d. Service level

Guidance: level 1

:: Data management ::

__________ is the ability of a physical product to remain functional, without requiring excessive maintenance or repair, when faced with the challenges of normal operation over its design lifetime. There are several measures of __________ in use, including years of life, hours of use, and number of operational cycles. In economics, goods with a long usable life are referred to as durable goods.

Exam Probability: **Medium**

36. *Answer choices:*

(see index for correct answer)

- a. Durability
- b. Master data
- c. Microsoft Office PerformancePoint Server
- d. SIGMOD Edgar F. Codd Innovations Award

Guidance: level 1

:: Production economics ::

_________ is the joint use of a resource or space. It is also the process of dividing and distributing. In its narrow sense, it refers to joint or alternating use of inherently finite goods, such as a common pasture or a shared residence. Still more loosely, " _________ " can actually mean giving something as an outright gift: for example, to "share" one`s food really means to give some of it as a gift. _________ is a basic component of human interaction, and is responsible for strengthening social ties and ensuring a person's well-being.

Exam Probability: **Low**

37. *Answer choices:*

(see index for correct answer)

- a. Product pipeline
- b. Peer production
- c. Marginal product
- d. Sharing

Guidance: level 1

:: Natural materials ::

_________ is a finely-grained natural rock or soil material that combines one or more _________ minerals with possible traces of quartz , metal oxides and organic matter. Geologic _________ deposits are mostly composed of phyllosilicate minerals containing variable amounts of water trapped in the mineral structure. _________ s are plastic due to particle size and geometry as well as water content, and become hard, brittle and non–plastic upon drying or firing. Depending on the soil`s content in which it is found, _________ can appear in various colours from white to dull grey or brown to deep orange-red.

Exam Probability: **High**

38. *Answer choices:*
(see index for correct answer)

- a. Expanded clay aggregate
- b. Clay
- c. Armenian bole
- d. Sorbent

Guidance: level 1

:: Production economics ::

_________ is the creation of a whole that is greater than the simple sum of its parts. The term _________ comes from the Attic Greek word sea synergia from synergos, , meaning "working together".

Exam Probability: **Low**

39. *Answer choices:*
(see index for correct answer)

- a. Marginal product of labor
- b. Sectoral output
- c. Limiting factor
- d. Transaction cost

Guidance: level 1

:: Elementary mathematics ::

In mathematics, a _________ is an enumerated collection of objects in which repetitions are allowed. Like a set, it contains members . The number of elements is called the length of the _________ . Unlike a set, the same elements can appear multiple times at different positions in a _________ , and order matters. Formally, a _________ can be defined as a function whose domain is either the set of the natural numbers or the set of the first n natural numbers . The position of an element in a _________ is its rank or index; it is the natural number from which the element is the image. It depends on the context or a specific convention, if the first element has index 0 or 1. When a symbol has been chosen for denoting a _________ , the nth element of the _________ is denoted by this symbol with n as subscript; for example, the nth element of the Fibonacci _________ is generally denoted Fn.

Exam Probability: **Medium**

40. *Answer choices:*

(see index for correct answer)

- a. Subsequence
- b. Periodic function
- c. Unit vector
- d. Constant function

Guidance: level 1

:: Planning ::

_________ is a high level plan to achieve one or more goals under conditions of uncertainty. In the sense of the "art of the general," which included several subsets of skills including tactics, siegecraft, logistics etc., the term came into use in the 6th century C.E. in East Roman terminology, and was translated into Western vernacular languages only in the 18th century. From then until the 20th century, the word " _________ " came to denote "a comprehensive way to try to pursue political ends, including the threat or actual use of force, in a dialectic of wills" in a military conflict, in which both adversaries interact.

Exam Probability: **Low**

41. *Answer choices:*

(see index for correct answer)

- a. Reproductive life plan
- b. Default effect
- c. Strategy
- d. Enterprise architecture planning

Guidance: level 1

:: Goods ::

In most contexts, the concept of _________ denotes the conduct that should be preferred when posed with a choice between possible actions. _________ is generally considered to be the opposite of evil, and is of interest in the study of morality, ethics, religion and philosophy. The specific meaning and etymology of the term and its associated translations among ancient and contemporary languages show substantial variation in its inflection and meaning depending on circumstances of place, history, religious, or philosophical context.

Exam Probability: **Low**

42. *Answer choices:*

(see index for correct answer)

- a. Global public good
- b. Refined goods
- c. Good
- d. Club good

Guidance: level 1

:: Management ::

A supply-chain network is an evolution of the basic supply chain. Due to rapid technological advancement, organisations with a basic supply chain can develop this chain into a more complex structure involving a higher level of interdependence and connectivity between more organisations, this constitutes a supply-chain network.

Exam Probability: **High**

43. *Answer choices:*

(see index for correct answer)

- a. Supply chain network

- b. Lead scoring
- c. Instruction creep
- d. Change advisory board

Guidance: level 1

:: Mereology ::

__________ , in the abstract, is what belongs to or with something, whether as an attribute or as a component of said thing. In the context of this article, it is one or more components , whether physical or incorporeal, of a person`s estate; or so belonging to, as in being owned by, a person or jointly a group of people or a legal entity like a corporation or even a society. Depending on the nature of the __________ , an owner of __________ has the right to consume, alter, share, redefine, rent, mortgage, pawn, sell, exchange, transfer, give away or destroy it, or to exclude others from doing these things, as well as to perhaps abandon it; whereas regardless of the nature of the __________ , the owner thereof has the right to properly use it , or at the very least exclusively keep it.

Exam Probability: **High**

44. *Answer choices:*

(see index for correct answer)

- a. Mereological essentialism
- b. Mereotopology
- c. Non-wellfounded mereology
- d. Meronomy

Guidance: level 1

:: Information systems ::

__________ is the process of creating, sharing, using and managing the knowledge and information of an organisation. It refers to a multidisciplinary approach to achieving organisational objectives by making the best use of knowledge.

Exam Probability: **Medium**

45. *Answer choices:*

(see index for correct answer)

- a. Knowledge management
- b. European Research Center for Information Systems
- c. Hospital information system
- d. Information Systems Security Association

Guidance: level 1

:: Business process ::

A _________ or business method is a collection of related, structured activities or tasks by people or equipment which in a specific sequence produce a service or product for a particular customer or customers. _________ es occur at all organizational levels and may or may not be visible to the customers. A _________ may often be visualized as a flowchart of a sequence of activities with interleaving decision points or as a process matrix of a sequence of activities with relevance rules based on data in the process. The benefits of using _________ es include improved customer satisfaction and improved agility for reacting to rapid market change. Process-oriented organizations break down the barriers of structural departments and try to avoid functional silos.

Exam Probability: **Low**

46. *Answer choices:*

(see index for correct answer)

- a. Business process
- b. ProcessEdge
- c. Outsourced document processing
- d. Knowledge process outsourcing

Guidance: level 1

:: Management ::

_________ is a term used in business and Information Technology to describe the in-depth process of capturing customer`s expectations, preferences and aversions. Specifically, the _________ is a market research technique that produces a detailed set of customer wants and needs, organized into a hierarchical structure, and then prioritized in terms of relative importance and satisfaction with current alternatives. _________ studies typically consist of both qualitative and quantitative research steps. They are generally conducted at the start of any new product, process, or service design initiative in order to better understand the customer`s wants and needs, and as the key input for new product definition, Quality Function Deployment , and the setting of detailed design specifications.

Exam Probability: **Low**

47. *Answer choices:*

(see index for correct answer)

- a. Voice of the customer
- b. Maryland StateStat
- c. Supervisory board
- d. Resource breakdown structure

Guidance: level 1

:: Management ::

_________ is a method of quality control which employs statistical methods to monitor and control a process. This helps to ensure that the process operates efficiently, producing more specification-conforming products with less waste . SPC can be applied to any process where the "conforming product" output can be measured. Key tools used in SPC include run charts, control charts, a focus on continuous improvement, and the design of experiments. An example of a process where SPC is applied is manufacturing lines.

Exam Probability: **Medium**

48. *Answer choices:*

(see index for correct answer)

- a. Situational crisis communication theory
- b. Inside job
- c. Statistical process control
- d. Commercial management

Guidance: level 1

:: Business planning ::

_________ is an organization`s process of defining its strategy, or direction, and making decisions on allocating its resources to pursue this strategy. It may also extend to control mechanisms for guiding the implementation of the strategy. _________ became prominent in corporations during the 1960s and remains an important aspect of strategic management. It is executed by strategic planners or strategists, who involve many parties and research sources in their analysis of the organization and its relationship to the environment in which it competes.

Exam Probability: **High**

49. *Answer choices:*

(see index for correct answer)

- a. Open Options Corporation
- b. Exit planning
- c. Community Futures
- d. Strategic planning

Guidance: level 1

:: Commerce ::

A _________ is an employee within a company, business or other organization who is responsible at some level for buying or approving the acquisition of goods and services needed by the company. Responsible for buying the best quality products, goods and services for their company at the most competitive prices, _________ s work in a wide range of sectors for many different organizations. The position responsibilities may be the same as that of a buyer or purchasing agent, or may include wider supervisory or managerial responsibilities. A _________ may oversee the acquisition of materials needed for production, general supplies for offices and facilities, equipment, or construction contracts. A _________ often supervises purchasing agents and buyers, but in small companies the _________ may also be the purchasing agent or buyer. The _________ position may also carry the title "Procurement Manager" or in the public sector, "Procurement Officer". He or she can come from both an Engineering or Economics background.

Exam Probability: **Medium**

50. *Answer choices:*

(see index for correct answer)

- a. Fixed price
- b. Purchasing manager
- c. Drawback
- d. Customs broking

Guidance: level 1

:: Industrial processes ::

__________ is a technique involving the condensation of vapors and the return of this condensate to the system from which it originated. It is used in industrial and laboratory distillations. It is also used in chemistry to supply energy to reactions over a long period of time.

Exam Probability: **Medium**

51. *Answer choices:*

(see index for correct answer)

- a. Reflux
- b. Vacuum forming
- c. Fluidized bed reactor
- d. Cathodic arc deposition

Guidance: level 1

:: Project management ::

Rolling-wave planning is the process of project planning in waves as the project proceeds and later details become clearer; similar to the techniques used in agile software development approaches like Scrum..

Exam Probability: **High**

52. *Answer choices:*

(see index for correct answer)

- a. Front-end loading
- b. Burn down chart
- c. Rolling Wave planning
- d. Product flow diagram

Guidance: level 1

:: Production and manufacturing ::

Automatic __________ in continuous production processes is a combination of control engineering and chemical engineering disciplines that uses industrial control systems to achieve a production level of consistency, economy and safety which could not be achieved purely by human manual control. It is implemented widely in industries such as oil refining, pulp and paper manufacturing, chemical processing and power generating plants.

Exam Probability: **Low**

53. *Answer choices:*

(see index for correct answer)

- a. Cycle time variation
- b. Process control
- c. Technological theory of social production
- d. Division of labour

Guidance: level 1

:: Finance ::

__________ is a financial estimate intended to help buyers and owners determine the direct and indirect costs of a product or system. It is a management accounting concept that can be used in full cost accounting or even ecological economics where it includes social costs.

Exam Probability: **Medium**

54. *Answer choices:*

(see index for correct answer)

- a. Electronic communication network
- b. Total cost of ownership
- c. Offshore trust
- d. Net insurance benefit

Guidance: level 1

:: Project management ::

A __________ is the approximation of the cost of a program, project, or operation. The __________ is the product of the cost estimating process. The __________ has a single total value and may have identifiable component values. A problem with a cost overrun can be avoided with a credible, reliable, and accurate __________ . A cost estimator is the professional who prepares __________ s. There are different types of cost estimators, whose title may be preceded by a modifier, such as building estimator, or electrical estimator, or chief estimator. Other professionals such as quantity surveyors and cost engineers may also prepare __________ s or contribute to __________ s. In the US, according to the Bureau of Labor Statistics, there were 185,400 cost estimators in 2010. There are around 75,000 professional quantity surveyors working in the UK.

Exam Probability: **Medium**

55. *Answer choices:*

(see index for correct answer)

- a. NetPoint
- b. Duration
- c. Deployment Plan
- d. Level of Effort

Guidance: level 1

:: Outsourcing ::

A __________ is a document that solicits proposal, often made through a bidding process, by an agency or company interested in procurement of a commodity, service, or valuable asset, to potential suppliers to submit business proposals. It is submitted early in the procurement cycle, either at the preliminary study, or procurement stage.

Exam Probability: **Low**

56. *Answer choices:*

(see index for correct answer)

- a. Request for proposal
- b. Talentica Software
- c. Affiliated Computer Services
- d. Sourcing agent

Guidance: level 1

:: Project management ::

A _________ is a source or supply from which a benefit is produced and it has some utility. _________ s can broadly be classified upon their availability—they are classified into renewable and non-renewable _________ s.Examples of non renewable _________ s are coal ,crude oil natural gas nuclear energy etc. Examples of renewable _________ s are air,water,wind,solar energy etc. They can also be classified as actual and potential on the basis of level of development and use, on the basis of origin they can be classified as biotic and abiotic, and on the basis of their distribution, as ubiquitous and localized . An item becomes a _________ with time and developing technology. Typically, _________ s are materials, energy, services, staff, knowledge, or other assets that are transformed to produce benefit and in the process may be consumed or made unavailable. Benefits of _________ utilization may include increased wealth, proper functioning of a system, or enhanced well-being. From a human perspective a natural _________ is anything obtained from the environment to satisfy human needs and wants. From a broader biological or ecological perspective a _________ satisfies the needs of a living organism .

Exam Probability: **Medium**

57. *Answer choices:*

(see index for correct answer)

- a. The Practice Standard for Scheduling
- b. Indian Institute of Project Management
- c. Project cancellation
- d. Resource allocation

Guidance: level 1

:: Unit operations ::

__________ is a discipline of thermal engineering that concerns the generation, use, conversion, and exchange of thermal energy between physical systems. __________ is classified into various mechanisms, such as thermal conduction, thermal convection, thermal radiation, and transfer of energy by phase changes. Engineers also consider the transfer of mass of differing chemical species, either cold or hot, to achieve __________ . While these mechanisms have distinct characteristics, they often occur simultaneously in the same system.

Exam Probability: **Medium**

58. *Answer choices:*

(see index for correct answer)

- a. Clearing factor
- b. Homogenization
- c. Solvent impregnated resin
- d. Heat transfer

Guidance: level 1

:: Manufacturing ::

__________ or lean production, often simply "lean", is a systematic method for the minimization of waste within a manufacturing system without sacrificing productivity, which can cause problems. Lean also takes into account waste created through overburden and waste created through unevenness in work loads . Working from the perspective of the client who consumes a product or service, "value" is any action or process that a customer would be willing to pay for.

Exam Probability: **Low**

59. *Answer choices:*

(see index for correct answer)

- a. Single-machine scheduling
- b. Enterprise appliance transaction module
- c. Motoman
- d. Lean manufacturing

Guidance: level 1

Commerce

Commerce relates to "the exchange of goods and services, especially on a large scale." It includes legal, economic, political, social, cultural and technological systems that operate in any country or internationally.

:: ::

_________ refers to a business or organization attempting to acquire goods or services to accomplish its goals. Although there are several organizations that attempt to set standards in the _________ process, processes can vary greatly between organizations. Typically the word " _________ " is not used interchangeably with the word "procurement", since procurement typically includes expediting, supplier quality, and transportation and logistics in addition to _________ .

Exam Probability: **Medium**

1. *Answer choices:*
(see index for correct answer)

- a. process perspective
- b. Purchasing
- c. information systems assessment
- d. similarity-attraction theory

Guidance: level 1

:: Management occupations ::

_________ ship is the process of designing, launching and running a new business, which is often initially a small business. The people who create these businesses are called _________ s.

Exam Probability: **Low**

2. *Answer choices:*

(see index for correct answer)

- a. City manager
- b. Legislator
- c. Entrepreneur
- d. Business magnate

Guidance: level 1

:: Trading posts of the Hanseatic League ::

_________ is a city and unitary authority area in North _________ shire, England, with a population of 208,200 as of 2017. Located at the confluence of the Rivers Ouse and Foss, it is the county town of the historic county of _________ shire and was the home of the House of _________ throughout its existence. The city is known for its famous historical landmarks such as _________ Minster and the city walls, as well as a variety of cultural and sporting activities, which makes it a popular tourist destination in England. The local authority is the City of _________ Council, a single tier governing body responsible for providing all local services and facilities throughout the city. The City of _________ local government district includes rural areas beyond the old city boundaries.

Exam Probability: **Medium**

3. *Answer choices:*

(see index for correct answer)

- a. Antwerp
- b. Pskov
- c. Kaunas
- d. Falsterbo

Guidance: level 1

:: Contract law ::

A __________ is a legally-binding agreement which recognises and governs the rights and duties of the parties to the agreement. A __________ is legally enforceable because it meets the requirements and approval of the law. An agreement typically involves the exchange of goods, services, money, or promises of any of those. In the event of breach of __________, the law awards the injured party access to legal remedies such as damages and cancellation.

Exam Probability: **High**

4. *Answer choices:*

(see index for correct answer)

- a. Culpa in contrahendo
- b. Pact ink
- c. Cohabitation agreement
- d. first refusal

Guidance: level 1

:: Manufacturing ::

A __________ is a building for storing goods. __________ s are used by manufacturers, importers, exporters, wholesalers, transport businesses, customs, etc. They are usually large plain buildings in industrial parks on the outskirts of cities, towns or villages.

Exam Probability: **Low**

5. *Answer choices:*

(see index for correct answer)

- a. Warehouse
- b. Gunsmith
- c. Manufacturing bill of materials
- d. Form, fit and function

Guidance: level 1

:: ::

An _________ is the production of goods or related services within an economy. The major source of revenue of a group or company is the indicator of its relevant _________ . When a large group has multiple sources of revenue generation, it is considered to be working in different industries. Manufacturing _________ became a key sector of production and labour in European and North American countries during the Industrial Revolution, upsetting previous mercantile and feudal economies. This came through many successive rapid advances in technology, such as the production of steel and coal.

Exam Probability: **Medium**

6. *Answer choices:*

(see index for correct answer)

- a. Industry
- b. co-culture
- c. open system
- d. hierarchical perspective

Guidance: level 1

:: Business ethics ::

_________ is a type of harassment technique that relates to a sexual nature and the unwelcome or inappropriate promise of rewards in exchange for sexual favors. _________ includes a range of actions from mild transgressions to sexual abuse or assault. Harassment can occur in many different social settings such as the workplace, the home, school, churches, etc. Harassers or victims may be of any gender.

Exam Probability: **Low**

7. *Answer choices:*

(see index for correct answer)

- a. Centre for Research on Multinational Corporations
- b. Sexual harassment
- c. Proceedings of the International Association for Business and Society
- d. Society for Business Ethics

Guidance: level 1

:: Marketing ::

__________ or stock is the goods and materials that a business holds for the ultimate goal of resale .

Exam Probability: **High**

8. *Answer choices:*

(see index for correct answer)

- a. Inventory
- b. Cult brand
- c. Market overhang
- d. Customer insight

Guidance: level 1

:: Commodities ::

In economics, a __________ is an economic good or service that has full or substantial fungibility: that is, the market treats instances of the good as equivalent or nearly so with no regard to who produced them. Most commodities are raw materials, basic resources, agricultural, or mining products, such as iron ore, sugar, or grains like rice and wheat. Commodities can also be mass-produced unspecialized products such as chemicals and computer memory.

Exam Probability: **Low**

9. *Answer choices:*

(see index for correct answer)

- a. Sample grade
- b. Commoditization
- c. Commodity
- d. IRely

Guidance: level 1

:: Fraud ::

In law, _________ is intentional deception to secure unfair or unlawful gain, or to deprive a victim of a legal right. _________ can violate civil law , a criminal law , or it may cause no loss of money, property or legal right but still be an element of another civil or criminal wrong. The purpose of _________ may be monetary gain or other benefits, for example by obtaining a passport, travel document, or driver`s license, or mortgage _________ , where the perpetrator may attempt to qualify for a mortgage by way of false statements.

Exam Probability: **Low**

10. *Answer choices:*

(see index for correct answer)

- a. Pharma fraud
- b. Hitler Diaries
- c. Regummed stamp
- d. Fraud

Guidance: level 1

:: Quality management ::

_________ ensures that an organization, product or service is consistent. It has four main components: quality planning, quality assurance, quality control and quality improvement. _________ is focused not only on product and service quality, but also on the means to achieve it. _________ , therefore, uses quality assurance and control of processes as well as products to achieve more consistent quality.What a customer wants and is willing to pay for it determines quality. It is written or unwritten commitment to a known or unknown consumer in the market . Thus, quality can be defined as fitness for intended use or, in other words, how well the product performs its intended function

Exam Probability: **Medium**

11. *Answer choices:*

(see index for correct answer)

- a. Quality management
- b. Quality management system
- c. Dana Ulery
- d. Informal Methods

Guidance: level 1

:: ::

__________ is the social science that studies the production, distribution, and consumption of goods and services.

Exam Probability: **High**

12. *Answer choices:*

(see index for correct answer)

- a. hierarchical
- b. Economics
- c. personal values
- d. cultural

Guidance: level 1

:: ::

__________ Corporation is an American multinational technology company with headquarters in Redmond, Washington. It develops, manufactures, licenses, supports and sells computer software, consumer electronics, personal computers, and related services. Its best known software products are the __________ Windows line of operating systems, the __________ Office suite, and the Internet Explorer and Edge Web browsers. Its flagship hardware products are the Xbox video game consoles and the __________ Surface lineup of touchscreen personal computers. As of 2016, it is the world`s largest software maker by revenue, and one of the world`s most valuable companies. The word " __________ " is a portmanteau of "microcomputer" and "software". __________ is ranked No. 30 in the 2018 Fortune 500 rankings of the largest United States corporations by total revenue.

Exam Probability: **Medium**

13. *Answer choices:*

(see index for correct answer)

- a. open system
- b. Microsoft
- c. surface-level diversity
- d. co-culture

Guidance: level 1

:: Business terms ::

The __________ or reception is an area where visitors arrive and first encounter a staff at a place of business. __________ staff will deal with whatever question the visitor has and put them in contact with a relevant person at the company. Broadly speaking, the __________ includes roles that affect the revenues of the business. The term __________ is in contrast to the term back office which refers to a company`s operations, personnel, accounting, payroll and financial departments which do not interact directly with customers.

Exam Probability: **Medium**

14. *Answer choices:*

(see index for correct answer)

- a. Mission statement
- b. Front office
- c. granular
- d. organic growth

Guidance: level 1

:: Production economics ::

In economics long run is a theoretical concept where all markets are in equilibrium, and all prices and quantities have fully adjusted and are in equilibrium. The long run contrasts with the __________ where there are some constraints and markets are not fully in equilibrium.

Exam Probability: **Low**

15. *Answer choices:*

(see index for correct answer)

- a. HMI quality
- b. Diminishing returns
- c. Productive capacity
- d. Short run

Guidance: level 1

:: Auctioneering ::

__________ are electronic auctions, which can be used by sellers to sell their items to many potential buyers. Sellers and buyers can be individuals, organizations etc.

Exam Probability: **High**

16. *Answer choices:*

(see index for correct answer)

- a. Demsetz auction
- b. Online trading community
- c. Forward auction
- d. Unique bid auction

Guidance: level 1

:: Direct marketing ::

__________ is a form of advertising where organizations communicate directly to customers through a variety of media including cell phone text messaging, email, websites, online adverts, database marketing, fliers, catalog distribution, promotional letters, targeted television, newspapers, magazine advertisements, and outdoor advertising. Among practitioners, it is also known as direct response marketing.

Exam Probability: **Low**

17. *Answer choices:*

(see index for correct answer)

- a. Warm market
- b. Direct Marketing Association
- c. Tupperware Brands
- d. DVD club

Guidance: level 1

:: Service industries ::

_________ is travel for pleasure or business; also the theory and practice of touring, the business of attracting, accommodating, and entertaining tourists, and the business of operating tours. _________ may be international, or within the traveller`s country. The World _________ Organization defines _________ more generally, in terms which go "beyond the common perception of _________ as being limited to holiday activity only", as people "traveling to and staying in places outside their usual environment for not more than one consecutive year for leisure and not less than 24 hours, business and other purposes".

Exam Probability: **High**

18. *Answer choices:*

(see index for correct answer)

- a. Maid service
- b. Association of Special Fares Agents
- c. Financial services in Singapore
- d. Tourism

Guidance: level 1

:: Dot-com bubble ::

_________ was an online grocery business that filed bankruptcy in 2001 after 3 years of operation and was later folded into Amazon.com. It was headquartered in Foster City, California, United States. It delivered products to customers` homes within a 30-minute window of their choosing. At its peak, it offered service in ten US markets: the San Francisco Bay Area; Dallas; Sacramento; San Diego; Los Angeles; Orange County, California; Chicago; Seattle; Portland, Oregon; and Atlanta, Georgia. The company had hoped to expand to 26 cities by 2001.

Exam Probability: **Low**

19. *Answer choices:*

(see index for correct answer)

- a. Webvan
- b. @Home Network
- c. Dot-com company
- d. E-Dreams

Guidance: level 1

:: ::

_________ is the practical authority granted to a legal body to administer justice within a defined field of responsibility, e.g., Michigan tax law. In federations like the United States, areas of _________ apply to local, state, and federal levels; e.g. the court has _________ to apply federal law.

Exam Probability: **High**

20. *Answer choices:*

(see index for correct answer)

- a. interpersonal communication
- b. imperative
- c. hierarchical
- d. Jurisdiction

Guidance: level 1

:: ::

A _________ or _________ s is a type of footwear and not a specific type of shoe. Most _________ s mainly cover the foot and the ankle, while some also cover some part of the lower calf. Some _________ s extend up the leg, sometimes as far as the knee or even the hip. Most _________ s have a heel that is clearly distinguishable from the rest of the sole, even if the two are made of one piece. Traditionally made of leather or rubber, modern _________ s are made from a variety of materials. _________ s are worn both for their functionality protecting the foot and leg from water, extreme cold, mud or hazards or providing additional ankle support for strenuous activities with added traction requirements , or may have hobnails on their undersides to protect against wear and to get better grip; and for reasons of style and fashion.

Exam Probability: **Medium**

21. *Answer choices:*

(see index for correct answer)

- a. hierarchical perspective
- b. Boot
- c. deep-level diversity
- d. functional perspective

Guidance: level 1

:: Commerce ::

An __________ is a bank that offers card association branded payment cards directly to consumers. The name is derived from the practice of issuing payment to the acquiring bank on behalf of its customer .

Exam Probability: **Low**

22. *Answer choices:*

(see index for correct answer)

- a. Customs broking
- b. Linestanding
- c. Acquiring bank
- d. Issuing bank

Guidance: level 1

:: Decision theory ::

Within economics the concept of __________ is used to model worth or value, but its usage has evolved significantly over time. The term was introduced initially as a measure of pleasure or satisfaction within the theory of utilitarianism by moral philosophers such as Jeremy Bentham and John Stuart Mill. But the term has been adapted and reapplied within neoclassical economics, which dominates modern economic theory, as a __________ function that represents a consumer`s preference ordering over a choice set. As such, it is devoid of its original interpretation as a measurement of the pleasure or satisfaction obtained by the consumer from that choice.

Exam Probability: **Low**

23. *Answer choices:*

(see index for correct answer)

- a. Utility
- b. Pignistic probability
- c. TOPSIS
- d. Rademacher complexity

Guidance: level 1

:: ::

_________ is an American restaurant chain and international franchise which was founded in 1958 by Dan and Frank Carney. The company is known for its Italian-American cuisine menu, including pizza and pasta, as well as side dishes and desserts. _________ has 18,431 restaurants worldwide as of December 31, 2018, making it the world`s largest pizza chain in terms of locations. It is a subsidiary of Yum! Brands, Inc., one of the world`s largest restaurant companies.

Exam Probability: **Medium**

24. *Answer choices:*

(see index for correct answer)

- a. deep-level diversity
- b. levels of analysis
- c. co-culture
- d. Pizza Hut

Guidance: level 1

:: Supply chain management ::

_________ is the removal of intermediaries in economics from a supply chain, or cutting out the middlemen in connection with a transaction or a series of transactions. Instead of going through traditional distribution channels, which had some type of intermediary , companies may now deal with customers directly, for example via the Internet. Hence, the use of factory direct and direct from the factory to mean the same thing.

Exam Probability: **Medium**

25. *Answer choices:*

(see index for correct answer)

- a. Gideon Hillman Consulting
- b. Dynamic discounting
- c. Disintermediation
- d. Demand sensing

Guidance: level 1

:: Information technology management ::

B2B is often contrasted with business-to-consumer . In B2B commerce, it is often the case that the parties to the relationship have comparable negotiating power, and even when they do not, each party typically involves professional staff and legal counsel in the negotiation of terms, whereas B2C is shaped to a far greater degree by economic implications of information asymmetry. However, within a B2B context, large companies may have many commercial, resource and information advantages over smaller businesses. The United Kingdom government, for example, created the post of Small Business Commissioner under the Enterprise Act 2016 to "enable small businesses to resolve disputes" and "consider complaints by small business suppliers about payment issues with larger businesses that they supply."

Exam Probability: **Medium**

26. *Answer choices:*

(see index for correct answer)

- a. XML/EDIFACT
- b. Enterprise portal
- c. Business-to-business
- d. Belarc

Guidance: level 1

:: ::

A _________ is any person who contracts to acquire an asset in return for some form of consideration.

Exam Probability: **Low**

27. *Answer choices:*

(see index for correct answer)

- a. functional perspective
- b. hierarchical perspective
- c. deep-level diversity
- d. interpersonal communication

Guidance: level 1

:: Business terms ::

_________ ning is an organization`s process of defining its strategy, or direction, and making decisions on allocating its resources to pursue this strategy. It may also extend to control mechanisms for guiding the implementation of the strategy. _________ ning became prominent in corporations during the 1960s and remains an important aspect of strategic management. It is executed by _________ ners or strategists, who involve many parties and research sources in their analysis of the organization and its relationship to the environment in which it competes.

Exam Probability: **Medium**

28. *Answer choices:*

(see index for correct answer)

- a. back office
- b. Mission statement
- c. customer base
- d. centralization

Guidance: level 1

:: ::

In marketing jargon, product lining is offering several related products for sale individually. Unlike product bundling, where several products are combined into one group, which is then offered for sale as a units, product lining involves offering the products for sale separately. A line can comprise related products of various sizes, types, colors, qualities, or prices. Line depth refers to the number of subcategories a category has. Line consistency refers to how closely related the products that make up the line are. Line vulnerability refers to the percentage of sales or profits that are derived from only a few products in the line.

Exam Probability: **Low**

29. *Answer choices:*

(see index for correct answer)

- a. Character
- b. functional perspective
- c. interpersonal communication
- d. personal values

Guidance: level 1

:: ::

__________ s and acquisitions are transactions in which the ownership of companies, other business organizations, or their operating units are transferred or consolidated with other entities. As an aspect of strategic management, M&A can allow enterprises to grow or downsize, and change the nature of their business or competitive position.

Exam Probability: **Low**

30. *Answer choices:*
(see index for correct answer)

- a. co-culture
- b. Merger
- c. functional perspective
- d. process perspective

Guidance: level 1

:: Dot-com bubble ::

__________, Inc., is a web search engine and web portal established in 1994, spun out of Carnegie Mellon University. __________ also encompasses a network of email, webhosting, social networking, and entertainment websites. The company is based in Waltham, Massachusetts, and is currently a subsidiary of Kakao.

Exam Probability: **Low**

31. *Answer choices:*
(see index for correct answer)

- a. Xoom
- b. Dot-com bubble
- c. Lycos
- d. Pay to surf

Guidance: level 1

:: Commerce ::

_________ relates to "the exchange of goods and services, especially on a large scale". It includes legal, economic, political, social, cultural and technological systems that operate in a country or in international trade.

Exam Probability: **Low**

32. *Answer choices:*

(see index for correct answer)

- a. Non-commercial
- b. Purchase discount
- c. TradeCard
- d. Jumble sale

Guidance: level 1

:: ::

_________ is a type of government support for the citizens of that society. _________ may be provided to people of any income level, as with social security , but it is usually intended to ensure that the poor can meet their basic human needs such as food and shelter. _________ attempts to provide poor people with a minimal level of well-being, usually either a free- or a subsidized-supply of certain goods and social services, such as healthcare, education, and vocational training.

Exam Probability: **Medium**

33. *Answer choices:*

(see index for correct answer)

- a. Welfare
- b. cultural
- c. deep-level diversity
- d. similarity-attraction theory

Guidance: level 1

:: Minimum wage ::

A __________ is the lowest remuneration that employers can legally pay their workers—the price floor below which workers may not sell their labor. Most countries had introduced __________ legislation by the end of the 20th century.

Exam Probability: **Medium**

34. *Answer choices:*

(see index for correct answer)

- a. Minimum wage in the United States
- b. Minimum wage
- c. Minimum Wage Fairness Act
- d. National Anti-Sweating League

Guidance: level 1

:: E-commerce ::

__________ is a method of e-commerce where shoppers` friends become involved in the shopping experience. __________ attempts to use technology to mimic the social interactions found in physical malls and stores. With the rise of mobile devices, __________ is now extending beyond the online world and into the offline world of shopping.

Exam Probability: **Medium**

35. *Answer choices:*

(see index for correct answer)

- a. Point of sale
- b. Social shopping
- c. Business-to-manager
- d. Want Button

Guidance: level 1

:: Project management ::

In political science, an _________ is a means by which a petition signed by a certain minimum number of registered voters can force a government to choose to either enact a law or hold a public vote in parliament in what is called indirect _________ , or under direct _________ , the proposition is immediately put to a plebiscite or referendum, in what is called a Popular initiated Referendum or citizen-initiated referendum).

Exam Probability: **Medium**

36. *Answer choices:*

(see index for correct answer)

- a. Costab
- b. Pmhub
- c. Social project management
- d. Initiative

Guidance: level 1

:: Stock market ::

The _________ of a corporation is all of the shares into which ownership of the corporation is divided. In American English, the shares are commonly known as " _________ s". A single share of the _________ represents fractional ownership of the corporation in proportion to the total number of shares. This typically entitles the _________ holder to that fraction of the company`s earnings, proceeds from liquidation of assets , or voting power, often dividing these up in proportion to the amount of money each _________ holder has invested. Not all _________ is necessarily equal, as certain classes of _________ may be issued for example without voting rights, with enhanced voting rights, or with a certain priority to receive profits or liquidation proceeds before or after other classes of shareholders.

Exam Probability: **High**

37. *Answer choices:*

(see index for correct answer)

- a. Barbell strategy
- b. Stock
- c. GXG Markets
- d. Sector rotation

Guidance: level 1

:: Market research ::

__________ is an organized effort to gather information about target markets or customers. It is a very important component of business strategy. The term is commonly interchanged with marketing research; however, expert practitioners may wish to draw a distinction, in that marketing research is concerned specifically about marketing processes, while __________ is concerned specifically with markets.

Exam Probability: **Medium**

38. *Answer choices:*

(see index for correct answer)

- a. Industry analyst
- b. Early adopter
- c. Landing page optimization
- d. Market research

Guidance: level 1

:: ::

__________ is a marketing communication that employs an openly sponsored, non-personal message to promote or sell a product, service or idea. Sponsors of __________ are typically businesses wishing to promote their products or services. __________ is differentiated from public relations in that an advertiser pays for and has control over the message. It differs from personal selling in that the message is non-personal, i.e., not directed to a particular individual. __________ is communicated through various mass media, including traditional media such as newspapers, magazines, television, radio, outdoor __________ or direct mail; and new media such as search results, blogs, social media, websites or text messages. The actual presentation of the message in a medium is referred to as an advertisement, or "ad" or advert for short.

Exam Probability: **High**

39. *Answer choices:*

(see index for correct answer)

- a. hierarchical
- b. imperative
- c. personal values

- d. Advertising

Guidance: level 1

:: Management ::

The term __________ refers to measures designed to increase the degree of autonomy and self-determination in people and in communities in order to enable them to represent their interests in a responsible and self-determined way, acting on their own authority. It is the process of becoming stronger and more confident, especially in controlling one`s life and claiming one`s rights. __________ as action refers both to the process of self- __________ and to professional support of people, which enables them to overcome their sense of powerlessness and lack of influence, and to recognize and use their resources. To do work with power.

Exam Probability: **Low**

40. *Answer choices:*

(see index for correct answer)

- a. Action item
- b. Goals Breakdown Structure
- c. Project management simulation
- d. Empowerment

Guidance: level 1

:: Warrants issued in Hong Kong Stock Exchange ::

__________ is a chemical element with symbol Ag and atomic number 47. A soft, white, lustrous transition metal, it exhibits the highest electrical conductivity, thermal conductivity, and reflectivity of any metal. The metal is found in the Earth`s crust in the pure, free elemental form , as an alloy with gold and other metals, and in minerals such as argentite and chlorargyrite. Most __________ is produced as a byproduct of copper, gold, lead, and zinc refining.

Exam Probability: **Low**

41. *Answer choices:*

(see index for correct answer)

- a. Hong Kong Exchanges and Clearing
- b. The Link REIT
- c. China Resources Cement
- d. Emperor International Holdings Limited

Guidance: level 1

:: Real property law ::

A __________ is the grant of authority or rights, stating that the granter formally recognizes the prerogative of the recipient to exercise the rights specified. It is implicit that the granter retains superiority , and that the recipient admits a limited status within the relationship, and it is within that sense that __________ s were historically granted, and that sense is retained in modern usage of the term.

Exam Probability: **High**

42. *Answer choices:*

(see index for correct answer)

- a. Registers of Scotland
- b. Charter
- c. Freehold
- d. Feu

Guidance: level 1

:: Business law ::

The __________ , first published in 1952, is one of a number of Uniform Acts that have been established as law with the goal of harmonizing the laws of sales and other commercial transactions across the United States of America through UCC adoption by all 50 states, the District of Columbia, and the Territories of the United States.

Exam Probability: **Medium**

43. *Answer choices:*

(see index for correct answer)

- a. Installment sale
- b. Uniform Commercial Code
- c. Recharacterisation
- d. Official Assignee

Guidance: level 1

:: Computer access control ::

__________ is the act of confirming the truth of an attribute of a single piece of data claimed true by an entity. In contrast with identification, which refers to the act of stating or otherwise indicating a claim purportedly attesting to a person or thing`s identity, __________ is the process of actually confirming that identity. It might involve confirming the identity of a person by validating their identity documents, verifying the authenticity of a website with a digital certificate, determining the age of an artifact by carbon dating, or ensuring that a product is what its packaging and labeling claim to be. In other words, __________ often involves verifying the validity of at least one form of identification.

Exam Probability: **Low**

44. *Answer choices:*

(see index for correct answer)

- a. Secure attention key
- b. Microsoft Fingerprint Reader
- c. Authentication
- d. Form-based authentication

Guidance: level 1

:: Management ::

__________ is the identification, evaluation, and prioritization of risks followed by coordinated and economical application of resources to minimize, monitor, and control the probability or impact of unfortunate events or to maximize the realization of opportunities.

Exam Probability: **Low**

45. *Answer choices:*

(see index for correct answer)

- a. Resource breakdown structure
- b. Change advisory board
- c. Managerialism
- d. Total Worker Health

Guidance: level 1

:: Generally Accepted Accounting Principles ::

In accounting, _________ is the income that a business have from its normal business activities, usually from the sale of goods and services to customers. _________ is also referred to as sales or turnover.Some companies receive _________ from interest, royalties, or other fees. _________ may refer to business income in general, or it may refer to the amount, in a monetary unit, earned during a period of time, as in "Last year, Company X had _________ of $42 million". Profits or net income generally imply total _________ minus total expenses in a given period. In accounting, in the balance statement it is a subsection of the Equity section and _________ increases equity, it is often referred to as the "top line" due to its position on the income statement at the very top. This is to be contrasted with the "bottom line" which denotes net income .

Exam Probability: **High**

46. *Answer choices:*

(see index for correct answer)

- a. Matching principle
- b. Revenue
- c. Net realizable value
- d. Statement of recommended practice

Guidance: level 1

:: Business law ::

A _________ is an arrangement where parties, known as partners, agree to cooperate to advance their mutual interests. The partners in a _________ may be individuals, businesses, interest-based organizations, schools, governments or combinations. Organizations may partner to increase the likelihood of each achieving their mission and to amplify their reach. A _________ may result in issuing and holding equity or may be only governed by a contract.

Exam Probability: **Medium**

47. *Answer choices:*

(see index for correct answer)

- a. Partnership
- b. Uniform Commercial Code
- c. Operating lease
- d. TRIPS Agreement

Guidance: level 1

:: Investment ::

In finance, the benefit from an _________ is called a return. The return may consist of a gain realised from the sale of property or an _________ , unrealised capital appreciation , or _________ income such as dividends, interest, rental income etc., or a combination of capital gain and income. The return may also include currency gains or losses due to changes in foreign currency exchange rates.

Exam Probability: **Medium**

48. *Answer choices:*
(see index for correct answer)

- a. IFund
- b. Juniperus Capital
- c. Investment
- d. Insurance bond

Guidance: level 1

:: Asset ::

In financial accounting, an _________ is any resource owned by the business. Anything tangible or intangible that can be owned or controlled to produce value and that is held by a company to produce positive economic value is an _________ . Simply stated, _________ s represent value of ownership that can be converted into cash . The balance sheet of a firm records the monetary value of the _________ s owned by that firm. It covers money and other valuables belonging to an individual or to a business.

Exam Probability: **Low**

49. *Answer choices:*
(see index for correct answer)

- a. Current asset

- b. Fixed asset

Guidance: level 1

:: Information retrieval ::

_________ is a technique used by recommender systems. _________ has two senses, a narrow one and a more general one.

Exam Probability: **Medium**

50. *Answer choices:*
(see index for correct answer)

- a. Information Retrieval Specialist Group
- b. Stemming
- c. Dynatext
- d. Collaborative filtering

Guidance: level 1

:: Strategic alliances ::

A _________ is an agreement between two or more parties to pursue a set of agreed upon objectives needed while remaining independent organizations. A _________ will usually fall short of a legal partnership entity, agency, or corporate affiliate relationship. Typically, two companies form a _________ when each possesses one or more business assets or have expertise that will help the other by enhancing their businesses. _________ s can develop in outsourcing relationships where the parties desire to achieve long-term win-win benefits and innovation based on mutually desired outcomes.

Exam Probability: **High**

51. *Answer choices:*
(see index for correct answer)

- a. Defensive termination
- b. Strategic alliance
- c. Management contract
- d. Bridge Alliance

Guidance: level 1

:: ::

__________ are electronic transfer of money from one bank account to another, either within a single financial institution or across multiple institutions, via computer-based systems, without the direct intervention of bank staff.

Exam Probability: **High**

52. *Answer choices:*

(see index for correct answer)

- a. Sarbanes-Oxley act of 2002
- b. co-culture
- c. cultural
- d. Electronic funds transfer

Guidance: level 1

:: ::

A trade fair is an exhibition organized so that companies in a specific industry can showcase and demonstrate their latest products and services, meet with industry partners and customers, study activities of rivals, and examine recent market trends and opportunities. In contrast to consumer fairs, only some trade fairs are open to the public, while others can only be attended by company representatives and members of the press, therefore __________ s are classified as either "public" or "trade only". A few fairs are hybrids of the two; one example is the Frankfurt Book Fair, which is trade only for its first three days and open to the general public on its final two days. They are held on a continuing basis in virtually all markets and normally attract companies from around the globe. For example, in the U.S., there are currently over 10,000 __________ s held every year, and several online directories have been established to help organizers, attendees, and marketers identify appropriate events.

Exam Probability: **High**

53. *Answer choices:*

(see index for correct answer)

- a. imperative
- b. Trade show

- c. corporate values
- d. interpersonal communication

Guidance: level 1

:: ::

__________ is the extraction of valuable minerals or other geological materials from the earth, usually from an ore body, lode, vein, seam, reef or placer deposit. These deposits form a mineralized package that is of economic interest to the miner.

Exam Probability: **High**

54. *Answer choices:*

(see index for correct answer)

- a. empathy
- b. imperative
- c. Mining
- d. Character

Guidance: level 1

:: Commerce ::

__________, Inc. is an American media-services provider headquartered in Los Gatos, California, founded in 1997 by Reed Hastings and Marc Randolph in Scotts Valley, California. The company`s primary business is its subscription-based streaming OTT service which offers online streaming of a library of films and television programs, including those produced in-house. As of April 2019, __________ had over 148 million paid subscriptions worldwide, including 60 million in the United States, and over 154 million subscriptions total including free trials. It is available almost worldwide except in mainland China as well as Syria, North Korea, and Crimea . The company also has offices in the Netherlands, Brazil, India, Japan, and South Korea. __________ is a member of the Motion Picture Association of America .

Exam Probability: **Medium**

55. *Answer choices:*

(see index for correct answer)

- a. Netflix
- b. Real prices and ideal prices
- c. V-commerce
- d. Country commercial guides

Guidance: level 1

:: E-commerce ::

A _________ is a hosted service offering that acts as an intermediary between business partners sharing standards based or proprietary data via shared business processes. The offered service is referred to as " _________ services".

Exam Probability: **Low**

56. *Answer choices:*

(see index for correct answer)

- a. Want Button
- b. Electronic Commerce Directive
- c. Value-added network
- d. TRADACOMS

Guidance: level 1

:: ::

_________ is the practice of deliberately managing the spread of information between an individual or an organization and the public. _________ may include an organization or individual gaining exposure to their audiences using topics of public interest and news items that do not require direct payment. This differentiates it from advertising as a form of marketing communications. _________ is the idea of creating coverage for clients for free, rather than marketing or advertising. But now, advertising is also a part of greater PR Activities.An example of good _________ would be generating an article featuring a client, rather than paying for the client to be advertised next to the article. The aim of _________ is to inform the public, prospective customers, investors, partners, employees, and other stakeholders and ultimately persuade them to maintain a positive or favorable view about the organization, its leadership, products, or political decisions. _________ professionals typically work for PR and marketing firms, businesses and companies, government, and public officials as PIOs and nongovernmental organizations, and nonprofit organizations. Jobs central to _________ include account coordinator, account executive, account supervisor, and media relations manager.

Exam Probability: **Medium**

57. *Answer choices:*

(see index for correct answer)

- a. process perspective
- b. information systems assessment
- c. Public relations
- d. open system

Guidance: level 1

:: ::

In Western musical notation, the staff or stave is a set of five horizontal lines and four spaces that each represent a different musical pitch or in the case of a percussion staff, different percussion instruments. Appropriate music symbols, depending on the intended effect, are placed on the staff according to their corresponding pitch or function. Musical notes are placed by pitch, percussion notes are placed by instrument, and rests and other symbols are placed by convention.

Exam Probability: **Low**

58. *Answer choices:*

(see index for correct answer)

- a. hierarchical
- b. hierarchical perspective
- c. functional perspective
- d. Staff position

Guidance: level 1

:: ::

Business is the activity of making one`s living or making money by producing or buying and selling products . Simply put, it is "any activity or enterprise entered into for profit. It does not mean it is a company, a corporation, partnership, or have any such formal organization, but it can range from a street peddler to General Motors."

Exam Probability: **Medium**

59. *Answer choices:*

(see index for correct answer)

- a. deep-level diversity
- b. interpersonal communication
- c. Firm
- d. imperative

Guidance: level 1

Business ethics

Business ethics (also known as corporate ethics) is a form of applied ethics or professional ethics, that examines ethical principles and moral or ethical problems that can arise in a business environment. It applies to all aspects of business conduct and is relevant to the conduct of individuals and entire organizations. These ethics originate from individuals, organizational statements or from the legal system. These norms, values, ethical, and unethical practices are what is used to guide business. They help those businesses maintain a better connection with their stakeholders.

:: Television terminology ::

A _________ organization , also known as a non-business entity, not-for-profit organization, or _________ institution, is dedicated to furthering a particular social cause or advocating for a shared point of view. In economic terms, it is an organization that uses its surplus of the revenues to further achieve its ultimate objective, rather than distributing its income to the organization`s shareholders, leaders, or members. _________ s are tax exempt or charitable, meaning they do not pay income tax on the money that they receive for their organization. They can operate in religious, scientific, research, or educational settings.

Exam Probability: **High**

1. *Answer choices:*

(see index for correct answer)

- a. distance learning
- b. not-for-profit
- c. multiplexing
- d. Nonprofit

Guidance: level 1

:: Leadership ::

_________ is leadership that is directed by respect for ethical beliefs and values and for the dignity and rights of others. It is thus related to concepts such as trust, honesty, consideration, charisma, and fairness.

Exam Probability: **Low**

2. *Answer choices:*

(see index for correct answer)

- a. Moral example
- b. Authentic leadership
- c. Integral leadership
- d. Leadership analysis

Guidance: level 1

:: Carbon finance ::

The _________ is an international treaty which extends the 1992 United Nations Framework Convention on Climate Change that commits state parties to reduce greenhouse gas emissions, based on the scientific consensus that global warming is occurring and it is extremely likely that human-made CO2 emissions have predominantly caused it. The _________ was adopted in Kyoto, Japan on 11 December 1997 and entered into force on 16 February 2005. There are currently 192 parties to the Protocol.

Exam Probability: **Low**

3. *Answer choices:*

(see index for correct answer)

- a. Kyoto Protocol
- b. Chinese national carbon trading scheme
- c. Carbon Clear
- d. Joint Implementation

Guidance: level 1

:: ::

_________ is a non-governmental environmental organization with offices in over 39 countries and an international coordinating body in Amsterdam, the Netherlands. _________ was founded in 1971 by Irving Stowe, and Dorothy Stowe, Canadian and US ex-pat environmental activists. _________ states its goal is to "ensure the ability of the Earth to nurture life in all its diversity" and focuses its campaigning on worldwide issues such as climate change, deforestation, overfishing, commercial whaling, genetic engineering, and anti-nuclear issues. It uses direct action, lobbying, research, and ecotage to achieve its goals. The global organization does not accept funding from governments, corporations, or political parties, relying on three million individual supporters and foundation grants. _________ has a general consultative status with the United Nations Economic and Social Council and is a founding member of the INGO Accountability Charter, an international non-governmental organization that intends to foster accountability and transparency of non-governmental organizations.

Exam Probability: **Medium**

4. *Answer choices:*

(see index for correct answer)

- a. hierarchical perspective
- b. corporate values
- c. Greenpeace
- d. imperative

Guidance: level 1

:: Business ethics ::

_________ is a type of harassment technique that relates to a sexual nature and the unwelcome or inappropriate promise of rewards in exchange for sexual favors. _________ includes a range of actions from mild transgressions to sexual abuse or assault. Harassment can occur in many different social settings such as the workplace, the home, school, churches, etc. Harassers or victims may be of any gender.

Exam Probability: **Medium**

5. *Answer choices:*

(see index for correct answer)

- a. Conscious business
- b. Cost the limit of price
- c. Sexual harassment
- d. Precarity

Guidance: level 1

:: Coal ::

_________ is a combustible black or brownish-black sedimentary rock, formed as rock strata called _________ seams. _________ is mostly carbon with variable amounts of other elements; chiefly hydrogen, sulfur, oxygen, and nitrogen. _________ is formed if dead plant matter decays into peat and over millions of years the heat and pressure of deep burial converts the peat into _________ . Vast deposits of _________ originates in former wetlands—called _________ forests—that covered much of the Earth`s tropical land areas during the late Carboniferous and Permian times.

Exam Probability: **Medium**

6. *Answer choices:*

(see index for correct answer)

- a. Azienda Nazionale Idrogenazione Combustibili
- b. Energy value of coal
- c. Coal
- d. Black coal equivalent

Guidance: level 1

:: Business ethics ::

__________ is a persistent pattern of mistreatment from others in the workplace that causes either physical or emotional harm. It can include such tactics as verbal, nonverbal, psychological, physical abuse and humiliation. This type of workplace aggression is particularly difficult because, unlike the typical school bully, workplace bullies often operate within the established rules and policies of their organization and their society. In the majority of cases, bullying in the workplace is reported as having been by someone who has authority over their victim. However, bullies can also be peers, and occasionally subordinates. Research has also investigated the impact of the larger organizational context on bullying as well as the group-level processes that impact on the incidence and maintenance of bullying behaviour. Bullying can be covert or overt. It may be missed by superiors; it may be known by many throughout the organization. Negative effects are not limited to the targeted individuals, and may lead to a decline in employee morale and a change in organizational culture. It can also take place as overbearing supervision, constant criticism, and blocking promotions.

Exam Probability: **High**

7. *Answer choices:*

(see index for correct answer)

- a. Workplace bullying
- b. Sweatshop
- c. Institute for Business and Professional Ethics
- d. Pension spiking

Guidance: level 1

:: ::

Cannabis, also known as __________ among other names, is a psychoactive drug from the Cannabis plant used for medical or recreational purposes. The main psychoactive part of cannabis is tetrahydrocannabinol , one of 483 known compounds in the plant, including at least 65 other cannabinoids. Cannabis can be used by smoking, vaporizing, within food, or as an extract.

Exam Probability: **High**

8. *Answer choices:*

(see index for correct answer)

- a. corporate values
- b. Character
- c. Marijuana
- d. hierarchical perspective

Guidance: level 1

:: Power (social and political) ::

_________ is a form of reverence gained by a leader who has strong interpersonal relationship skills. _________ , as an aspect of personal power, becomes particularly important as organizational leadership becomes increasingly about collaboration and influence, rather than command and control.

Exam Probability: **High**

9. *Answer choices:*

(see index for correct answer)

- a. Referent power
- b. Expert power
- c. need for power

Guidance: level 1

:: Types of marketing ::

_________ is an advertisement strategy in which a company uses surprise and/or unconventional interactions in order to promote a product or service. It is a type of publicity. The term was popularized by Jay Conrad Levinson`s 1984 book _________ .

Exam Probability: **Low**

10. *Answer choices:*

(see index for correct answer)

- a. Proximity marketing
- b. Menu engineering
- c. Social pull marketing
- d. Guerrilla Marketing

Guidance: level 1

:: Data management ::

__________ is a form of intellectual property that grants the creator of an original creative work an exclusive legal right to determine whether and under what conditions this original work may be copied and used by others, usually for a limited term of years. The exclusive rights are not absolute but limited by limitations and exceptions to __________ law, including fair use. A major limitation on __________ on ideas is that __________ protects only the original expression of ideas, and not the underlying ideas themselves.

Exam Probability: **Medium**

11. *Answer choices:*

(see index for correct answer)

- a. Database schema
- b. Learning object metadata
- c. Copyright
- d. ISO/IEC JTC 1/SC 32

Guidance: level 1

:: Business ethics ::

__________ is a type of international private business self-regulation. While once it was possible to describe CSR as an internal organisational policy or a corporate ethic strategy, that time has passed as various international laws have been developed and various organisations have used their authority to push it beyond individual or even industry-wide initiatives. While it has been considered a form of corporate self-regulation for some time, over the last decade or so it has moved considerably from voluntary decisions at the level of individual organisations, to mandatory schemes at regional, national and even transnational levels.

Exam Probability: **Medium**

12. *Answer choices:*

(see index for correct answer)

- a. Jewish business ethics
- b. Wheelmen
- c. Sullivan principles
- d. Corporate social responsibility

Guidance: level 1

:: ::

A _________ is a problem offering two possibilities, neither of which is unambiguously acceptable or preferable. The possibilities are termed the horns of the _________ , a clichéd usage, but distinguishing the _________ from other kinds of predicament as a matter of usage.

Exam Probability: **Medium**

13. *Answer choices:*

(see index for correct answer)

- a. surface-level diversity
- b. Dilemma
- c. Character
- d. empathy

Guidance: level 1

:: United States law ::

The ABA _________ , created by the American Bar Association , are a set of rules that prescribe baseline standards of legal ethics and professional responsibility for lawyers in the United States. They were promulgated by the ABA House of Delegates upon the recommendation of the Kutak Commission in 1983. The rules are merely recommendations, or models, and are not themselves binding. However, having a common set of Model Rules facilitates a common discourse on legal ethics, and simplifies professional responsibility training as well as the day-to-day application of such rules. As of 2015, 49 states and four territories have adopted the rules in whole or in part, of which the most recent to do so was the Commonwealth of the Northern Mariana Islands in March 2015. California is the only state that has not adopted the ABA Model Rules, while Puerto Rico is the only U.S. jurisdiction outside of confederation has not adopted them but instead has its own Código de Ética Profesional.

Exam Probability: **High**

14. *Answer choices:*

(see index for correct answer)

- a. judgment notwithstanding the verdict

- b. Pro se

Guidance: level 1

:: Patent law ::

A __________ is generally any statement intended to specify or delimit the scope of rights and obligations that may be exercised and enforced by parties in a legally recognized relationship. In contrast to other terms for legally operative language, the term __________ usually implies situations that involve some level of uncertainty, waiver, or risk.

Exam Probability: **High**

15. *Answer choices:*

(see index for correct answer)

- a. Disclaimer
- b. Claim
- c. Patent prosecution
- d. Triadic patent

Guidance: level 1

:: Electronic waste ::

__________ or e-waste describes discarded electrical or electronic devices. Used electronics which are destined for refurbishment, reuse, resale, salvage, recycling through material recovery, or disposal are also considered e-waste. Informal processing of e-waste in developing countries can lead to adverse human health effects and environmental pollution.

Exam Probability: **High**

16. *Answer choices:*

(see index for correct answer)

- a. Global waste trade
- b. Computer liquidator
- c. World Reuse, Repair and Recycling Association
- d. Digger gold

Guidance: level 1

:: ::

In regulatory jurisdictions that provide for it , _________ is a group of laws and organizations designed to ensure the rights of consumers as well as fair trade, competition and accurate information in the marketplace. The laws are designed to prevent the businesses that engage in fraud or specified unfair practices from gaining an advantage over competitors. They may also provides additional protection for those most vulnerable in society. _________ laws are a form of government regulation that aim to protect the rights of consumers. For example, a government may require businesses to disclose detailed information about products—particularly in areas where safety or public health is an issue, such as food.

Exam Probability: **Medium**

17. *Answer choices:*

(see index for correct answer)

- a. open system
- b. process perspective
- c. Consumer Protection
- d. levels of analysis

Guidance: level 1

:: ::

A _________ is a proceeding by a party or parties against another in the civil court of law.The archaic term "suit in law" is found in only a small number of laws still in effect today.The term " _________ " is used in reference to a civil action brought in a court of law in which a plaintiff, a party who claims to have incurred loss as a result of a defendant's actions, demands a legal or equitable remedy. The defendant is required to respond to the plaintiff's complaint. If the plaintiff is successful, judgment is in the plaintiff's favor, and a variety of court orders may be issued to enforce a right, award damages, or impose a temporary or permanent injunction to prevent an act or compel an act. A declaratory judgment may be issued to prevent future legal disputes.

Exam Probability: **High**

18. *Answer choices:*

(see index for correct answer)

- a. Lawsuit
- b. information systems assessment
- c. functional perspective
- d. imperative

Guidance: level 1

:: Business ethics ::

A _________ is a person who exposes any kind of information or activity that is deemed illegal, unethical, or not correct within an organization that is either private or public. The information of alleged wrongdoing can be classified in many ways: violation of company policy/rules, law, regulation, or threat to public interest/national security, as well as fraud, and corruption. Those who become _________ s can choose to bring information or allegations to surface either internally or externally. Internally, a _________ can bring his/her accusations to the attention of other people within the accused organization such as an immediate supervisor. Externally, a _________ can bring allegations to light by contacting a third party outside of an accused organization such as the media, government, law enforcement, or those who are concerned. _________ s, however, take the risk of facing stiff reprisal and retaliation from those who are accused or alleged of wrongdoing.

Exam Probability: **Low**

19. *Answer choices:*

(see index for correct answer)

- a. Jewish business ethics
- b. Sherpa
- c. Whistleblower
- d. Electronic retailing self-regulation program

Guidance: level 1

:: Reputation management ::

_________ or image of a social entity is an opinion about that entity, typically as a result of social evaluation on a set of criteria.

Exam Probability: **Medium**

20. *Answer choices:*

(see index for correct answer)

- a. Distrust
- b. Meta-moderation system
- c. Reputation
- d. Reputation management

Guidance: level 1

:: ::

_________ Corporation was an American energy, commodities, and services company based in Houston, Texas. It was founded in 1985 as a merger between Houston Natural Gas and InterNorth, both relatively small regional companies. Before its bankruptcy on December 3, 2001, _________ employed approximately 29,000 staff and was a major electricity, natural gas, communications and pulp and paper company, with claimed revenues of nearly $101 billion during 2000. Fortune named _________ "America`s Most Innovative Company" for six consecutive years.

Exam Probability: **High**

21. *Answer choices:*

(see index for correct answer)

- a. Character
- b. hierarchical perspective
- c. interpersonal communication
- d. Enron

Guidance: level 1

:: Social responsibility ::

The United Nations Global Compact is a non-binding United Nations pact to encourage businesses worldwide to adopt sustainable and socially responsible policies, and to report on their implementation. The _________ is a principle-based framework for businesses, stating ten principles in the areas of human rights, labor, the environment and anti-corruption. Under the Global Compact, companies are brought together with UN agencies, labor groups and civil society. Cities can join the Global Compact through the Cities Programme.

Exam Probability: **High**

22. *Answer choices:*
(see index for correct answer)

- a. Social impact
- b. Footprints network
- c. UN Global Compact
- d. Socially responsible business

Guidance: level 1

:: Pyramid and Ponzi schemes ::

__________ was an Italian swindler and con artist in the U.S. and Canada. His aliases include Charles Ponci, Carlo, and Charles P. Bianchi. Born and raised in Italy, he became known in the early 1920s as a swindler in North America for his money-making scheme. He promised clients a 50% profit within 45 days or 100% profit within 90 days, by buying discounted postal reply coupons in other countries and redeeming them at face value in the United States as a form of arbitrage. In reality, Ponzi was paying earlier investors using the investments of later investors. While this type of fraudulent investment scheme was not originally invented by Ponzi, it became so identified with him that it now is referred to as a "Ponzi scheme". His scheme ran for over a year before it collapsed, costing his "investors" $20 million.

Exam Probability: **High**

23. *Answer choices:*
(see index for correct answer)

- a. Success University
- b. WinCapita
- c. Valerie Red-Horse
- d. Charles Ponzi

Guidance: level 1

:: Business ::

__________ , or built-in obsolescence, in industrial design and economics is a policy of planning or designing a product with an artificially limited useful life, so that it becomes obsolete after a certain period of time. The rationale behind this strategy is to generate long-term sales volume by reducing the time between repeat purchases .

Exam Probability: **High**

24. *Answer choices:*

(see index for correct answer)

- a. Professional services
- b. Resource slack
- c. Operating subsidiary
- d. Planned obsolescence

Guidance: level 1

:: ::

The __________ , the Calvinist work ethic or the Puritan work ethic is a work ethic concept in theology, sociology, economics and history that emphasizes that hard work, discipline and frugality are a result of a person`s subscription to the values espoused by the Protestant faith, particularly Calvinism. The phrase was initially coined in 1904–1905 by Max Weber in his book The Protestant Ethic and the Spirit of Capitalism.

Exam Probability: **Medium**

25. *Answer choices:*

(see index for correct answer)

- a. co-culture
- b. Protestant work ethic
- c. Sarbanes-Oxley act of 2002
- d. levels of analysis

Guidance: level 1

:: Public relations terminology ::

_________ , also called "green sheen", is a form of spin in which green PR or green marketing is deceptively used to promote the perception that an organization`s products, aims or policies are environmentally friendly. Evidence that an organization is _________ often comes from pointing out the spending differences: when significantly more money or time has been spent advertising being "green" , than is actually spent on environmentally sound practices. _________ efforts can range from changing the name or label of a product to evoke the natural environment on a product that contains harmful chemicals to multimillion-dollar marketing campaigns portraying highly polluting energy companies as eco-friendly.Publicized accusations of _________ have contributed to the term`s increasing use.

Exam Probability: **High**

26. *Answer choices:*

(see index for correct answer)

- a. Crisis communication
- b. Photo op
- c. PR Gallery
- d. Junk science

Guidance: level 1

:: ::

A _________ service is an online platform which people use to build social networks or social relationship with other people who share similar personal or career interests, activities, backgrounds or real-life connections.

Exam Probability: **High**

27. *Answer choices:*

(see index for correct answer)

- a. cultural
- b. personal values
- c. corporate values
- d. empathy

Guidance: level 1

:: Hazard analysis ::

Broadly speaking, a _________ is the combined effort of 1. identifying and analyzing potential events that may negatively impact individuals, assets, and/or the environment ; and 2. making judgments "on the tolerability of the risk on the basis of a risk analysis" while considering influencing factors . Put in simpler terms, a _________ analyzes what can go wrong, how likely it is to happen, what the potential consequences are, and how tolerable the identified risk is. As part of this process, the resulting determination of risk may be expressed in a quantitative or qualitative fashion. The _________ is an inherent part of an overall risk management strategy, which attempts to, after a _________ , "introduce control measures to eliminate or reduce" any potential risk-related consequences.

Exam Probability: **Low**

28. *Answer choices:*
(see index for correct answer)

- a. Hazard
- b. Hazard identification
- c. Swiss cheese model
- d. Hazardous Materials Identification System

Guidance: level 1

:: ::

_________ Ltd. is the world's 2nd largest offshore drilling contractor and is based in Vernier, Switzerland. The company has offices in 20 countries, including Switzerland, Canada, United States, Norway, Scotland, India, Brazil, Singapore, Indonesia and Malaysia.

Exam Probability: **Medium**

29. *Answer choices:*
(see index for correct answer)

- a. levels of analysis
- b. personal values
- c. cultural
- d. Transocean

Guidance: level 1

:: Ethical banking ::

A _________ or community development finance institution - abbreviated in both cases to CDFI - is a financial institution that provides credit and financial services to underserved markets and populations, primarily in the USA but also in the UK. A CDFI may be a community development bank, a community development credit union , a community development loan fund , a community development venture capital fund , a microenterprise development loan fund, or a community development corporation.

Exam Probability: **Medium**

30. *Answer choices:*

(see index for correct answer)

- a. Community development financial institution
- b. Charity Bank
- c. JAK Members Bank
- d. Triodos Bank

Guidance: level 1

:: Labor rights ::

The _________ is the concept that people have a human _________ , or engage in productive employment, and may not be prevented from doing so. The _________ is enshrined in the Universal Declaration of Human Rights and recognized in international human rights law through its inclusion in the International Covenant on Economic, Social and Cultural Rights, where the _________ emphasizes economic, social and cultural development.

Exam Probability: **High**

31. *Answer choices:*

(see index for correct answer)

- a. The Hyatt 100
- b. China Labor Watch
- c. Kim Bobo
- d. Right to work

Guidance: level 1

:: Criminal law ::

_________ is the body of law that relates to crime. It proscribes conduct perceived as threatening, harmful, or otherwise endangering to the property, health, safety, and moral welfare of people inclusive of one`s self. Most _________ is established by statute, which is to say that the laws are enacted by a legislature. _________ includes the punishment and rehabilitation of people who violate such laws. _________ varies according to jurisdiction, and differs from civil law, where emphasis is more on dispute resolution and victim compensation, rather than on punishment or rehabilitation. Criminal procedure is a formalized official activity that authenticates the fact of commission of a crime and authorizes punitive or rehabilitative treatment of the offender.

Exam Probability: **Low**

32. *Answer choices:*
(see index for correct answer)

- a. Mala in se
- b. Mala prohibita
- c. Self-incrimination
- d. Criminal law

Guidance: level 1

:: Human resource management ::

_________ encompasses values and behaviors that contribute to the unique social and psychological environment of a business. The _________ influences the way people interact, the context within which knowledge is created, the resistance they will have towards certain changes, and ultimately the way they share knowledge. _________ represents the collective values, beliefs and principles of organizational members and is a product of factors such as history, product, market, technology, strategy, type of employees, management style, and national culture; culture includes the organization`s vision, values, norms, systems, symbols, language, assumptions, environment, location, beliefs and habits.

Exam Probability: **Medium**

33. *Answer choices:*
(see index for correct answer)

- a. Workforce modeling
- b. Organizational culture

- c. Human resource consulting
- d. Reward management

Guidance: level 1

:: ::

__________ is the study and management of exchange relationships. __________ is the business process of creating relationships with and satisfying customers. With its focus on the customer, __________ is one of the premier components of business management.

Exam Probability: **Low**

34. *Answer choices:*

(see index for correct answer)

- a. personal values
- b. cultural
- c. Character
- d. Marketing

Guidance: level 1

:: Business law ::

A __________ is an arrangement where parties, known as partners, agree to cooperate to advance their mutual interests. The partners in a __________ may be individuals, businesses, interest-based organizations, schools, governments or combinations. Organizations may partner to increase the likelihood of each achieving their mission and to amplify their reach. A __________ may result in issuing and holding equity or may be only governed by a contract.

Exam Probability: **High**

35. *Answer choices:*

(see index for correct answer)

- a. Commercial law
- b. Statutory liability
- c. Partnership
- d. Wrongful trading

Guidance: level 1

:: United States federal trade legislation ::

The _________ of 1914 established the Federal Trade Commission. The Act, signed into law by Woodrow Wilson in 1914, outlaws unfair methods of competition and outlaws unfair acts or practices that affect commerce.

Exam Probability: **Low**

36. *Answer choices:*

(see index for correct answer)

- a. Tariff of 1824
- b. Federal Trade Commission Act
- c. Bell Trade Act
- d. International Emergency Economic Powers Act

Guidance: level 1

:: Real estate ::

_________ s serve several societal needs – primarily as shelter from weather, security, living space, privacy, to store belongings, and to comfortably live and work. A _________ as a shelter represents a physical division of the human habitat and the outside .

Exam Probability: **Low**

37. *Answer choices:*

(see index for correct answer)

- a. Family farm
- b. Building
- c. Real estate investment club
- d. Frontage

Guidance: level 1

:: Social philosophy ::

The __________ describes the unintended social benefits of an individual`s self-interested actions. Adam Smith first introduced the concept in The Theory of Moral Sentiments, written in 1759, invoking it in reference to income distribution. In this work, however, the idea of the market is not discussed, and the word "capitalism" is never used.

Exam Probability: **High**

38. *Answer choices:*

(see index for correct answer)

- a. Veil of Ignorance
- b. Societal attitudes towards abortion
- c. Invisible hand
- d. vacancy chain

Guidance: level 1

:: Auditing ::

__________ refers to the independence of the internal auditor or of the external auditor from parties that may have a financial interest in the business being audited. Independence requires integrity and an objective approach to the audit process. The concept requires the auditor to carry out his or her work freely and in an objective manner.

Exam Probability: **Low**

39. *Answer choices:*

(see index for correct answer)

- a. Walk-through test
- b. Joint audit
- c. Environmental audit
- d. Auditor independence

Guidance: level 1

:: Social philosophy ::

The " _________ " is a method of determining the morality of issues. It asks a decision-maker to make a choice about a social or moral issue, and assumes that they have enough information to know the consequences of their possible decisions for everyone but would not know, or would not take into account, which person he or she is. The theory contends that not knowing one`s ultimate position in society would lead to the creation of a just system, as the decision-maker would not want to make decisions which benefit a certain group at the expense of another, because the decision-maker could theoretically end up in either group. The idea has been present in moral philosophy at least since the eighteenth century. The _________ is part of a long tradition of thinking in terms of a social contract that includes the writings of Immanuel Kant, Thomas Hobbes, John Locke, Jean Jacques Rousseau, and Thomas Jefferson. Prominent modern names attached to it are John Harsanyi and John Rawls.

Exam Probability: **Medium**

40. *Answer choices:*

(see index for correct answer)

- a. Societal attitudes towards abortion
- b. Invisible hand
- c. vacancy chain
- d. Freedom to contract

Guidance: level 1

:: United States federal defense and national security legislation ::

The USA _________ is an Act of the U.S. Congress that was signed into law by President George W. Bush on October 26, 2001. The title of the Act is a contrived three letter initialism preceding a seven letter acronym , which in combination stand for Uniting and Strengthening America by Providing Appropriate Tools Required to Intercept and Obstruct Terrorism Act of 2001. The acronym was created by a 23 year old Congressional staffer, Chris Kyle.

Exam Probability: **High**

41. *Answer choices:*

(see index for correct answer)

- a. Patriot Act
- b. USA PATRIOT Act

Guidance: level 1

:: Labour law ::

An __________ is special or specified circumstances that partially or fully exempt a person or organization from performance of a legal obligation so as to avoid an unreasonable or disproportionate burden or obstacle.

Exam Probability: **Low**

42. *Answer choices:*

(see index for correct answer)

- a. Danish Vacation Law
- b. Michele Tiraboschi
- c. Occupational disease
- d. Undue hardship

Guidance: level 1

:: International trade ::

__________ involves the transfer of goods or services from one person or entity to another, often in exchange for money. A system or network that allows __________ is called a market.

Exam Probability: **Medium**

43. *Answer choices:*

(see index for correct answer)

- a. Trade
- b. Foreign trade multiplier
- c. Global financial system
- d. Hosuk Lee-Makiyama

Guidance: level 1

:: Monopoly (economics) ::

A _________ is a form of intellectual property that gives its owner the legal right to exclude others from making, using, selling, and importing an invention for a limited period of years, in exchange for publishing an enabling public disclosure of the invention. In most countries _________ rights fall under civil law and the _________ holder needs to sue someone infringing the _________ in order to enforce his or her rights. In some industries _________s are an essential form of competitive advantage; in others they are irrelevant.

Exam Probability: **High**

44. *Answer choices:*

(see index for correct answer)

- a. Patent
- b. Dominance
- c. Monopoly
- d. Monopsony

Guidance: level 1

:: Human resource management ::

_________ is the ethics of an organization, and it is how an organization responds to an internal or external stimulus. _________ is interdependent with the organizational culture. Although it is akin to both organizational behavior and industrial and organizational psychology as well as business ethics on the micro and macro levels, _________ is neither OB or I/O psychology, nor is it solely business ethics . _________ express the values of an organization to its employees and/or other entities irrespective of governmental and/or regulatory laws.

Exam Probability: **Low**

45. *Answer choices:*

(see index for correct answer)

- a. Progressive discipline
- b. Vendor on premises
- c. Cross-cultural capital
- d. Occupational burnout

Guidance: level 1

:: ::

__________ is "property consisting of land and the buildings on it, along with its natural resources such as crops, minerals or water; immovable property of this nature; an interest vested in this an item of real property, buildings or housing in general. Also: the business of __________ ; the profession of buying, selling, or renting land, buildings, or housing." It is a legal term used in jurisdictions whose legal system is derived from English common law, such as India, England, Wales, Northern Ireland, United States, Canada, Pakistan, Australia, and New Zealand.

Exam Probability: **Low**

46. *Answer choices:*

(see index for correct answer)

- a. corporate values
- b. hierarchical perspective
- c. Character
- d. Real estate

Guidance: level 1

:: Renewable energy ::

__________ is the conversion of energy from sunlight into electricity, either directly using photovoltaics , indirectly using concentrated __________ , or a combination. Concentrated __________ systems use lenses or mirrors and tracking systems to focus a large area of sunlight into a small beam. Photovoltaic cells convert light into an electric current using the photovoltaic effect.

Exam Probability: **Medium**

47. *Answer choices:*

(see index for correct answer)

- a. Wind power
- b. Solar power
- c. Deep water source cooling
- d. Biofuel

Guidance: level 1

:: ::

__________ generally refers to a focus on the needs or desires of one`s self. A number of philosophical, psychological, and economic theories examine the role of __________ in motivating human action.

Exam Probability: **Medium**

48. *Answer choices:*

(see index for correct answer)

- a. Self-interest
- b. personal values
- c. cultural
- d. hierarchical

Guidance: level 1

:: Supply chain management terms ::

In business and finance, __________ is a system of organizations, people, activities, information, and resources involved inmoving a product or service from supplier to customer. __________ activities involve the transformation of natural resources, raw materials, and components into a finished product that is delivered to the end customer. In sophisticated __________ systems, used products may re-enter the __________ at any point where residual value is recyclable. __________s link value chains.

Exam Probability: **Low**

49. *Answer choices:*

(see index for correct answer)

- a. Supply Chain
- b. Price look-up code
- c. Direct shipment
- d. Work in process

Guidance: level 1

:: ::

__________ ism is a form of government characterized by strong central power and limited political freedoms. Individual freedoms are subordinate to the state and there is no constitutional accountability and rule of law under an __________ regime. __________ regimes can be autocratic with power concentrated in one person or it can be more spread out between multiple officials and government institutions. Juan Linz`s influential 1964 description of __________ ism characterized __________ political systems by four qualities.

Exam Probability: **High**

50. *Answer choices:*
(see index for correct answer)

- a. deep-level diversity
- b. Authoritarian
- c. open system
- d. similarity-attraction theory

Guidance: level 1

:: ::

__________ is a cognitive process that elicits emotion and rational associations based on an individual`s moral philosophy or value system. __________ stands in contrast to elicited emotion or thought due to associations based on immediate sensory perceptions and reflexive responses, as in sympathetic central nervous system responses. In common terms, __________ is often described as leading to feelings of remorse when a person commits an act that conflicts with their moral values. An individual`s moral values and their dissonance with familial, social, cultural and historical interpretations of moral philosophy are considered in the examination of cultural relativity in both the practice and study of psychology. The extent to which __________ informs moral judgment before an action and whether such moral judgments are or should be based on reason has occasioned debate through much of modern history between theories of modern western philosophy in juxtaposition to the theories of romanticism and other reactionary movements after the end of the Middle Ages.

Exam Probability: **Medium**

51. *Answer choices:*
(see index for correct answer)

- a. co-culture
- b. open system
- c. empathy
- d. corporate values

Guidance: level 1

:: Fraud ::

In law, __________ is intentional deception to secure unfair or unlawful gain, or to deprive a victim of a legal right. __________ can violate civil law , a criminal law , or it may cause no loss of money, property or legal right but still be an element of another civil or criminal wrong. The purpose of __________ may be monetary gain or other benefits, for example by obtaining a passport, travel document, or driver`s license, or mortgage __________ , where the perpetrator may attempt to qualify for a mortgage by way of false statements.

Exam Probability: **Medium**

52. *Answer choices:*
(see index for correct answer)

- a. Fraud
- b. Credit card fraud
- c. Health care fraud
- d. World Luxury Association

Guidance: level 1

:: ::

__________ in the United States is a federal and state program that helps with medical costs for some people with limited income and resources. __________ also offers benefits not normally covered by Medicare, including nursing home care and personal care services. The Health Insurance Association of America describes __________ as "a government insurance program for persons of all ages whose income and resources are insufficient to pay for health care." __________ is the largest source of funding for medical and health-related services for people with low income in the United States, providing free health insurance to 74 million low-income and disabled people as of 2017. It is a means-tested program that is jointly funded by the state and federal governments and managed by the states, with each state currently having broad leeway to determine who is eligible for its implementation of the program. States are not required to participate in the program, although all have since 1982. __________ recipients must be U.S. citizens or qualified non-citizens, and may include low-income adults, their children, and people with certain disabilities. Poverty alone does not necessarily qualify someone for __________ .

Exam Probability: **Medium**

53. *Answer choices:*

(see index for correct answer)

- a. deep-level diversity
- b. information systems assessment
- c. Medicaid
- d. hierarchical

Guidance: level 1

:: Majority–minority relations ::

It was established as axiomatic in anthropological research by Franz Boas in the first few decades of the 20th century and later popularized by his students. Boas first articulated the idea in 1887: "civilization is not something absolute, but ... is relative, and ... our ideas and conceptions are true only so far as our civilization goes". However, Boas did not coin the term.

Exam Probability: **Low**

54. *Answer choices:*
(see index for correct answer)

- a. Affirmative action
- b. cultural dissonance
- c. Cultural relativism

Guidance: level 1

:: ::

The _________ to Fight AIDS, Tuberculosis and Malaria is an international financing organization that aims to "attract, leverage and invest additional resources to end the epidemics of HIV/AIDS, tuberculosis and malaria to support attainment of the Sustainable Development Goals established by the United Nations." A public-private partnership, the organization maintains its secretariat in Geneva, Switzerland. The organization began operations in January 2002. Microsoft founder Bill Gates was one of the first private foundations among many bilateral donors to provide seed money for the partnership.

Exam Probability: **High**

55. *Answer choices:*
(see index for correct answer)

- a. hierarchical
- b. open system
- c. Character
- d. Global Fund

Guidance: level 1

:: ::

The _________ of 1977 is a United States federal law known primarily for two of its main provisions: one that addresses accounting transparency requirements under the Securities Exchange Act of 1934 and another concerning bribery of foreign officials. The Act was amended in 1988 and in 1998, and has been subject to continued congressional concerns, namely whether its enforcement discourages U.S. companies from investing abroad.

Exam Probability: **High**

56. *Answer choices:*
(see index for correct answer)

- a. open system
- b. empathy
- c. similarity-attraction theory
- d. information systems assessment

Guidance: level 1

:: ::

A _________ is a set of rules, often written, with regards to clothing. _________ s are created out of social perceptions and norms, and vary based on purpose, circumstances and occasions. Different societies and cultures are likely to have different _________ s.

Exam Probability: **Low**

57. *Answer choices:*
(see index for correct answer)

- a. co-culture
- b. Dress code
- c. corporate values
- d. personal values

Guidance: level 1

:: Workplace ::

In business management, _________ is a management style whereby a manager closely observes and/or controls the work of his/her subordinates or employees.

Exam Probability: **High**

58. *Answer choices:*
(see index for correct answer)

- a. Workplace revenge
- b. Workplace friendship
- c. Work etiquette
- d. Micromanagement

Guidance: level 1

:: ::

The Catholic Church, also known as the Roman Catholic Church, is the largest Christian church, with approximately 1.3 billion baptised Catholics worldwide as of 2017. As the world`s oldest continuously functioning international institution, it has played a prominent role in the history and development of Western civilisation. The church is headed by the Bishop of Rome, known as the pope. Its central administration, the Holy See, is in the Vatican City, an enclave within the city of Rome in Italy.

Exam Probability: **High**

59. *Answer choices:*

(see index for correct answer)

- a. functional perspective
- b. open system
- c. Catholicism
- d. Character

Guidance: level 1

Accounting

Accounting or accountancy is the measurement, processing, and communication of financial information about economic entities such as businesses and corporations. The modern field was established by the Italian mathematician Luca Pacioli in 1494. Accounting, which has been called the "language of business", measures the results of an organization's economic activities and conveys this information to a variety of users, including investors, creditors, management, and regulators.

:: Generally Accepted Accounting Principles ::

In accrual accounting, the revenue recognition principle states that expenses should be recorded during the period in which they are incurred, regardless of when the transfer of cash occurs. Conversely, cash basis accounting calls for the recognition of an expense when the cash is paid, regardless of when the expense was actually incurred.

Exam Probability: **Medium**

1. *Answer choices:*

(see index for correct answer)

- a. Normal balance
- b. Operating income before depreciation and amortization
- c. Net realizable value
- d. Matching principle

Guidance: level 1

:: ::

An _________ is an asset that lacks physical substance. It is defined in opposition to physical assets such as machinery and buildings. An _________ is usually very hard to evaluate. Patents, copyrights, franchises, goodwill, trademarks, and trade names. The general interpretation also includes software and other intangible computer based assets are all examples of _________ s. _________ s generally—though not necessarily—suffer from typical market failures of non-rivalry and non-excludability.

Exam Probability: **High**

2. *Answer choices:*

(see index for correct answer)

- a. Sarbanes-Oxley act of 2002
- b. corporate values
- c. process perspective
- d. Intangible asset

Guidance: level 1

:: Taxation ::

A _________ is a person or organization subject to pay a tax. _________ s have an Identification Number, a reference number issued by a government to its citizens.

Exam Probability: **Low**

3. *Answer choices:*

(see index for correct answer)

- a. Language tax
- b. Value capture
- c. Effective marginal tax rate
- d. Taxpayer

Guidance: level 1

:: Business law ::

An __________ is a natural person, business, or corporation that provides goods or services to another entity under terms specified in a contract or within a verbal agreement. Unlike an employee, an __________ does not work regularly for an employer but works as and when required, during which time they may be subject to law of agency. __________ s are usually paid on a freelance basis. Contractors often work through a limited company or franchise, which they themselves own, or may work through an umbrella company.

Exam Probability: **Low**

4. *Answer choices:*
(see index for correct answer)

- a. Country of origin
- b. Independent contractor
- c. TRIPS Agreement
- d. Advertising regulation

Guidance: level 1

:: Accounting in the United States ::

__________ were documents issued by the Committee on Accounting Procedure between 1938 and 1959 on various accounting problems. They were discontinued with the dissolution of the Committee in 1959 under a recommendation from the Special Committee on Research Program. In all, 17 bulletins were issued; however, the lack of binding authority over AICPA's membership reduced the influence of, and compliance with the content of the bulletins. The __________ have all been superseded by the Accounting Standards Codification .

Exam Probability: **Medium**

5. *Answer choices:*
(see index for correct answer)

- a. Joseph Eve, Certified Public Accountants
- b. Accounting Research Bulletins
- c. Comprehensive Performance Assessment
- d. Accounting Today

Guidance: level 1

:: ::

An inheritance or _________ is a tax paid by a person who inherits money or property or a levy on the estate of a person who has died.

Exam Probability: **Medium**

6. *Answer choices:*

(see index for correct answer)

- a. open system
- b. corporate values
- c. Estate tax
- d. similarity-attraction theory

Guidance: level 1

:: Accounting in the United States ::

_________ refers to a Memorandum of Understanding signed in September 2002 between the Financial Accounting Standards Board , the US standard setter, and the International Accounting Standards Board . The agreement is so called as it was reached in Norwalk.

Exam Probability: **Low**

7. *Answer choices:*

(see index for correct answer)

- a. Norwalk Agreement
- b. Governmental Accounting Standards Board
- c. Clean Energy Bank
- d. Federal Accounting Standards Advisory Board

Guidance: level 1

:: Accounting source documents ::

A _________ is a commercial document and first official offer issued by a buyer to a seller indicating types, quantities, and agreed prices for products or services. It is used to control the purchasing of products and services from external suppliers. _________ s can be an essential part of enterprise resource planning system orders.

Exam Probability: **Low**

8. *Answer choices:*

(see index for correct answer)

- a. Parcel audit
- b. Credit memorandum
- c. Banknote
- d. Purchase order

Guidance: level 1

:: Tax reform ::

_________ is the process of changing the way taxes are collected or managed by the government and is usually undertaken to improve tax administration or to provide economic or social benefits. _________ can include reducing the level of taxation of all people by the government, making the tax system more progressive or less progressive, or simplifying the tax system and making the system more understandable or more accountable.

Exam Probability: **Medium**

9. *Answer choices:*

(see index for correct answer)

- a. Tax reform
- b. Enterprise Value Tax
- c. Equity of condition
- d. Goods and Services Tax

Guidance: level 1

:: Project management ::

_________ is the widespread practice of collecting information and attempting to spot a pattern. In some fields of study, the term " _________ " has more formally defined meanings.

Exam Probability: **Low**

10. *Answer choices:*

(see index for correct answer)

- a. Theme-centered interaction
- b. ISO 10006

- c. The Practice Standard for Scheduling
- d. Trend analysis

Guidance: level 1

:: Project management ::

In economics, _________ is the assignment of available resources to various uses. In the context of an entire economy, resources can be allocated by various means, such as markets or central planning.

Exam Probability: **High**

11. *Answer choices:*

(see index for correct answer)

- a. Project manager
- b. Project plan
- c. Association for Project Management
- d. Resource allocation

Guidance: level 1

:: Pricing ::

_________ is the difference between a lower selling price and a higher purchase price, resulting in a financial loss for the seller.

Exam Probability: **Medium**

12. *Answer choices:*

(see index for correct answer)

- a. Capital loss
- b. Reference price
- c. Relationship-based pricing
- d. Base point pricing

Guidance: level 1

:: Management accounting ::

__________ , or dollar contribution per unit, is the selling price per unit minus the variable cost per unit. "Contribution" represents the portion of sales revenue that is not consumed by variable costs and so contributes to the coverage of fixed costs. This concept is one of the key building blocks of break-even analysis.

Exam Probability: **Medium**

13. *Answer choices:*
(see index for correct answer)

- a. Chartered Institute of Management Accountants
- b. Environmental full-cost accounting
- c. Contribution margin
- d. Factory overhead

Guidance: level 1

:: United States Generally Accepted Accounting Principles ::

In a companies` financial reporting, __________ "includes all changes in equity during a period except those resulting from investments by owners and distributions to owners". Because that use excludes the effects of changing ownership interest, an economic measure of __________ is necessary for financial analysis from the shareholders` point of view

Exam Probability: **Low**

14. *Answer choices:*
(see index for correct answer)

- a. GASB 34
- b. Comprehensive annual financial report
- c. Comprehensive income
- d. GASB 45

Guidance: level 1

:: Accounting software ::

__________ is an accounting software package developed and marketed by Intuit. __________ products are geared mainly toward small and medium-sized businesses and offer on-premises accounting applications as well as cloud-based versions that accept business payments, manage and pay bills, and payroll functions.

Exam Probability: **Medium**

15. *Answer choices:*
(see index for correct answer)

- a. AME Accounting Software
- b. Open Systems Accounting Software
- c. PyBookie
- d. Wave Accounting

Guidance: level 1

:: ::

__________ is capital that is contributed to a corporation by investors by purchase of stock from the corporation, the primary market, not by purchase of stock in the open market from other stockholders . It includes share capital as well as additional __________ .

Exam Probability: **High**

16. *Answer choices:*
(see index for correct answer)

- a. co-culture
- b. open system
- c. similarity-attraction theory
- d. levels of analysis

Guidance: level 1

:: Economic globalization ::

__________ is an agreement in which one company hires another company to be responsible for a planned or existing activity that is or could be done internally,and sometimes involves transferring employees and assets from one firm to another.

Exam Probability: **Low**

17. *Answer choices:*

(see index for correct answer)

- a. Outsourcing
- b. global financial

Guidance: level 1

:: Accounting terminology ::

Accounts are typically defined by an identifier and a caption or header and are coded by account type. In computerized accounting systems with computable quantity accounting, the accounts can have a quantity measure definition.

Exam Probability: **High**

18. *Answer choices:*

(see index for correct answer)

- a. Impairment cost
- b. General ledger
- c. Chart of accounts
- d. Capital expenditure

Guidance: level 1

:: Valuation (finance) ::

__________ refers to an assessment of the viability, stability, and profitability of a business, sub-business or project.

Exam Probability: **Low**

19. *Answer choices:*

(see index for correct answer)

- a. Chepakovich valuation model
- b. Diminution in value
- c. Financial analysis
- d. International Valuation Standards Council

Guidance: level 1

:: Management accounting ::

__________ accounting is a traditional cost accounting method introduced in the 1920s, as an alternative for the traditional cost accounting method based on historical costs.

Exam Probability: **Low**

20. *Answer choices:*
(see index for correct answer)

- a. Net present value
- b. Fixed cost
- c. Institute of Cost and Management Accountants of Bangladesh
- d. Standard cost

Guidance: level 1

:: Financial ratios ::

In finance, the __________ , also known as the acid-test ratio is a type of liquidity ratio which measures the ability of a company to use its near cash or quick assets to extinguish or retire its current liabilities immediately. Quick assets include those current assets that presumably can be quickly converted to cash at close to their book values. It is the ratio between quickly available or liquid assets and current liabilities.

Exam Probability: **Medium**

21. *Answer choices:*
(see index for correct answer)

- a. EV/EBITDA
- b. Quick ratio
- c. Expense ratio
- d. Accounting liquidity

Guidance: level 1

:: Options (finance) ::

A _________ bond is a type of bond that allows the issuer of the bond to retain the privilege of redeeming the bond at some point before the bond reaches its date of maturity. In other words, on the call date, the issuer has the right, but not the obligation, to buy back the bonds from the bond holders at a defined call price. Technically speaking, the bonds are not really bought and held by the issuer but are instead cancelled immediately.

Exam Probability: **High**

22. *Answer choices:*

(see index for correct answer)

- a. Chooser option
- b. Real options valuation
- c. Callable
- d. Credit default option

Guidance: level 1

:: Mathematical finance ::

In economics and finance, _________ , also known as present discounted value, is the value of an expected income stream determined as of the date of valuation. The _________ is always less than or equal to the future value because money has interest-earning potential, a characteristic referred to as the time value of money, except during times of negative interest rates, when the _________ will be more than the future value. Time value can be described with the simplified phrase, "A dollar today is worth more than a dollar tomorrow". Here, `worth more` means that its value is greater. A dollar today is worth more than a dollar tomorrow because the dollar can be invested and earn a day`s worth of interest, making the total accumulate to a value more than a dollar by tomorrow. Interest can be compared to rent. Just as rent is paid to a landlord by a tenant without the ownership of the asset being transferred, interest is paid to a lender by a borrower who gains access to the money for a time before paying it back. By letting the borrower have access to the money, the lender has sacrificed the exchange value of this money, and is compensated for it in the form of interest. The initial amount of the borrowed funds is less than the total amount of money paid to the lender.

Exam Probability: **Low**

23. *Answer choices:*

(see index for correct answer)

- a. Inverse demand function
- b. Present value
- c. Snell envelope
- d. Delta neutral

Guidance: level 1

:: ::

_________ science is the application of science to criminal and civil laws, mainly—on the criminal side—during criminal investigation, as governed by the legal standards of admissible evidence and criminal procedure.

Exam Probability: **Low**

24. *Answer choices:*

(see index for correct answer)

- a. corporate values
- b. empathy
- c. Forensic
- d. deep-level diversity

Guidance: level 1

:: Management accounting ::

_________ is a professional business study of Accounts and management in which we learn importance of accounts in our management system.

Exam Probability: **Medium**

25. *Answer choices:*

(see index for correct answer)

- a. Management accounting
- b. Direct material total variance
- c. Invested capital
- d. Institute of Certified Management Accountants

Guidance: level 1

:: Macroeconomics ::

__________ is a change in a price of a good or product, or especially of a currency, in which case it is specifically an official rise of the value of the currency in relation to a foreign currency in a fixed exchange rate system. Under floating exchange rates, by contrast, a rise in a currency's value is an appreciation. Altering the face value of a currency without changing its purchasing power is a redenomination, not a __________ .

Exam Probability: **Low**

26. *Answer choices:*

(see index for correct answer)

- a. Matching theory
- b. Austrian business cycle theory
- c. Revaluation
- d. SIMIC

Guidance: level 1

:: Financial statements ::

In financial accounting, a __________ or statement of financial position or statement of financial condition is a summary of the financial balances of an individual or organization, whether it be a sole proprietorship, a business partnership, a corporation, private limited company or other organization such as Government or not-for-profit entity. Assets, liabilities and ownership equity are listed as of a specific date, such as the end of its financial year. A __________ is often described as a "snapshot of a company's financial condition". Of the four basic financial statements, the __________ is the only statement which applies to a single point in time of a business' calendar year.

Exam Probability: **High**

27. *Answer choices:*

(see index for correct answer)

- a. Statement of retained earnings
- b. Emphasis of matter
- c. Balance sheet
- d. Statement on Auditing Standards No. 70: Service Organizations

Guidance: level 1

:: Hazard analysis ::

Broadly speaking, a _________ is the combined effort of 1. identifying and analyzing potential events that may negatively impact individuals, assets, and/or the environment ; and 2. making judgments "on the tolerability of the risk on the basis of a risk analysis" while considering influencing factors . Put in simpler terms, a _________ analyzes what can go wrong, how likely it is to happen, what the potential consequences are, and how tolerable the identified risk is. As part of this process, the resulting determination of risk may be expressed in a quantitative or qualitative fashion. The _________ is an inherent part of an overall risk management strategy, which attempts to, after a _________ , "introduce control measures to eliminate or reduce" any potential risk-related consequences.

Exam Probability: **Low**

28. *Answer choices:*

(see index for correct answer)

- a. Swiss cheese model
- b. Hazard
- c. Hazard identification
- d. Risk assessment

Guidance: level 1

:: Generally Accepted Accounting Principles ::

Financial statements prepared and presented by a company typically follow an external standard that specifically guides their preparation. These standards vary across the globe and are typically overseen by some combination of the private accounting profession in that specific nation and the various government regulators. Variations across countries may be considerable, making cross-country evaluation of financial data challenging.

Exam Probability: **Medium**

29. *Answer choices:*

(see index for correct answer)

- a. French generally accepted accounting principles

- b. Generally Accepted Accounting Principles
- c. Earnings before interest and taxes
- d. Chinese accounting standards

Guidance: level 1

:: Management accounting ::

In __________ or managerial accounting, managers use the provisions of accounting information in order to better inform themselves before they decide matters within their organizations, which aids their management and performance of control functions.

Exam Probability: **Low**

30. *Answer choices:*

(see index for correct answer)

- a. Institute of Cost and Management Accountants of Bangladesh
- b. Certified Management Accountants of Canada
- c. Total benefits of ownership
- d. Management accounting

Guidance: level 1

:: Inventory ::

__________ is a system of inventory in which updates are made on a periodic basis. This differs from perpetual inventory systems, where updates are made as seen fit.

Exam Probability: **High**

31. *Answer choices:*

(see index for correct answer)

- a. Order picking
- b. Cost of goods sold
- c. Ending inventory
- d. Specific identification

Guidance: level 1

:: Budgets ::

__________ is a method of budgeting in which all expenses must be justified and approved for each new period. Developed by Peter Pyhrr in the 1970s, __________ starts from a "zero base" at the beginning of every budget period, analyzing needs and costs of every function within an organization and allocating funds accordingly, regardless of how much money has previously been budgeted to any given line item.

Exam Probability: **Medium**

32. *Answer choices:*

(see index for correct answer)

- a. Programme budgeting
- b. Budget set
- c. Budgeted cost of work scheduled
- d. Railway Budget

Guidance: level 1

:: Accounting terminology ::

In accounting/accountancy, __________ are journal entries usually made at the end of an accounting period to allocate income and expenditure to the period in which they actually occurred. The revenue recognition principle is the basis of making __________ that pertain to unearned and accrued revenues under accrual-basis accounting. They are sometimes called Balance Day adjustments because they are made on balance day.

Exam Probability: **Low**

33. *Answer choices:*

(see index for correct answer)

- a. Adjusting entries
- b. Accounting equation
- c. Basis of accounting
- d. Capital appreciation

Guidance: level 1

:: Types of accounting ::

Various __________ systems are used by various public sector entities. In the United States, for instance, there are two levels of government which follow different accounting standards set forth by independent, private sector boards. At the federal level, the Federal Accounting Standards Advisory Board sets forth the accounting standards to follow. Similarly, there is the __________ Standards Board for state and local level government.

Exam Probability: **High**

34. *Answer choices:*

(see index for correct answer)

- a. Governmental accounting
- b. Product control
- c. Personal environmental impact accounting

Guidance: level 1

:: Accounting in the United States ::

Established in 1988, the __________ is a professional organization of fraud examiners. Its activities include producing fraud information, tools and training. The ACFE grants the professional designation of Certified Fraud Examiner. The ACFE is the world's largest anti-fraud organization and is a provider of anti-fraud training and education, with more than 85,000 members.

Exam Probability: **High**

35. *Answer choices:*

(see index for correct answer)

- a. International Qualification Examination
- b. Association of Certified Fraud Examiners
- c. Legal liability of certified public accountants
- d. Other comprehensive income

Guidance: level 1

:: ::

A __________ is an individual or institution that legally owns one or more shares of stock in a public or private corporation. __________ s may be referred to as members of a corporation. Legally, a person is not a __________ in a corporation until their name and other details are entered in the corporation`s register of __________ s or members.

Exam Probability: **High**

36. *Answer choices:*

(see index for correct answer)

- a. Shareholder
- b. cultural
- c. functional perspective
- d. interpersonal communication

Guidance: level 1

:: Debt ::

A __________ is a monetary amount owed to a creditor that is unlikely to be paid and, or which the creditor is not willing to take action to collect for various reasons, often due to the debtor not having the money to pay, for example due to a company going into liquidation or insolvency. There are various technical definitions of what constitutes a __________, depending on accounting conventions, regulatory treatment and the institution provisioning. In the USA, bank loans with more than ninety days` arrears become "problem loans". Accounting sources advise that the full amount of a __________ be written off to the profit and loss account or a provision for __________ s as soon as it is foreseen.

Exam Probability: **High**

37. *Answer choices:*

(see index for correct answer)

- a. Debt management plan
- b. Legal liability
- c. Bad debt
- d. Credit

Guidance: level 1

:: Accounting terminology ::

__________ is money owed by a business to its suppliers shown as a liability on a company`s balance sheet. It is distinct from notes payable liabilities, which are debts created by formal legal instrument documents.

Exam Probability: **Low**

38. *Answer choices:*

(see index for correct answer)

- a. Fair value accounting
- b. Total absorption costing
- c. Basis of accounting
- d. Accounts payable

Guidance: level 1

:: Commerce ::

Continuation of an entity as a __________ is presumed as the basis for financial reporting unless and until the entity`s liquidation becomes imminent. Preparation of financial statements under this presumption is commonly referred to as the __________ basis of accounting. If and when an entity`s liquidation becomes imminent, financial statements are prepared under the liquidation basis of accounting .

Exam Probability: **High**

39. *Answer choices:*

(see index for correct answer)

- a. Non-commercial
- b. Purchasing manager
- c. Social gravity
- d. Return merchandise authorization

Guidance: level 1

:: Stock market ::

A _________ , securities exchange or bourse, is a facility where stock brokers and traders can buy and sell securities, such as shares of stock and bonds and other financial instruments. _________ s may also provide for facilities the issue and redemption of such securities and instruments and capital events including the payment of income and dividends. Securities traded on a _________ include stock issued by listed companies, unit trusts, derivatives, pooled investment products and bonds. _________ s often function as "continuous auction" markets with buyers and sellers consummating transactions via open outcry at a central location such as the floor of the exchange or by using an electronic trading platform.

Exam Probability: **Medium**

40. *Answer choices:*
(see index for correct answer)

- a. CNBC World
- b. Wash trade
- c. Box spread
- d. Stock Exchange

Guidance: level 1

:: Legal terms ::

A _________ is a gathering of people who have been invited by a host for the purposes of socializing, conversation, recreation, or as part of a festival or other commemoration of a special occasion. A _________ will typically feature food and beverages, and often music and dancing or other forms of entertainment. In many Western countries, parties for teens and adults are associated with drinking alcohol such as beer, wine, or distilled spirits.

Exam Probability: **High**

41. *Answer choices:*
(see index for correct answer)

- a. Party
- b. Legal nullity
- c. Public service company
- d. Intentional harassment, alarm or distress

Guidance: level 1

:: Inventory ::

Costs are associated with particular goods using one of the several formulas, including specific identification, first-in first-out , or average cost. Costs include all costs of purchase, costs of conversion and other costs that are incurred in bringing the inventories to their present location and condition. Costs of goods made by the businesses include material, labor, and allocated overhead. The costs of those goods which are not yet sold are deferred as costs of inventory until the inventory is sold or written down in value.

Exam Probability: **High**

42. *Answer choices:*

(see index for correct answer)

- a. Perpetual inventory
- b. Cost of goods sold
- c. Reorder point
- d. Specific identification

Guidance: level 1

:: Generally Accepted Accounting Principles ::

__________ , or non-current liabilities, are liabilities that are due beyond a year or the normal operation period of the company. The normal operation period is the amount of time it takes for a company to turn inventory into cash. On a classified balance sheet, liabilities are separated between current and __________ to help users assess the company`s financial standing in short-term and long-term periods. __________ give users more information about the long-term prosperity of the company, while current liabilities inform the user of debt that the company owes in the current period. On a balance sheet, accounts are listed in order of liquidity, so __________ come after current liabilities. In addition, the specific long-term liability accounts are listed on the balance sheet in order of liquidity. Therefore, an account due within eighteen months would be listed before an account due within twenty-four months. Examples of __________ are bonds payable, long-term loans, capital leases, pension liabilities, post-retirement healthcare liabilities, deferred compensation, deferred revenues, deferred income taxes, and derivative liabilities.

Exam Probability: **Medium**

43. *Answer choices:*

(see index for correct answer)

- a. Earnings before interest and taxes
- b. Long-term liabilities
- c. Revenue
- d. Financial position of the United States

Guidance: level 1

:: ::

__________ are electronic transfer of money from one bank account to another, either within a single financial institution or across multiple institutions, via computer-based systems, without the direct intervention of bank staff.

Exam Probability: **High**

44. *Answer choices:*

(see index for correct answer)

- a. process perspective
- b. cultural
- c. levels of analysis
- d. Electronic funds transfer

Guidance: level 1

:: E-commerce ::

__________ is an e-commerce payment system used in the Netherlands, based on online banking. Introduced in 2005, this payment method allows customers to buy on the Internet using direct online transfers from their bank account.

Exam Probability: **Low**

45. *Answer choices:*

(see index for correct answer)

- a. Online auction tools
- b. IDEAL
- c. Plantify
- d. SAScon

Guidance: level 1

:: ::

The U.S. _________ is an independent agency of the United States federal government. The SEC holds primary responsibility for enforcing the federal securities laws, proposing securities rules, and regulating the securities industry, the nation`s stock and options exchanges, and other activities and organizations, including the electronic securities markets in the United States.

Exam Probability: **High**

46. *Answer choices:*

(see index for correct answer)

- a. open system
- b. empathy
- c. Securities and Exchange Commission
- d. information systems assessment

Guidance: level 1

:: ::

_________ is a means of protection from financial loss. It is a form of risk management, primarily used to hedge against the risk of a contingent or uncertain loss

Exam Probability: **Low**

47. *Answer choices:*

(see index for correct answer)

- a. hierarchical
- b. functional perspective
- c. Insurance
- d. Character

Guidance: level 1

:: Labor terms ::

__________ , often called DI or disability income insurance, or income protection, is a form of insurance that insures the beneficiary`s earned income against the risk that a disability creates a barrier for a worker to complete the core functions of their work. For example, the worker may suffer from an inability to maintain composure in the case of psychological disorders or an injury, illness or condition that causes physical impairment or incapacity to work. It encompasses paid sick leave, short-term disability benefits , and long-term disability benefits . Statistics show that in the US a disabling accident occurs, on average, once every second. In fact, nearly 18.5% of Americans are currently living with a disability, and 1 out of every 4 persons in the US workforce will suffer a disabling injury before retirement.

Exam Probability: **Medium**

48. *Answer choices:*

(see index for correct answer)

- a. Strike action
- b. Absence rate
- c. Capital services
- d. Disability insurance

Guidance: level 1

:: Taxation in the United States ::

The Modified Accelerated Cost Recovery System is the current tax depreciation system in the United States. Under this system, the capitalized cost of tangible property is recovered over a specified life by annual deductions for depreciation. The lives are specified broadly in the Internal Revenue Code. The Internal Revenue Service publishes detailed tables of lives by classes of assets. The deduction for depreciation is computed under one of two methods at the election of the taxpayer, with limitations. See IRS Publication 946 for a 120-page guide to __________ .

Exam Probability: **Low**

49. *Answer choices:*

(see index for correct answer)

- a. MACRS
- b. Charitable remainder unitrust
- c. United States Department of Justice Tax Division

- d. Itemized

Guidance: level 1

:: Business law ::

A __________ is a form of partnership similar to a general partnership except that while a general partnership must have at least two general partners, a __________ must have at least one GP and at least one limited partner.

Exam Probability: **Medium**

50. *Answer choices:*
(see index for correct answer)

- a. Bulk transfer
- b. Forward-looking statement
- c. WIPO Copyright Treaty
- d. Limited partnership

Guidance: level 1

:: Accounting terminology ::

__________ is an accounting system for recording resources whose use has been limited by the donor, grant authority, governing agency, or other individuals or organisations or by law. It emphasizes accountability rather than profitability, and is used by Nonprofit organizations and by governments. In this method, a fund consists of a self-balancing set of accounts and each are reported as either unrestricted, temporarily restricted or permanently restricted based on the provider-imposed restrictions.

Exam Probability: **Low**

51. *Answer choices:*
(see index for correct answer)

- a. Fund accounting
- b. Capital appreciation
- c. Fair value accounting
- d. Cash flow management

Guidance: level 1

:: Financial ratios ::

The __________ is a liquidity ratio that measures whether a firm has enough resources to meet its short-term obligations. It compares a firm`s current assets to its current liabilities, and is expressed as follows.

Exam Probability: **Medium**

52. *Answer choices:*

(see index for correct answer)

- a. Current ratio
- b. Sustainable growth rate
- c. Market-to-book
- d. Beta

Guidance: level 1

:: Financial markets ::

__________ s are monetary contracts between parties. They can be created, traded, modified and settled. They can be cash , evidence of an ownership interest in an entity , or a contractual right to receive or deliver cash .

Exam Probability: **Low**

53. *Answer choices:*

(see index for correct answer)

- a. Secondary market
- b. Payment schedule
- c. Financial instrument
- d. Faroese Securities Market

Guidance: level 1

:: ::

A __________ is a form of public administration which, in a majority of contexts, exists as the lowest tier of administration within a given state. The term is used to contrast with offices at state level, which are referred to as the central government, national government, or federal government and also to supranational government which deals with governing institutions between states. __________ s generally act within powers delegated to them by legislation or directives of the higher level of government. In federal states, __________ generally comprises the third tier of government, whereas in unitary states, __________ usually occupies the second or third tier of government, often with greater powers than higher-level administrative divisions.

Exam Probability: **High**

54. *Answer choices:*

(see index for correct answer)

- a. Local government
- b. information systems assessment
- c. interpersonal communication
- d. cultural

Guidance: level 1

:: ::

__________ is the process of making predictions of the future based on past and present data and most commonly by analysis of trends. A commonplace example might be estimation of some variable of interest at some specified future date. Prediction is a similar, but more general term. Both might refer to formal statistical methods employing time series, cross-sectional or longitudinal data, or alternatively to less formal judgmental methods. Usage can differ between areas of application: for example, in hydrology the terms "forecast" and " __________ " are sometimes reserved for estimates of values at certain specific future times, while the term "prediction" is used for more general estimates, such as the number of times floods will occur over a long period.

Exam Probability: **Medium**

55. *Answer choices:*

(see index for correct answer)

- a. deep-level diversity
- b. open system
- c. levels of analysis
- d. cultural

Guidance: level 1

:: Financial ratios ::

The _________ or dividend-price ratio of a share is the dividend per share, divided by the price per share. It is also a company's total annual dividend payments divided by its market capitalization, assuming the number of shares is constant. It is often expressed as a percentage.

Exam Probability: **Low**

56. *Answer choices:*

(see index for correct answer)

- a. Statutory liquidity ratio
- b. Price/cash flow ratio
- c. Debtor days
- d. Cash flow return on investment

Guidance: level 1

:: Business models ::

A _________ , _________ company or daughter company is a company that is owned or controlled by another company, which is called the parent company, parent, or holding company. The _________ can be a company, corporation, or limited liability company. In some cases it is a government or state-owned enterprise. In some cases, particularly in the music and book publishing industries, subsidiaries are referred to as imprints.

Exam Probability: **Low**

57. *Answer choices:*

(see index for correct answer)

- a. Brainsworking
- b. Entreship
- c. Strategy map
- d. Subsidiary

Guidance: level 1

:: Notes (finance) ::

A __________ , sometimes referred to as a note payable, is a legal instrument , in which one party promises in writing to pay a determinate sum of money to the other , either at a fixed or determinable future time or on demand of the payee, under specific terms.

Exam Probability: **Low**

58. *Answer choices:*

(see index for correct answer)

- a. Interest Bearing Note
- b. Large-sized note
- c. Promissory note
- d. Demand Note

Guidance: level 1

:: Financial ratios ::

The __________ is a financial ratio indicating the relative proportion of equity used to finance a company`s assets. The two components are often taken from the firm`s balance sheet or statement of financial position , but the ratio may also be calculated using market values for both, if the company`s equities are publicly traded.

Exam Probability: **Medium**

59. *Answer choices:*

(see index for correct answer)

- a. Sterling ratio
- b. Operating leverage
- c. Short interest ratio
- d. Days payable outstanding

Guidance: level 1

INDEX: Correct Answers

Foundations of Business

1. b: Gross domestic product

2. a: Economic Development

3. c: Import

4. : Health

5. b: Entrepreneur

6. : Selling

7. b: Currency

8. d: Industrial Revolution

9. c: Security

10. a: Project management

11. d: Brainstorming

12. a: Analysis

13. d: Balance sheet

14. d: Small business

15. d: Building

16. c: Interview

17. a: Social security

18. : Trade

19. c: Image

20. : Credit

21. c: Committee

22. c: Specification

23. d: Money

24. b: Marketing strategy

25. a: Cash flow

26. b: Sustainability

27. a: Recession

28. a: Training

29. d: Sony

30. b: System

31. d: Logistics

32. b: Income statement

33. b: Stock market

34. c: Trade agreement

35. d: Customs

36. d: Economies of scale

37. b: Availability

38. : Restructuring

39. : Business model

40. d: Copyright

41. b: Internal control

42. d: Meeting

43. d: Capital market

44. : Tariff

45. b: Bias

46. : Firm

47. : Pattern

48. b: Market segmentation

49. a: Internal Revenue Service

50. : Interest

51. : Quality management

52. : Protection

53. c: Limited liability

54. a: SWOT analysis

55. : Benchmarking

56. d: Focus group

57. c: Fraud

58. c: Opportunity cost

59. c: ASEAN

Management

1. b: Resource management

2. : Interaction

3. b: Enabling

4. d: Raw material

5. c: Hotel

6. : Strategic management

7. b: Vendor

8. b: General manager

9. a: Self-assessment

10. a: Case study

11. : Management system

12. a: Risk management

13. c: Glass ceiling

14. a: Situational leadership

15. b: Labor force

16. a: Recession

17. : Interview

18. d: Creativity

19. a: Management

20. b: Absenteeism

21. d: Decentralization

22. a: Officer

23. d: Total cost

24. : Question

25. a: Human resource management

26. a: Outsourcing

27. d: Inventory control

28. d: Strategic alliance

29. c: Best practice

30. d: Entrepreneurship

31. c: Joint venture

32. c: Insurance

33. d: Problem

34. c: Entrepreneur

35. c: Industrial Revolution

36. b: Proactive

37. d: Statistic

38. c: Feedback

39. c: Specification

40. c: Board of directors

41. : Problem solving

42. d: Logistics

43. : Training and development

44. c: Patent

45. b: Virtual team

46. b: Transactional leadership

47. b: Compromise

48. a: Integrity

49. d: Industry

50. : Evaluation

51. b: Strategy

52. d: Six Sigma

53. a: Organization chart

54. b: Restructuring

55. c: Efficiency

56. b: Choice

57. d: Schedule

58. d: Human resources

59. c: Mission statement

Business law

1. d: Mortgage

2. d: Voidable contract

3. c: Duress

4. a: Ford

5. b: Arbitration clause

6. : Jury

7. d: Certiorari

8. b: Clayton Act

9. a: Surety

10. a: Resource

11. b: Holder in due course

12. a: Computer fraud

13. d: Judicial review

14. a: Relevant market

15. c: False imprisonment

16. a: Commercial speech

17. c: Mirror image rule

18. a: Limited liability

19. b: Adverse possession

20. a: Deed

21. d: Substantive law

22. d: Option contract

23. b: Criminal law

24. d: Buyer

25. b: Employment discrimination

26. d: Securities Act

27. : Opening statement

28. b: Treaty

29. : Affidavit

30. d: Probate

31. a: Mens rea

32. c: Standing

33. d: Corporation

34. : Social responsibility

35. : Warranty

36. : Credit

37. : Creditor

38. b: Federal government

39. c: Competitor

40. b: Consideration

41. b: Cooperative

42. d: Perfection

43. b: Bailee

44. c: Offeror

45. d: Firm

46. : Specific performance

47. a: Personal property

48. a: Merger

49. d: Cyberspace

50. b: Tort

51. : Mediation

52. c: Patent

53. b: Ratification

54. a: Manufacturing

55. : Bankruptcy

56. b: Corruption

57. b: Complaint

58. b: Interest

59. b: Bill of lading

Finance

1. : Credit card

2. d: Income tax

3. a: Brand

4. b: Technology

5. b: Asset

6. c: Total cost

7. a: Financial market

8. : Promissory note

9. : Relevance

10. c: Commercial bank

11. c: Incentive

12. d: Manufacturing

13. : Ending inventory

14. c: Capital lease

15. a: Sinking fund

16. b: Mutual fund

17. a: Residual value

18. : Certified Public Accountant

19. c: Issuer

20. b: Working capital

21. b: Financial management

22. a: Volume

23. d: Goldman Sachs

24. a: Futures contract

25. d: Social security

26. d: Capital stock

27. a: Purchasing

28. a: Utility

29. c: Secondary market

30. c: Limited liability

31. : Ledger

32. c: Discounting

33. b: Patent

34. b: Dividend yield

35. b: Pension

36. : Yield to maturity

37. c: Revenue recognition

38. : Capital expenditure

39. c: Intangible asset

40. b: Cash management

41. b: Historical cost

42. : Worksheet

43. b: Finance

44. a: Debenture

45. d: Factory

46. : Source document

47. c: Face

48. c: Bad debt

49. c: Fiscal year

50. b: INDEX

51. b: Finished good

52. c: Restructuring

53. c: Variable Costing

54. c: Currency

55. c: Activity-based costing

56. c: Forecasting

57. b: Payback period

58. a: Management accounting

59. a: Preference

Human resource management

1. d: Locus of control

2. c: Job sharing

3. a: Realistic job preview

4. d: Job analysis

5. b: Merit pay

6. c: Asset

7. b: Right to work

8. : Overlearning

9. c: Balanced scorecard

10. c: Business game

11. a: Distance learning

12. c: Layoff

13. c: Union shop

14. a: Organizational learning

15. c: Open shop

16. d: Test validity

17. d: Action learning

18. b: Content validity

19. a: Knowledge worker

20. b: Body language

21. b: Human resource management

22. b: Cover letter

23. c: Flexible spending account

24. d: Industrial relations

25. c: Knowledge management

26. b: Enforcement

27. b: Global sourcing

28. d: Severance package

29. b: Global workforce

30. : Assessment center

31. c: Public administration

32. a: Labor union

33. a: National Association of Colleges and Employers

34. c: Efficiency wage

35. : Occupational Safety and Health Act

36. d: Partnership

37. a: Adaptive

38. d: Arbitration

39. d: Referent power

40. c: Training and development

41. c: Conformity

42. d: Organizational commitment

43. c: Workforce planning

44. d: Independent contractor

45. a: Transformational leadership

46. b: Workplace violence

47. a: Emotional intelligence

48. c: Concurrent validity

49. : Performance appraisal

50. d: Organizational structure

51. c: Labor force

52. b: Retraining

53. d: Evidence-based

54. d: Profit sharing

55. b: Organizational chart

56. d: Career development

57. d: Wage

58. c: Lilly Ledbetter

59. d: Collective bargaining

Information systems

1. c: Payment Card Industry Data Security Standard

2. a: Database management system

3. : Big data

4. c: Statistics

5. c: Virtual team

6. : Government-to-business

7. : Decision-making

8. : System

9. a: Reputation management

10. d: Peer production

11. c: Consumer-to-consumer

12. : Economies of scale

13. c: Click-through rate

14. b: Netscape

15. : World Wide Web

16. b: Data element

17. a: Data redundancy

18. : Web mining

19. b: Web analytics

20. c: Security controls

21. a: Balanced scorecard

22. d: Data

23. c: Vulnerability

24. d: Government-to-citizen

25. b: Information privacy

26. c: Downtime

27. a: Enterprise application

28. c: Microprocessor

29. d: Data cleansing

30. c: Strategic information system

31. : Availability

32. d: Blog

33. d: Data file

34. : Transaction processing

35. : Dashboard

36. b: Analytics

37. b: Folksonomy

38. a: Privacy policy

39. : Freemium

40. : Entity-relationship

41. a: Positioning system

42. d: Questionnaire

43. : Electronic funds transfer

44. : Wide Area Network

45. c: Help desk

46. c: PeopleSoft

47. d: Data center

48. : Payment system

49. a: Census

50. a: Master data

51. b: Extranet

52. c: Joint application design

53. a: Mobile commerce

54. b: Botnet

55. d: System software

56. b: Query by Example

57. : Drill down

58. b: Network management

59. b: Transport Layer Security

Marketing

1. a: Problem Solving

2. a: Perception

3. c: Logo

4. c: Patent

5. a: Sales

6. b: Exchange rate

7. d: Fixed cost

8. c: Advertising campaign

9. c: Shares

10. b: Buyer

11. b: Business Week

12. a: Customer experience

13. c: Product line

14. d: Star

15. d: Corporation

16. : Total Quality Management

17. b: Security

18. b: Auction

19. c: Frequency

20. b: Need

21. d: Consideration

22. c: Monopoly

23. a: Questionnaire

24. : Copyright

25. a: Life

26. b: Noise

27. : Sales promotion

28. c: Psychographic

29. a: Tangible

30. c: Audit

31. : Database

32. c: New product development

33. b: Derived demand

34. d: Organizational structure

35. c: Product manager

36. d: Vendor

37. d: Intranet

38. a: Secondary data

39. b: Logistics

40. : Brainstorming

41. d: Personnel

42. c: Shopping

43. c: Project

44. b: Entrepreneur

45. b: Empowerment

46. c: Public

47. : Bottom line

48. a: Product concept

49. : Marketing research

50. d: North American Free Trade Agreement

51. : INDEX

52. c: Microsoft

53. a: Choice

54. d: Sales management

55. c: Credit

56. b: Competitive advantage

57. d: Creative brief

58. : Unique selling proposition

59. d: Focus group

Manufacturing

1. a: Process engineering

2. d: Distillation

3. c: Sputnik

4. b: Asset

5. a: PDCA

6. a: Chemical reaction

7. d: Pattern

8. c: Ball

9. d: Project

10. a: Planning

11. a: Supplier relationship management

12. : Initiative

13. b: Scope statement

14. : Cost reduction

15. : Heat treating

16. : Vendor

17. : Remanufacturing

18. d: Assembly line

19. a: Paper

20. a: Metal

21. b: Goal

22. : Project team

23. b: Financial plan

24. a: Prize

25. : Kaizen

26. c: Quality audit

27. a: Tool

28. b: Performance

29. : Zero Defects

30. : Blanket

31. : Process capability

32. b: Sensitivity analysis

33. b: Downtime

34. : Control limits

35. d: Service level

36. a: Durability

37. d: Sharing

38. b: Clay

39. : Synergy

40. : Sequence

41. c: Strategy

42. c: Good

43. a: Supply chain network

44. : Property

45. a: Knowledge management

46. a: Business process

47. a: Voice of the customer

48. c: Statistical process control

49. d: Strategic planning

50. b: Purchasing manager

51. a: Reflux

52. c: Rolling Wave planning

53. b: Process control

54. b: Total cost of ownership

55. : Cost estimate

56. a: Request for proposal

57. : Resource

58. d: Heat transfer

59. d: Lean manufacturing

Commerce

1. b: Purchasing

2. c: Entrepreneur

3. : York

4. : Contract

5. a: Warehouse

6. a: Industry

7. b: Sexual harassment

8. a: Inventory

9. c: Commodity

10. d: Fraud

11. a: Quality management

12. b: Economics

13. b: Microsoft

14. b: Front office

15. d: Short run

16. c: Forward auction

17. : Direct marketing

18. d: Tourism

19. a: Webvan

20. d: Jurisdiction

21. b: Boot

22. d: Issuing bank

23. a: Utility

24. d: Pizza Hut

25. c: Disintermediation

26. c: Business-to-business

27. : Buyer

28. : Strategic plan

29. : Product mix

30. b: Merger

31. c: Lycos

32. : Commerce

33. a: Welfare

34. b: Minimum wage

35. b: Social shopping

36. d: Initiative

37. b: Stock

38. d: Market research

39. d: Advertising

40. d: Empowerment

41. : Silver

42. b: Charter

43. b: Uniform Commercial Code

44. c: Authentication

45. : Risk management

46. b: Revenue

47. a: Partnership

48. c: Investment

49. c: Asset

50. d: Collaborative filtering

51. b: Strategic alliance

52. d: Electronic funds transfer

53. b: Trade show

54. c: Mining

55. a: Netflix

56. c: Value-added network

57. c: Public relations

58. d: Staff position

59. c: Firm

Business ethics

1. d: Nonprofit

2. : Ethical leadership

3. a: Kyoto Protocol

4. c: Greenpeace

5. c: Sexual harassment

6. c: Coal

7. a: Workplace bullying

8. c: Marijuana

9. a: Referent power

10. d: Guerrilla Marketing

11. c: Copyright

12. d: Corporate social responsibility

13. b: Dilemma

14. c: Model Rules of Professional Conduct

15. a: Disclaimer

16. : Electronic waste

17. c: Consumer Protection

18. a: Lawsuit

19. c: Whistleblower

20. c: Reputation

21. d: Enron

22. c: UN Global Compact

23. d: Charles Ponzi

24. d: Planned obsolescence

25. b: Protestant work ethic

26. : Greenwashing

27. : Social networking

28. : Risk assessment

29. d: Transocean

30. a: Community development financial institution

31. d: Right to work

32. d: Criminal law

33. b: Organizational culture

34. d: Marketing

35. c: Partnership

36. b: Federal Trade Commission Act

37. b: Building

38. c: Invisible hand

39. d: Auditor independence

40. : Veil of ignorance

41. a: Patriot Act

42. d: Undue hardship

43. a: Trade

44. a: Patent

45. : Organizational ethics

46. d: Real estate

47. b: Solar power

48. a: Self-interest

49. a: Supply Chain

50. b: Authoritarian

51. : Conscience

52. a: Fraud

53. c: Medicaid

54. c: Cultural relativism

55. d: Global Fund

56. : Foreign Corrupt Practices Act

57. b: Dress code

58. d: Micromanagement

59. c: Catholicism

Accounting

1. d: Matching principle

2. d: Intangible asset

3. d: Taxpayer

4. b: Independent contractor

5. b: Accounting Research Bulletins

6. c: Estate tax

7. a: Norwalk Agreement

8. d: Purchase order

9. a: Tax reform

10. d: Trend analysis

11. d: Resource allocation

12. a: Capital loss

13. c: Contribution margin

14. c: Comprehensive income

15. : QuickBooks

16. : Paid-in capital

17. a: Outsourcing

18. c: Chart of accounts

19. c: Financial analysis

20. d: Standard cost

21. b: Quick ratio

22. c: Callable

23. b: Present value

24. c: Forensic

25. : Accounting management

26. c: Revaluation

27. c: Balance sheet

28. d: Risk assessment

29. b: Generally Accepted Accounting Principles

30. d: Management accounting

31. : Periodic inventory

32. : Zero-based budgeting

33. a: Adjusting entries

34. a: Governmental accounting

35. b: Association of Certified Fraud Examiners

36. a: Shareholder

37. c: Bad debt

38. d: Accounts payable

39. : Going concern

40. d: Stock Exchange

41. a: Party

42. b: Cost of goods sold

43. b: Long-term liabilities

44. d: Electronic funds transfer

45. b: IDEAL

46. c: Securities and Exchange Commission

47. c: Insurance

48. d: Disability insurance

49. a: MACRS

50. d: Limited partnership

51. a: Fund accounting

52. a: Current ratio

53. c: Financial instrument

54. a: Local government

55. : Forecasting

56. : Dividend yield

57. d: Subsidiary

58. c: Promissory note

59. : Equity ratio

CPSIA information can be obtained
at www.ICGtesting.com
Printed in the USA
LVHW051624301019
635718LV00005B/730/P

9 781538 863404